"Work or Fight!"

"Work or Fight!"

Race, Gender, and the Draft in World War One

Gerald E. Shenk

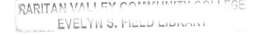

palgrave
macmillan

First published in 2005 by
PALGRAVE MACMILLAN™
175 Fifth Avenue, New York, N.Y. 10010 and
Houndmills, Basingstoke, Hampshire, England RG21 6XS
Companies and representatives throughout the world.

PALGRAVE MACMILLAN is the global academic imprint of the Palgrave Macmillan division of St. Martin's Press, LLC and of Palgrave Macmillan Ltd. Macmillan® is a registered trademark in the United States, United Kingdom and other countries. Palgrave is a registered trademark in the European Union and other countries.

ISBN 1–4039–6175–1
ISBN 1–4039–6177–8 (pbk.)

Library of Congress Cataloging-in-Publication Data

Shenk, Gerald E.
    "Work or fight!" : race, gender, and the draft in World War One / by Gerald E. Shenk.
        p. cm.
    Includes bibliographical references and index.
    ISBN 1–4039–6175–1—ISBN 1–4039–6177–8 (pbk.)
        1. United States—Armed Forces—Recruiting, enlistment, etc.—World War, 1914–1918. 2. United States. Selective Service System—History. 3. United States—Social conditions—1865–1918. I. Title.

D570.8.R4S54 2005
940.3'73—dc22   2005047658

A catalogue record for this book is available from the British Library.

Design by Newgen Imaging Systems (P) Ltd., Chennai, India.

First edition: December 2005

10 9 8 7 6 5 4 3 2 1

Printed in the United States of America.

For Emily Brackbill Shenk

CONTENTS

Acknowledgments

This book reflects many years of activism, study, and engagement with friends and colleagues inside and outside of academia. I first became interested in studying the Selective Service System in 1969 when as a conscientious objector during the U.S. war in Vietnam I went to work for the National Interreligious Service Board for Conscientious Objectors (NISBCO) in Washington, D.C. And so, I must first thank, John Lapp, a history professor at Eastern Mennonite College, who taught me how to think critically about war and society, and who inspired me to take that job. My co-workers at NISBCO, and then at the National Council to Repeal the Draft, The Church of the Brethren Washington Office, the Public Law Education Institute, and the Central Committee for Conscientious Objectors gave me the basic foundation for understanding the Selective Service System. Inadvertently, I am certain, public officials whom I met during my years in Washington, D.C., helped me understand how the actions of administrators in large governmental bureaucracies may reinforce systems of inequality based on race, gender, and class. Between the years 1969 and 1973, I had the opportunity to meet Selective Service officials in the National Headquarters, as well as members of Congress or their legislative assistants to discuss the draft. These included long-time Director of Selective Service, General Lewis B. Hershey and his successor, Curtis Tarr, and James Woolsey, future CIA Director, but then legislative assistant to the Chair of the Senate Armed Services Committee, Senator John Stennis. I doubt any of these officials would agree with much of my analysis, but I thank them, nevertheless, for their unwitting contributions to this study.

Without the generous help of quite a number of my colleagues, students, and friends I would never have completed this work. Akasha Hull's insightful suggestions on the final draft helped me immeasurably. Students who read all or parts of the manuscript and provided valuable feedback included: Kevin Miller, Cenan Pirani, John Klein, Theresa Mendoza, Moses Nagata, Miguel Gomez, and Shane Bauer. Kevin Miller also assisted with the research on the Selective Service System in California, and composed the index. Over several years my colleague David Takacs helped me to fine tune my arguments and clarify the writing. Fellow Carnegie Scholars, Mary Romero, Vernon Burton, Jane Aikman, and Patti Owen-Smith commented on an early version. Ilene Feinman, Angie Tran, Fran Ansley, and Roberto Corrada helped me think through knotty theoretical problems.

I am also grateful to those many individuals who assisted me with feedback and encouragement many years ago when this work was in dissertation form. I continue to discover ways in which my advisor, Steven Hahn, inspired and helped me build the skills and intellectual curiosity necessary for good historical scholarship. Over the years, John Chambers II of Rutgers University, who is our leading historian of the draft, has provided valuable feedback and encouraged me to continue with this project. Other faculty and colleagues mostly at the University of California, San Diego, in the 1980s who helped in various ways include: Michael Gorman, Kris Webb, Chris D'Arpa, Jeannie Wayne, Ross Frank, Mary Hoogterp, Jewell Spangler, Cynthia Radding, James Sabbs, Tom Summerhill, Eric Van Young, Michael Parrish, Robert Ritchie, Rachel Klein, Julie Saville, Thomas Dublin, and Ramón Gutierrez. Dan Carter, Pete Daniel, John Inscoe, Ted Ownby, Jacquelyn Dowd Hall, Stephanie McCurry, Alex Lichtenstein, and Mel McKiven all commented on sections. Abe Shragge directed me to sources on San Diego. Farrell Evans not only read and commented on everything I sent him, but along with Raul Ramirez, regularly prodded me to see this through to the finish. My brother Dan and his wife Naomi often provided an ideal writing environment at their secluded cabin in the Virginia mountains.

Various archivists and librarians helped me along the way. Dale Couch and Virginia Shaderon at the Georgia Department of Archives and History not only helped with archival documents, but significantly influenced my thinking about the intersections of race and gender. Numerous other staff assisted me as well at the Washington National Records Center, both at Suitland and College Park, Maryland, the regional National Archives Branches at Atlanta, Chicago, Bayonne, New Jersey, Laguna Niguel and San Bruno, California, the Paterson, New Jersey, Free Public Library, the Newnan-Coweta Genealogical Society, Newnan, Georgia, the Quincy and Adams County Historical Society, Quincy, Illinois, the UC, San Diego, Historical Network, and the Mandeville Special Collections at the UC, San Diego University Library.

Finally, this would never have been completed had not my original editor at Palgrave, Deborah Gershenowitz, had the vision to see how an unwieldy six hundred page manuscript could be transformed into a book of sensible length without diluting its message, and had not Mark Glick negotiated the details of the contract. I am also grateful to new staff at Palgrave who took over this project at the very end of the process. History editor Alessandra Bastagli, and her assistant Petrina Crockford, as well as production coordinator, Yasmin Mathew, offered exactly the right assistance at the right time. It was a pleasure to work with them. Despite the well-intentioned efforts of everyone who has assisted me along the way, I alone am responsible for whatever flaws may remain in the finished work.

INTRODUCTION

I have been given to understand that whiteness is the ownership of the earth, forever and ever, Amen.

—W. E. B. Du Bois[1]

Milton Brackbill, at the age of ninety-one, sat with his wife Ruth in the relative safety of their Florida retirement home and described how he once stood up to threats from a "gang" of local men during World War I. The United States had entered the European War in the spring of 1917, and began drafting men in September. In the fall of 1917, Brackbill was a young husband and the father of a newborn baby girl. He and Ruth, both raised in the pacifist traditions of the Mennonite Church, now managed a farm near the Philadelphia "Mainline" town of Paoli. In the midst of a gathering war fever, their German ethnicity and pacifist beliefs made the young couple and their daughter Emily, vulnerable to community disapproval. Had he been called in the draft, Milton probably would have been inducted as a conscientious objector and sent to an army training camp where officers and other soldiers would have tried to intimidate him into accepting combat training. But because he was a father and the manager of a significant agricultural enterprise, local officials of the Selective Service System gave Milton an exemption. This, however, created community pressure on him to support the war in other ways. With few other Mennonites nearby, the Brackbill family stood relatively alone in its refusal to support the war. Paoli was two or three hours away from the large Mennonite communities of Lancaster and Bucks Counties in southern Pennsylvania.[2]

"One day," probably in October, "A whole gang of men came to the farm," said Brackbill. "It was kind of a threatening thing. They got after us to buy Liberty Bonds. . . . We took it as a threat. They made it pretty bad for [us]." They used terms like "yellowbellies." The men, whom Brackbill recognized as being from the towns of Paoli and Malvern, represented the "Mainline Christian concept that supported the war." But instead of being intimidated, Brackbill tried to talk with them about the "Sermon on the Mount," which is the foundation of the Mennonite belief that Christians can never participate in war. Milton Brackbill lived assiduously according to Christ's commands to love those who curse you, do good to those who spitefully use you, and to love your enemy as yourself. Yet seventy years later, you could still see a twinge of anger in his eyes as he described the men. "I'm kind of amazed at the stand I took," he told me, "because we had no preparation for this. I mean, nobody was thinking what would you do if this would happen. We weren't prepared for it.

But there must have been enough of a conviction in those things that came to me through my mother." Although the "gang" of Liberty Bond promoters left promising to return, they never did.

Milton and Ruth Brackbill were my grandparents, and their daughter Emily is my mother. I write this history of the Selective Service System during World War I as one whose Mennonite family on both sides has resisted the wartime demands of the United States for generations. But the men of my family have walked a fine line between open resistance and accommodation. Historian Gyan Prakash calls this "practice and negotiation."[3] Subordinate groups in most societies pick their way through the demands of the dominant group, mostly compromising and living according to social expectations, saving outright resistance only for those times when asked to betray their most basic convictions. Milton Brackbill took a principled stand when he refused to contribute to the war effort, by either fighting or paying for it. Still, he compromised with the wartime state when he registered for the draft and accepted an exemption. According to Selective Service policy, men like Milton Brackbill who were married, had dependent children, and produced significant agricultural goods contributed more to the war by staying at home, whether or not they purchased Liberty Bonds. In order to fight the war, the nation needed to have fewer than ten percent of its draft age men actually in the armed forces. What its political leaders wanted with equal urgency was that millions of other men and women work to sustain the existing social order and productive capacity. In this respect, Milton and Ruth Brackbill were not much different from millions of other families who supported the war simply by continuing to carry on their lives as before. With the exception of his refusal to purchase Liberty Bonds, Milton performed as the state expected all white men to: he took control over the course of his own life; he married; with his wife Ruth, he raised five daughters; he became the owner of productive land; and he built a profitable motel business along one of the main highways leading into Philadelphia.

For their part, the "gang" of white men who threatened my grandfather also walked a fine line of practice and negotiation. Going door to door and pressuring residents to purchase Liberty Bonds was one way white men could prove both their whiteness and their manhood, and consequently their entitlement to all the privileges of citizenship. Whiteness and manhood were intersecting identities that, for all practical purposes, defined who was a citizen and who was not at this time in U.S. history. Women of any race did not yet have the right to vote in most states. Black men had recently lost voting rights throughout the South. Federal law denied nonwhite immigrants the right to become naturalized citizens. American Indians only had rights of citizenship if they gave up their collective identities as Indians and assumed private and individual ownership of land. Recent immigrants, coming by the millions from southern and eastern Europe in the two decades before World War I, were forced through a process of cultural cleansing known as "Americanization," after which they might be considered white and their men permitted to exercise the rights of citizens. Yet neither whiteness nor manhood were automatically granted to people who looked white and were biologically male. White men achieved and sustained this status only through continuous performances, through constant vigilance, through struggles for control of productive processes, and by acquiring the power to influence the behavior of others. Christopher Capozzola argues that historically, an "obligation of citizenship" in the United States has been that private citizens participate in "collective policing [for] community defense." But this practice often turned into vigilantism. During World War I, President Woodrow Wilson tried to distinguish between "vigilance" and "vigilantism."[4] To step over the bounds of the former into the latter brought into question one's fitness for citizenship, but so did failure to be sufficiently vigilant. And so the "gang" from Malvern or Paoli was, perhaps, vigilant from the perspective of those who supported the war. But their tactics, verging on vigilantism, diminished them as men in my grandfather's view. He spoke of them with more than a hint of ridicule by referring to them repeatedly as a "gang," and on one occasion as "thugs."

I write this at a time when each U.S. resident must again consider the ways in which our daily choices support or resist U.S. wars abroad. While the nation wages a war with "volunteers," male residents of the United States must still register with the Selective Service System when they reach age eighteen. While there is evidence this volunteer armed force depends heavily on what is in effect an economic draft, eighteen-year-old males require proof of Selective Service registration in order to receive federal financial aid for college. It makes them, in effect, a reserve army, at the same time more privileged than their peers who have joined the armed forces because it's their best economic choice. The Selective Service System remains in place as an institution, lacking only the authority to issue induction orders. Rumors wax and wane from week to week that Congress may resurrect the president's authority to order inductions under the Selective Service System. It is my hope that the histories offered here provide readers a context and new ways of thinking about the deeper personal and collective meanings of these contemporary issues.

The system of military conscription approved by Congress and implemented by the War Department in 1917 helps us to understand the multifaceted nature of U.S. citizenship in the early twentieth century.[5] This plan adopted in May of that year did much more than draft men into the armed forces. It created an elaborate system of exemptions, discharges, and furloughs. By the end of the war, draft officials had classified a majority of the adult male population in the United States, prescribing exactly what function, military or civilian, they wanted each man to perform in service to the wartime state. Over the course of the first year after passage of the Selective Service Act, officials increasingly referred to the fundamental principle of this system as "Work or Fight." Simply put, each able-bodied man between the ages of twenty-one and thirty (or forty-five after September, 1918) must either find civilian employment in work that Selective Service officials approved of or be drafted. In operation, it was much more complex than that. But the slogan itself became a kind of blunt instrument that local police, federal marshals, and private vigilante groups could use to control specific men, teenage boys, and in the South, black women.[6]

This is the first major study of the World War I draft in the United States that examines it at the level of state and local operations. The one important book on the World War I draft published in the past half century, *To Raise an Army: The Draft Comes to Modern America*, by John Whiteclay Chambers II offers an excellent analysis of the Selective Service System at the national level. It provides important political context for understanding what the draft meant to national leaders at that time. I do not attempt here to redo what Chambers has already done so well. Rather, I hope to provide a multilayered portrayal and analysis of what the draft meant to Americans of all kinds where they lived their daily lives in their homes and communities.

The extent to which people had the power to determine their own and others' fate within this system was, in part, a measure of both their manliness and their whiteness. In this system, small groups of white men (tens of thousands of draft officials) made decisions that affected the lives of most other men, and many women, throughout the nation. The Selective Service System dramatically expanded the opportunities for individuals to act out or perform in ways that affirmed both their manhood and their whiteness. These individuals may have been among the tens of thousands who worked as volunteer registrars in June 1917. Or they may have served on one of 4,648 local boards, of which there was at least one for each county, one of the 155 district boards, one for each federal court district, one of the 1,319 medical advisory boards, or in one of 52 state headquarters, including one for each U.S. territory.[7] Or they may have participated in one of the many private or semiofficial citizens' organizations created to help enforce compliance with both the letter and the spirit of the principle of "work or fight."

Technically, the president appointed members of local boards, district boards, and medical advisory boards. But in reality, state governors or their adjutants general made the selections, usually from lists provided by their political contacts in local communities. This meant that, for the most part, local and district draft boards reflected and represented the interests of the existing political and social elite in each community and each state. In principle, service on a draft board was intended to be uncompensated, but the law allowed for special circumstances in which members could be paid for their time. As the national administrator of the system, Provost Marshal General Enoch Crowder, wrote:

> [A]s the duty of all selection boards was to go into American homes and take out for the service of the Nation [sic] our strongest and best young men to send them to the battle lines to incur the risks of a sacrifice which is not and can not be measured in terms of money compensation, so the duty of selection boards ought to be given the aspect of service of the same sort; and that as far as possible this service should be rendered without compensation.[8]

Although federal officials set policy and coordinated the overall operations of the draft from Washington, D.C., state and local officials did the real work of the Selective Service System. Governors supervised "all matters arising in the execution of the selective draft within their states." In fulfilling this responsibility they relied heavily on their adjutants general, who as heads of the respective state National Guards, were the top state military officials. Selective Service regulations gave local and district boards "exclusive jurisdiction" over "the determination of exemptions and deferred classifications," "subject only to review by the President."[9]

For draft-age men, the Selective Service process involved several steps. For most these were: (1) registration; (2) physical examination and interview; (3) classification; and (4) either exemption or induction into the army. Unlike later versions of the Selective Service System in which men registered when they reached draft age (which has usually been eighteen), the World War I system held nationwide registration days. In the first registration, on June 5, 1917, volunteer registrars signed up nearly ten million men. On the registration cards they recorded names, birth dates, places of birth, occupation, "race or nationality," marital status, whether they claimed any dependents, and whether they claimed any significant physical limitations. Another registration day was held a year later to capture all the men who had reached the age of twenty-one since June 1917, and two more were held in August and September 1918. The four registrations yielded nearly twenty-four million registrants. When the local or "exemption" board received the registration cards, its first job was to assign each a serial number. Officials in Washington, D.C., then held a series of public lotteries in which they drew serial numbers ranging from 1 to 10,500, the latter figure being the maximum number of registrants within any one local board juris-diction. The order in which these serial numbers were drawn determined the order in which men would be called by their local draft boards.

The War Department determined how many men it hoped to draft in each of a series of draft calls. Using this number and United States Census population figures for each locality, Selective Service officials in Washington assigned most local draft board two "quotas," or the number of "white" and "colored" men it needed to induct and ship to army training camps. Local boards then called the men in one by one, gave them physical examinations, and interviewed them about their claims for exemption, deferment, or furlough. If a man claimed an exemption on the grounds he worked in an essential industrial or agricultural enterprise, the board would make a recommendation and forward the case to a district board, which had original juris-diction in these cases. Local boards ruled on all other cases. These consisted primarily of claims for exemption based on physical disabilities or that someone else was dependent on them for economic support. A registrant could appeal a local board decision to the district board, and could appeal a district board decision to a presidential appeal board, provided the district board decision was not unanimous.[10]

The law defined two types of Selective Service violators—delinquents and deserters. Men who failed to register or who failed to comply with some other requirement of the Selective Service System prior to actually receiving a notice to report for induc-tion would be reported as "delinquent." Once a local board issued an induction order to a man, officials regarded him to be in the army. Thus, if he did not respond to his induction order, the board would report him as a "deserter." But unlike men who had already reported to the army and then deserted, men who failed to respond to induc-tion orders would not be prosecuted in courts martial, but in civilian federal courts by United States District Attorneys. By the end of the war, local boards had reported hundreds of thousands of men to U.S. attorneys as either delinquent, or deserters who failed to answer induction orders. In the face of such overwhelming numbers, the Justice Department simply ignored all but the most egregious or publicly visible of these cases.[11]

This was a system of and about men, but women (perhaps tens of thousands) found ways to use the system to their advantage. It was also an explicitly racialized system that privileged whiteness. In the communities studied here, all Selective Service officials were white, and it is likely that this was true everywhere. The law mandated separate quotas for "white" and "colored" men, and a complex system of exemptions or discharges based on such things as marital status, fatherhood, and occupation. This meant that the influence that men, as well as women, had over the Selective

Service System was largely determined by their race, gender, and class, or, in other words, by their position within a white heterosexual patriarchal society. Individuals needed to make their interactions with Selective Service officials into scripted performances of race, gender, and sexuality as they jostled with one another and with officials to get what they wanted. Draft registrants should be manly, act white, and show that whatever decision they sought would promote the welfare of a white, male-headed, heterosexual (wives and children were essential) household. This system implicitly racialized manhood as white, explicitly sexualized it as heterosexual (in that married men were privileged over single), implicitly classed it as economically independent (it privileged owners of productive property). While white "manhood" characterized the only people guaranteed the full rights of citizenship, not all white men got what they wanted from the Selective Service System. But draft officials only recognized white men (or white women defending white men) as individuals capable of acting in their own name under the law. Draft officials everywhere assumed that poor white men (especially those who owned no property), nonwhite men, non-Americanized immigrants, and women in general lacked competency to act on their own behalf. Whiteness, manhood, and therefore full citizenship at this time in U.S. history equaled the right to meaningful participation in the decisions that significantly affected one's life. It did not necessarily equal either being a soldier or getting an exemption. President Wilson himself implicitly recognized the inherent contradictions between possessing the agency inherent to white manhood and being a draftee when he tried to downplay the coercive nature of the draft. He denied that the Selective Service System was conscription at all, but rather, in his words, "a selection of the willing."

As a federal system, Selective Service reflected the social order and cultural values prized by property-owning married white men within their respective communities or states. As such, it is an ideal vehicle for comparing connections between race, class, gender, and citizenship in different regions of the country. In addition, decisions about who should be sent to war and who should be kept on the home front were invariably based on material, or economic considerations. White men who owned, or who helped control, the nation's economic resources selected other men for the draft. They did so largely on the basis of three criteria: their physical fitness; their role in the production of material goods for markets; and their position within or in relation to an acceptable white family.

In analyzing the records of the Selective Service System, I have asked basically two big questions: (1) What do these records tell us about race, gender, and class in the United States? (2) How did local histories and traditions relating to race, gender, and class affect the operations of the Selective Service System? This study will show that in the context of the Selective Service System white manhood was tied to control of the material world. The primary function of the state was to provide a social structure that made white manhood synonymous with mastery over the material world (nature), and over other humans whose race, gender, sexuality, or other characteristics marked them as unsuitable for the role of master of the material world. I have tried to take to heart Peter Kolchin's plea that studies of whiteness "include greater attention to historical and geographical context, [and] more precision in delineating the multiple meanings of 'whiteness.' ". . . [12] The evidence in government documents, and other sources on race, gender, and sexuality, that has been left to us from the places and times I explore here can be read as either prescriptions for action, or as the descriptions of things done that constituted performances of race and gender.

This book focuses on four states, Georgia, Illinois, New Jersey, and California, and on four communities within those states. I look at two structural levels of the Selective Service System, the local draft boards, and the state-level apparatus for administering the draft. I examine the social relations of the wartime state as seen through the records of local draft boards, district appeals boards, and the offices of the governor and state adjutants general. I first analyze in detail the political processes by which the Selective Service System was established at the county or city level and how each local draft board went about examining, classifying, and drafting men. Second, I examine the operations of the Selective Service System statewide in Georgia, Illinois, New Jersey, and California, respectively. This permits us to see a larger political and economic environment in which management of the labor force and the control of material production was central to both the war effort and to the struggles between local elites and statewide officials. Here we see how the bodily presence of propertied white men in specific geographic spaces affected their abilities to manage other people and control the production and distribution of material goods. And we see how those who were not propertied white males struggled to acquire a modicum of independence within the framework of this unstable contest among privileged white men. In each of these states the records of the Selective Service System reveal the existence of a paradigm in which property owning, rational, white males personified the state. That state in turn protected their private property rights to the earth and to the labor of others. While there are tremendous variations in the specific ways in which this paradigm was manifested, the paradigm itself was rarely, if ever, challenged even by those whom it most oppressed.

In the last chapter, I examine the final report of the Director of the Selective Service System at the end of World War I. Here I find that the language, content, and structure of this official document confirm my analyses of local and state draft records. In this report, Provost Marshal General, Enoch Crowder, took great pleasure in the scientific nature of his findings. It was explicitly the science of this work that enabled him to represent the economically successful, white, married man who worked in obedient partnership with the state, as the universal human, and the person most fully eligible to exercise the privileges of citizenship in the United States. Through an array of prescribed performances, individuals who exhibited the qualities of white manhood proved they merited these privileges. What counted as meritorious also happened to be what counted as whiteness and manhood.

Prologue: The Local in National Context

From the autumn of 1915 to the spring of 1917, Americans flocked to theaters to see D. W. Griffith's motion picture spectacle, *Birth of a Nation*. Large cities and small towns received the show with civic celebrations as it arrived at train stations in two railroad cars—one a sixty-foot baggage car containing scenic props, and the other a passenger car with twenty or so orchestra musicians who would perform the musical score live as the silent film played. The film told an heroic story of the founding of the Ku Klux Klan at the end of the Civil War. It depicted black men as violent beasts whose insatiable sexual appetites constituted a perpetual threat to southern white women. In this account, white men of the KKK arrived to save white women from black male lust and the American nation from the evils of Black Reconstruction. After watching a private showing at the White House, President Woodrow Wilson proclaimed that every man who sees *Birth of a Nation* is "a southern partisan for life."[13] The film and Wilson's sentiments fused white-middle-class ideologies of manhood, white supremacy, and 100 percent Americanism, and revealed the central role many white men believed the state played in constructing manhood, white supremacy, and enforcing social conformity.[14]

White male supremacy is the bedrock upon which the United States as a nation was founded, and it gave power and legitimacy to the military draft during World War I. It appears starkly and indisputably in early-twentieth-century Georgia. But, as Woodrow Wilson so readily affirmed, it existed virtually everywhere in the United States during the Progressive Era. Woodrow Wilson's statement in 1915 that every American man was a southerner at heart, assumed that all American men were white, and that the Americans who counted were men. The phrase "American man" seems at first glance to refer universally to all citizens, but viewed in its context as a comment on *Birth of a Nation* it is clear that it refers only to particular people, and those people are exclusively white, and male, and proudly racist. In context, there is no room in his brief sentence for women, for people of color, or, for that matter, for white men who lived their lives in poverty or in opposition to the social regimes of race and gender. Wilson, in effect, equated being American with the particular performances of white manhood that either promoted or acquiesced in the supremacy of propertied white males.

Each of the communities studied here had its own specific historical traditions by which propertied white men had established themselves as masters over the natural world, women, and men of color. And as masters they would bring their values, experience, and power to bear on the Selective Service System. In 1917, Coweta County, Georgia, was fifty-seven percent black. It was a primarily rural county dependent on the commercial cultivation of cotton, but with a significant industrial base of cotton textile mills in the County seat of Newnan. Poor white and black people alike in Coweta County, Georgia, labored in cotton fields and textile mills under a system that kept them in perpetual debt and made a small number of local white men exceedingly wealthy. These well-to-do white men unabashedly used the powers of local, state, and national government to maintain this system. Those who resisted often met violent ends. Most people in Adams County, Illinois, depended in some way on commercial agriculture in corn and hogs. Nearly everyone was white, but a large population of recent German immigrants, many of whom belonged to pacifist sects, suffered harassment during the war. In Adams County, white men had used the state to remove the indigenous people and impose a new regime of corn and hog farming that depended upon taming the Mississippi River. The propertied white men of Adams County saw the government as a necessary and beneficial partner. Influential white women helped construct the racial myths that made white men innocent of the violent history that gave them this land. Paterson, New Jersey, is one of the oldest industrial towns in the United States. By 1900 its primary industry was silk manufacturing, which employed large numbers of recent immigrants from southern and eastern Europe. Propertied white men in Paterson mastered their worlds through iron, textile, and silk industries, and a city government bent on increasing control of the lives of adolescent boys, immigrant men and women, and working-class white people. San Diego was the oldest European settlement in California, but the newest of its coastal cities in 1900. It was growing rapidly, its economy driven by real estate speculation, truck farming, and militarization. A majority of the population was white. White men there had struggled for more than a century to master American Indians, Mexicans, Chinese, and Japanese, by treating them as extensions of a complex and dangerous landscape. In San Diego, propertied white men struggled with each other to claim ownership of water that legally belonged to California Indians. This struggle ultimately revolves around one man in particular, who used his role as draft official as leverage in his battle to control water.

A final note about the organization of this book may be necessary to help the reader understand what appears to be some repetition in content. The focus on state and local operations assumes that political boundaries and jurisdictions profoundly shape relations of power—not only those that involve the direct application of governmental authority, but informal social relations as well. In the context of modern nations and states, people function within bounded space. Boundaries, such as city limits, county lines, state boundaries, and international borders greatly affected people's experiences with the Selective Service System during World War I. It is easy to see how such boundaries confined or limited activity. But the presence of such political and legal boundaries also offered individuals opportunities to transgress the law or social expectations. When they passed from one state to another, or crossed an international border it could change what options they had under the Selective Service System. In this respect, draft registrants perhaps had greater agency than draft officials whose official powers were limited to well-defined geographic spaces.

Chapter One
"The Darkness in Georgia"

Historians call the early twentieth century in the United States the "Progressive Era." And indeed, if the records of the Selective Service System reflect the times, nearly everyone in charge of any business or governmental entity seemed to think of themselves as "Progressive." In Georgia, as elsewhere, the basic principles of Progressivism infused the operations of the Selective Service System at every level. Men and women usually appealed to Progressive ideals in their communications with draft boards. A "Progressive" man or woman believed in teamwork and cooperative enterprises and rejected selfish individualism; deferred to the judgment of recognized experts and distrusted raw democracy; believed in the ability of well-organized institutions, whether private or governmental, to solve social and economic problems; admired technology and science, and especially believed that the scientific categorization and classification of all things was essential for understanding the world. In short, they believed that people working through organization and categorization applying the best wisdom of acknowledged experts could bring about "progress" on virtually any problem. It was, in a way, a comfortable new suit of clothes for the old familiar characters of white supremacy and southern patriarchy in the State of Georgia. However Georgia still had a core of rough-hewn individualists—some still in leadership positions—who resisted Progressivism. The Selective Service System in Georgia reveals the nature of these ideological conflicts while showing how compatible Progressivism was with a social order that sustained propertied white males in positions of dominance over everyone else.

By placing federal authority in the hands of state and local officials and then failing to articulate and enforce consistent selection policies, Selective Service officials in Washington enhanced in some ways the existing powers of the white male planter class in rural Georgia. In other ways it transferred power to white men in towns and cities, particularly the capital city of Atlanta. But decentralization and confusion within the Selective Service System combined with the peculiar conditions of wartime to create fissures in the structures of white patriarchy through which black men and women, as well as poor whites, might be able to escape the harsh conditions of racial caste and social class in Georgia. A complex admixture of factors determined who would wield power in wartime Georgia. Geographic location in the countryside, for example, enhanced the power of white male planters over sharecroppers, both black and white, but distance from Atlanta and Washington disadvantaged them in the articulation of policies. But most of all it was the status of manhood that conferred the potential to participate as an effective agent through state institutions. Manhood, as a claimed and selectively attributed identity, functioned as synecdoche, invoking qualities and status positions that placed certain individuals on the privileged sides of dyads of sex, race, and class. To be white rather than black, male rather than female, and in control of significant wealth and the labor of others rather than economically dependent, was to be a man.[1]

The story of two white women who owned a plantation in east-central Georgia may illustrate the possibilities as well as limitations for those who were able to achieve some, but not all, of the benefits of white manhood in Georgia. Pink Anderson and her mother initially welcomed Selective Service policies that seemed to favor the interests of planters. But they soon became angered that the system failed to recognize their right to laborers whom they conceived of as belonging to them. Although the Wilkes County draft board may have recommended exemptions for black share-croppers working on land belonging to the Anderson women, a district board in Atlanta ordered that the men be inducted into the army. The two women engaged in a losing battle with a variety of state Selective Service officials to keep the men working on their small cotton plantation. Thus, Mrs. F. H. Anderson complained to Governor Hugh Dorsey that "Pink had had [four negroes] put in deferred status last March, and we were assured that we could keep them until next November." Apologizing for having "so many young negroes," she explained that their families had been on her plantation since the Civil War. They had put in great crops, "so when the Government offered us these appeal cards we appealed for them." "Why," she demanded, "didn't this Board get my consent before they could reclassify my negroes?" She appended a "List of negroes taken from my farm," demanding that the government return them to her so that their crops would not go to waste.[2]

In many ways the Anderson women behaved as typical planters. They expressed a paternalistic concern for their "negroes," but they also made a proprietary claim on the bodies of black men living on their plantation. They assumed, as did other Georgia planters, that the history they shared with their "negroes" ("since the Civil War") on a common geographic spot gave them the prerogative to speak for them within the public arena of the state. The words and actions of the Anderson women seem to rest on something like the legal concept of coverture, giving heads of households both the right and the responsibility to act in the public sphere for their dependents, despite the fact that in 1918 women in Georgia could neither vote, nor hold elective office. The Anderson women, as women, lacked legal rights to exercise political power even as their ownership of valuable property and control of the labor of dependent laborers gave them some of the independence that many white southerners associated with manhood. If being women weakened their influence with Selective Service Officials, they were then less able than white men of their class to take full advantage of the economic benefits of the wartime state.[3] Neither the privileges of class, nor race were sufficient to secure full access to power or independence of action. Although whiteness and property ownership gave them a bit of a platform from which to defend their interests, they lacked maleness. To be biologically male was an essential element that white property owners needed in order to become empowered with the qualities of "manhood." Only those fully invested with all the elements of manliness could act as citizens fully entitled to compete with other white men in the public arena.

The Anderson case, and many others contained in the wartime Georgia records, demonstrate variations in access to power and capacities for self-determination, which were controlled by interdependent hierarchies based on sex, race, and class in Progressive Era Georgia. Various mixes of these status categories engendered people in relation to the state in very specific ways that largely determined their access to formal systems of power. As in the Anderson case, except in the city of Atlanta, "Negroes," meaning African American men, had virtually no access to formal instruments of power. White persons in Georgia rarely expected, or invited, them to participate in the legal battles over their draft status. To white Georgians, African Americans, male and female, were assumed to be incompetent to act either in their own cause or on their own in the interests of the general polity. The official actors in the case at hand were the Anderson women (because they were white property-owners), the local lawyer (by virtue of sex, race, and class), and members of the local and district boards (all white propertyowning males). On the other hand, the racial status of African American men gendered them as inherently unmanly in the eyes of white officials. To be sexually male did not imply manhood. To white officials, "negroes," by definition lacked capacity for manhood because, among other imputed attributes, they were presumed to be in a perpetual state of political and economic dependency. Black males thus had few avenues for achieving the benefits otherwise accruing to manhood in the South.[4] Yet their presence, more than any other single factor, drove the prime actors in this system to make the choices they made. While many white men also lived in conditions of dependency and political powerlessness in Progressive Era Georgia, nothing conjured up the image of an emasculated male quite as effectively as the word "negro," or its harsher derivative.[5] Repeatedly, it was by reference to the "negro" (and to a lesser extent, to poor white men and white women) that white men of power and wealth defined what they were, what they were not, and defended their rights to high status. In her analysis of racial lynchings in the South during this period, Jacquelyn Dowd Hall observes:

> In a culture that insisted upon work, instinctual repression, and acquisitive behavior, men struggled to separate themselves from nature; what James Madison called "the black race within our bosom [and] the red on our borders" became the repositories for those parts of the self which, in the process, had to be conquered and repressed.[6]

As well, poor white men and white women looked to their nonblackness as an important constituent of what made them special. Thus, their voices speak frequently in the records of the Selective Service System and its related wartime institutions. They call attention to themselves in explicit contrast to "Negroes," against whom they construct an identity of claimed privilege and authority.[7]

In the beginning, the Georgia planter class, and its political henchmen, the county sheriffs, eyed the draft with suspicion as a threat to local prerogatives. In fact, the Wilson Administration threatened many local officials in rural Georgia with criminal prosecution for their refusal to carry out provisions of the Selective Service Act.[8] The principle of selectivity meant that all un-drafted men between the ages of twenty-one and thirty-one would be classified and channeled into government-approved activities.

Revisions in 1918 would further extend the law's reach to nearly every working male over the age of eighteen. It was, in a very real sense, a labor draft as well as a military draft, and planters, to whom labor control was crucial, feared it would intrude on that control. That fear, as it turned out, was unfounded. The peculiar ways in which the Selective Service System functioned with respect to class, sex, and race were well-suited to the needs and desires of rural Georgia's most privileged white men.

Coweta County: The Community and its Local Draft Board

For nearly one hundred years after the Civil War, in the early spring of every year in Coweta County one could see thousands of sharecroppers and tenant farmers toiling behind mules, struggling to control heavy iron plows as they inched across vast fields of red clay and sand. At the start of the twentieth century, as people said, "cotton was king" in Coweta County.[9] Driven by the logic of a market economy and the imperatives of private property, it would have been difficult for anyone simply to subsist on the land as the indigenous Creeks had done only decades before the Civil War. Virtually all farmers grew cotton, whether they chose it for themselves, or whether it was chosen for them by the landowners. Some aspect of the cultivation and processing of cotton provided a living for all but a handful of the county's inhabitants. The demands of cotton cultivation and marketing shaped the relationships of people to one another as well as their relationships to nature. It alienated people from the land, made climate and wild animals the adversaries of humanity, and was the ideological as well as practical foundation for the alienating hierarchies of race, gender, and class. From the household of the poorest sharecropping family, to the formal structures of government; from the ties between planter and sharecropper, to those between tax-payer and public official, the personal and impersonal connections that gave meaning to people's lives all served the cause of men who acquired wealth and power, or of families forced to seek mere survival, through cotton.

The land on which propertied white men imposed the rigid social and environmental order of commercial cotton had been privatized by the white male state through processes of war, the forced removal of the Creek people, and the redistribution of land to mostly poor white men by means of a lottery. Through this process, the state created private property for the exclusive enjoyment and enrichment of white men. As Cheryl Harris writes, "Indians experienced the property laws of the colonizers and the emergent American nation as acts of violence perpetuated by the exercise of power and ratified through the rule of law." The practical and ongoing effect, she says, was nothing less than the establishment, through the constitutional guarantee of property rights to white men at the expense of Indians, of a legal "valorization of whiteness."[10]

A legally free yet economically dependent and practically unfree labor force in late-nineteenth-century Coweta County had its roots in the history of slavery, the Civil War, and Reconstruction. This labor force, constituting a majority of people in the county, sustained the power and well-being of propertied white males. Between 1827 and 1860 the slave population of Coweta County had grown to nearly half the total population. After the end of slavery, the black population continued to grow, comprising fifty-seven percent of the county population by World War I. Most black, and a large portion of white, families made their living cultivating cotton. Most owned no land, and were forced into economic dependency, working as wage laborers, or as tenant farmers perpetually indebted to white men who owned the land and provided subsistence goods on credit. Willie Lynch described the system this way:

> All of my people was farmers. My uncles and aunts, and so forth. Very few owned. Most of the people rented, and that was the reason I never liked farming. That was from listening to the farmers, the black farmers talk about—they used the term settling up at the end of the year, after your cotton had been picked and corn gathered. Corn and cotton then. Cotton was king then as I'd hear them say. . . . But corn was a part of it too. And everything was gathered. Then you went in and settled. So many of the black men, I would hear them saying that whatever you made they took back, you owed, and when you're in the process of putting it in the ground, then you had to go to the people that they had rented their farm from. It required money, you would get food and supplies. So few were able to keep any record of whatever the white man said.[11]

The devastation of the Civil War had also forced many white men who owned small amounts of land to go into debt to northern merchants for basic supplies. When prices paid for cotton were insufficient to pay their debts they lost their land and joined the ranks of indebted tenant farmers and sharecroppers.[12] This was Coweta County's rural labor force in 1917. For all practical purposes, their labor had become the property of their creditors. It was property guaranteed to its owners by the state, as we shall see shortly.

The commercial cultivation of cotton, especially in west-central Georgia where it is a non-native plant, requires intense labor to force the existing environment of native plants, soil, water, insects, and animals to yield to sufficient numbers of cotton plants to make it commercially viable. It is literally a war against nature, although the whole process depends upon nature.[13] Labor in the cotton fields is most intense in the early spring, when cotton is planted, and throughout the fall when it is harvested. But throughout the intense heat and humidity of the summer, cotton requires continuous chopping (thinning of the plants), and hoeing of weeds that would choke them out. It is such miserable work that few would do it without some form of coercion.

The harsh cycle of debt that imposed economic dependency upon many white and black families was sufficient to support the power of the propertied white males most of the time. As Willie Lynch remembered, it just seemed impossible for most sharecroppers to escape their indebtedness to the white men who owned the land, or the white men who advanced them seed, fertilizer, and food, clothing, and shelter for their families on credit until the cotton crop was harvested. They were dependent upon the landowner, the cotton gin owner, and merchants to determine the value of their harvest and to calculate the debt. "You never could quite get enough for your cotton to pay your debts," said Lynch, and so the man who gave you credit last year would offer it for the next on the condition that you planted cotton again.[14]

Preparing for War

Springtime, 1917, found residents of Coweta County facing a war on two fronts, one against the forces of nature, the other against what the nation's leaders told them was a German juggernaut. Cotton farmers, who already suffered from serious drought conditions, now also feared the impending arrival of the boll weevil, an insect that had devastated cotton crops in Alabama and Mississippi the previous year. By May, some were plowing under their rain-starved cotton crops and replanting. Corn planting had been halted to wait for rain.[15] The rains, but not the boll weevil, would eventually come that year, resulting in record harvests about one month later than usual. These vagaries of nature and human responses to them would help shape how Coweta's residents would respond to Woodrow Wilson's selective system for conscripting men to fight in the Great War.

The prospect that the United States might join the European war was not surprising to anyone who read the newspaper in Newnan, Georgia. As early as 1915, Wilson had abandoned the diplomatic efforts of his Secretary of State, William Jennings Bryan, after German a U-Boat sank the British ocean-liner, the Lusitania. Hundreds of Americans on board died. Still, two years had passed, and those who favored U.S. entry into the war knew there was strong sentiment against it, especially among many Democrats, and former Populist followers of Bryan and his southern counterpart from Georgia, Senator Tom Watson. Nevertheless, with the renewal of German U-boat action in the Atlantic in early 1917, it now seemed clear to many that America's entry into the European War was imminent. The propertied white men of Newnan, whose interests and ideology were reflected in the *Newnan Herald*, shifted their public attention from the problems of cotton cultivation and textile manufacturing to patriotic preparations for war. By May, the *Herald* had drummed up significant wartime frenzy among the white middle class and Newnan's wealthiest citizens.[16]

The *Herald* began a daily barrage of stories detailing German barbarities, bemoaning England's weakness against the dreaded Huns, and calling on all patriotic citizens to prepare for war. Newspaper accounts suggest that war fever had seized the town of Newnan. A few white men formed ad hoc militia groups. An officer of the "Newnan Guards," a local white militia group, announced that he would begin "training the young men of the town in the elements of military tactics." (As always then and frequently still, "young men" meant young white men. Even where blacks were the majority as in Coweta County, the language normalized whiteness.) The *Newnan Herald* proposed that men who were too old for the draft form a "Law and Order League for the protection of the town." To lead the League it nominated I. J. Stephens, known as "Uncle Ike," a Confederate veteran "with a war record as long as your arm." Others were advised, "if you can't tote a gun, float a flag." It was reported that the local Medical Association offered some coal deposits it apparently owned in Alabama. Churches, both black and white, said the *Herald*, rallied to the war cause as well. The minister at Central Baptist Church announced a sermon that would tell "How to Meet the War as Christians."[17]

Echoing local ministers, the *Herald* editorialized against people who thought war and Christianity incompatible. It asserted that, "Jesus was not a pacifist." Drawing from an article in *American Magazine* the newspaper recounted the story of Jesus casting money-changers out of the temple in Jerusalem. Jesus here fit the "Progressive" ideology of manhood. Angry at the injustices represented by the "exactions and oppression of the priests . . . he strode into that temple and stood like a young giant among that noisy crowd. . . . His blood boiled. . . . His eyes flashing fire, his little whip rising and falling across the backs of the skulking crew before him, he drove them forward, through the court, under the gates, out in the city streets." It was a show of masculine strength of both brawn and courage against evil people who responded with a most unmanly behavior characterized as "skulking." But that was not all that made him a manly man. Jesus had stood against "the stronghold of special privilege and won."[18] This was the old rallying cry of the Populist movement placed in the mouth of a man who fit the mold of a Theodore Roosevelt. One might imagine the same man charging fearlessly up a San Juan Hill, or looking a Hessian in the eye without flinching. Like any true man, he embraced wholeheartedly a dualistic view of the world that confidently draws sharp lines between good and evil, and then stands courageously with the good in opposition to evil. Recognition of moral ambiguities or the complexities of human behavior leads inevitably to hesitation and an inability to act quickly and decisively in any battle. In the view of propertied white men, such qualities carried both gendered and racial meanings. Weak or indecisive males were both gendered as less than men and racialized as less than white. A pacifist Jesus would have been neither manly nor white. There was no room for ambiguous moral positions or subtle attention to subjective value differences within either the manhood defined by the "Lost Cause" or Progressive war-making.[19] Here the South's elite white men were in accord with the most prominent national leaders. As Oliver Wendell Holmes had said in a Memorial Day address at Harvard in 1895, any man worthy of being called "gentleman" is always ready to go to war when his nation calls, whether or not he understands or agrees with the particular cause at hand. For Holmes and many of his contemporaries the best evidence of manhood had become a man's willingness to go to war even and perhaps especially, when one could not understand the cause. Men like Bryan and Watson, who clung to the old fashioned idea that manliness meant thinking for one's self, would undergo ruthless questioning of their manhood when they opposed U.S. involvement in the war.

Nevertheless, in Coweta County, the antithesis of white manhood was neither unmanly white males nor white womanhood, but rather African American men. White women, especially those attached to propertied white men as their wives, mothers, sisters, and daughters, were essential to and extensions of manhood. White middle-class women positioned themselves in the vanguard of local mobilizations for the war. They acted as essential elements in a racial patriarchy rooted in whiteness, heterosexuality, and private property. White-middle-class women organized and ran a wide range of war efforts including, most notably, the Coweta County Council of Defense. They also functioned as icons in the cultural production of support for the war. For, as posters, political speeches, and other wartime propaganda revealed, masculinization came not merely from fighting, but from fighting in defense of women and their sphere—the home. Posters, especially, presented a visual imagery of war as necessary to the protection of women. Often an idealized female representation symbolized the nation itself for which men died and killed.[20]

"Negroes," on the other hand, represented all that was unmanly to the southern white man. White men perceived them as subservient, not able to control their passions, and lacking in courage and a sense of duty. It is not surprising, then, that African American men were objects of suspicion when white people became concerned about wartime subversion. The newspaper warned people to be on the lookout for "Negroes" posing as Bible salesmen and ministers who had been seen in Birmingham, Alabama, attempting to incite disloyalty among their own people. Readers should keep a close watch for such "alleged ministers."[21] Significantly, however, this warning applied to unknown, unseen "negroes" from another state. As brutal as the effects of racial caste could be in Coweta County, white and black Cowetans lived in close proximity to each other. And while they might not ever have really known their black neighbors, white people in Coweta felt they did. And in the absence of an extreme event like murder or suspected rape, it was not easy to generate serious white suspicions that local "negroes" were a threat comparable to Germans.

Coweta's patriotic white middle class initially focused its xenophobia on the nearly invisible population of Germans among them. Public pronouncements carefully constructed persons of German ancestry as inferior, and therefore dangerous, forms of whiteness. The mass of Germans, as the national propaganda characterized them, resembled southern Negroes in that they were easily dominated by powerful men with evil intentions. But the German leaders, rather than being portrayed as unmanly, were characterized as subhuman monsters. Clearly, neither whiteness nor manhood depended primarily on physical features or biology. You couldn't distinguish a German man from any other white man by looking at him. But German men in Germany had performed in ways that showed them to be deformed representations of whiteness and manhood. And although there was no evidence that German men in Coweta County behaved similarly, a last name could be enough to raise suspicions. Their very physical invisibility made it even easier to incite public paranoia about the silent Germans in the community. Accordingly, the Newnan Bakery fired its German baker, and placed a notice in the paper to respond to rumors that a German baker still worked there. "We haven't had a German baker in 17 months," said the ad. "Our baker is an Irishman. To prove this, try a loaf of his milk bread."[22]

The public display of patriotism in Newnan reached its most emotional peak when a local theater booked what it touted as "D. W. Griffith's big military spectacle, *Birth of a Nation*, for the second week in May. No effort was spared to make this an event to match its showings in the nation's major cities. A twenty-piece orchestra was engaged, and the theater brought numerous additional scenic props to town in a "sixty-foot baggage car." The pageantry surrounding the showing of *Birth of a Nation* became part of the general mood of nationalistic celebrations during the month of May, 1917. The film surely reinforced a tendency of white Cowetans to fuse the ideologies of manhood, white supremacy and "100% Americanism." Viewers witnessed the triumph of all that was white, manly, pure and good against the vilest forces of evil—an effective model for the vilification of the German monster.[23] The association made by the Newnan press between the German as beast and the black man portrayed as beast by Griffith was surely more than coincidental. For just as *Birth of a Nation* asserted that it was the brutish character of the "Negro" politicians that led them to establish the oppressive Reconstruction regime, so the beastliness of German men made them a threat to white men's freedom and democracy. Griffith, of course, provided evidence of that brutish character in the black man's supposed insatiable sexual desire for white women. Thus, local elites attempted to use the same white fears that justified lynchings of black men across the South, including the famous lynching of Sam Hose in Coweta County in 1899, to drum up support for the War.[24]

But how was it that white men could use white racial fears of black men to generate fear of Germans, who by any physical criteria were certainly white? I believe the answer lies in the performative nature of racial identity. Whatever a person's bodily features, skin color, or genealogy, one had to perform whiteness in order to be white. The elites of Coweta County and the local press joined their counterparts elsewhere in the country in cataloguing the inherently uncivilized, and therefore less than white, nature of the German people. The use of Griffith's racist film to generate antagonism for Germany said clearly that Germans simply had failed to perform as white people should. First, as so much of the "100% Americanization" movement indicates, living in the United States and acting as a good American citizen was frequently equated with being white.[25] So in that sense, whiteness was synonymous with Americanism. Before the end of 1917 many German Americans gave up speaking German or eating sauerkraut to prove their American-ness/whiteness. Second, Germans posed an immediate danger to [white] America. In fact, images of Germans that appeared in the U.S. press seem remarkably similar to the images of black men portrayed as threats to white people in *Birth of a Nation*. According to Frederick C. Luebke, Americans "read lurid stories of . . . how innocent Belgium was raped and pillaged; . . . defenseless civilians had been massacred, fiends in German uniforms had amputated the breasts of Belgian women with the stroke of a sword." Such accounts, writes Luebke, were frequently either wholly fabricated, or distorted or embellished.[26] The analogy is not completely appropriate, since there can be no question that World War I saw some of the most egregious examples of pure brutality on both sides in the history of warfare. But President Wilson brought the images to the home front, warning in his December, 1915, State of the Union Address against "infinitely malignant hyphenates, creatures of passion and anarchy [who] preach and practice disloyalty."[27] What is instructive here is the way in which non-culpable "others" within U.S. society were constructed as monstrous dangers to whiteness, especially to white womanhood. Both cases made it a duty of white men to rescue of white womanhood in violent and repressive ways.

The president had publicly legitimized a kind of national social othering that was familiar to middle-class white Cowetans. They would embrace it enthusiastically. A few days before Congress declared war on Germany the Newnan City Council passed a prowar resolution referring to "unlawful and reprehensible aggressions of the imperial German government." Stating that "the rights of the nation and people of the United States can only be protected and maintained by armed intervention," the council urged Congress "to take immediate action to protect [those rights] against said aggressions." Then on April 6, 1917, the day of the declaration of war, the *Herald* praised President Wilson's war message, calling Germany's behavior "intolerable," and "insolent." "Germany's wanton disregard of our rights as a neutral nation [has] reached the limit of endurance," editorialized the newspaper. It went on to predict that with current preparations underway and new ones about to begin the American armed forces would become "a force of such formidableness as will command the respect of even so insolent an enemy as Germany."[28]

During the month of May, 1917, as national preparations for war intensified, the town leaders of Newnan and neighboring communities took steps to see that everyone knew that life-as-usual would be suspended for the duration of the war. Merchants and banks changed their hours of operation. Officials announced that the local baseball league had decided to suspend the season "on account of conditions caused by the war." The weekly sports headlines that had occupied so prominent a place in the newspaper were replaced with headlines of similar wording that now described the real thing.[29]

The attributes of manhood, however, that were promoted in the *Herald*, in public speeches, in theaters, and other formal institutions of elite society did not necessarily represent the ideals and self-image of most young men, white or black, in Coweta County at the outset of the war. It is not easy to determine the attitudes toward the war of those most likely to be asked to fight. But a variety of responses reported in the local newspaper reveal that they had, at the very least, mixed feelings. Some seemed anxious to see combat. Others sought to demonstrate their patriotism in ways less likely to result in injury or death. Still others, the vast majority, made whatever case they could for exemption and waited passively for the local draft board to have its way. What becomes evident in these responses is that a number of other kinds of performance could function to construct a manly identity for many white men even while they served to protect them from having to experience the dangers of war. These included: (1) acting as agents of the state or engaging in other civic activities associated with governing; (2) successfully managing large property holdings in a public manner; and (3) exercising control over dependent individuals, such as women and children, or adults deemed inferior, such as black men and women, or poor whites.

Putting the Local System in Place

On Tuesday, June 5, 1917, with a great patriotic display, the town of Newnan celebrated draft registration day. That morning, Sheriff J. D. Brewster began the ceremonies by raising a U.S. flag over the court house. Until now the court house had not had a flag, but Brewster helped to organize a fund-raising drive to purchase this flag specifically for draft registration day. Unwilling to let pass an opportunity to promote local pride, Brewster and the local company that constructed the flag pole made sure that it was taller than any in Atlanta. As the newspaper reported, the pole was "one inch taller than Atlanta's famous flag-pole at Five Points, about which the newspapers of that puffed-up town have been making so much fuss of late." A crowd estimated by the *Herald* at four or five hundred had turned out. "As the graceful folds of 'Old Glory' floated out in the breeze," reported the newspaper, "a shout went up from the crowd, which mingled with the martial strains of 'Dixie,' tinged the occasion with the spirit of patriotism that would have caused President Wilson to smile clear around to the back of his neck. . . ." With bowed heads the people then listened to a local minister say an invocation. The recently elected state legislator, Stanford Arnold, of draft age himself, then delivered an "eloquent and patriotic address." Nearly twenty-four hundred Coweta men between the ages of twenty-one and thirty registered for the draft that day. Fifty-five percent of them were African Americans.[30]

But few of the men who registered witnessed the patriotic rally that marked the start of registration day in Newnan. Largely rural laborers and farmers, they registered instead with locally appointed registrars located throughout the county.

The draft seemed to bring the power of the U.S. government directly into each home, for an average of one person per household registered for the draft in Coweta County. The U.S. government became a palpable presence in each home with the real potential to alter its material well-being. Certainly the decentralization of Selective Service registration guaranteed that all but the most remote families would know at least one man involved in conducting the registration. From two to four registrars were appointed for each of fourteen militia districts in the county. This meant that few men would have had to travel more than two or three miles to register.

In reality, as with most other government activity, the draft was yet another instance of the influence and power of the town-based middle class and wealthy white men over poorer or economically dependent rural men. The registrars were all white. They were nearly all middle or upper class in their outlook, economic position, and occupation. With new local government positions created by the Selective Service System more middle-class-white men in Coweta County were able to engage in the manly rituals of the state. Once registration was completed, the administration of the draft was left to a local draft board of three, operating in Newnan, and its medical appeal and legal advisory boards, also in Newnan. The social and economic profile of these officials was similar to that of the registrars—white, male, and owners of property.

Although less than twenty percent of the county population lived in towns, nearly all of the men who administered and enforced Selective Service law in the County lived in or very near the county seat of Newnan.[31] Of the eight men who served at one time or another on the Coweta local draft board or its legal and medical boards in 1917 and 1918, only one did not live within the limits of the fifth militia district that encompassed most of the town of Newnan. Twelve of the fourteen militia districts that made up the county had no one appointed to an official draft position other than registrar. An attorney from the Sixth District, W. A. Post, who was a member of the legal advisory board, was the only permanent draft official not living in Newnan. None of these permanent officials made their living exclusively, or even predominantly, from farming, although most received some income from farm operations. The profiles of draft officials contrasted sharply with the majority of Coweta's draft registrants who were black, rural, and landless.[32] More than three-quarters were engaged in farming; fewer than three in ten owned real property.

Thus, each of the white men who administered conscription in Coweta County had personal and political interests in the cultivation of cotton. On the other hand, none of them actually farmed, and the farm land they owned was small compared with the really large landowners.[33] All could be called middle class as well as middlemen in the total system of cotton cultivation and manufacturing. They were professionals, merchants, or politicians. The draft thus became part of a larger process through which the men of the political and economic elite secured the loyalty and cooperation of less prominent yet ambitious middle-class-white men.

Throughout the summer in preparation for the first draft call the local newspaper provided a steady stream of boilerplate and local news clearly designed to inspire patriotism and support for the war and to incite ridicule against those who opposed the war or resisted the draft. The *Newnan Herald* lavishly praised those men who helped to administer the draft. It published the names of those who contributed to the Red Cross Fund and who bought Liberty Bonds, listing the amount of their contribution. Newnan readers learned that "The manly man is the country's need. . . . The world delights in the manly man, and the weak and evil flee / When the manly man goes forth to hold his own on land or sea." But for those who opposed the war or failed to support it with either time or money the *Herald* showed contempt. It targeted Democratic Party leader and former Populist Tom Watson, and Tom Hardwick, a Georgia Congressman, accusing them of "both fighting the Wilson Administration tooth and nail. . . . They have become political bedfellows at last," declared the newspaper. "Now beat the Tom-Toms." It added that any member of Congress "who opposes the Administration in a grave emergency such as now confronts the country is worse than a slacker. He is a traitor."[34]

The term "slacker," while popular nationwide, combined ridicule and moral condemnation. It initially applied simply to men who sought to evade conscription. But it quickly took on broader implications—a label for any man who did not support the war. It suggested that he was loose, lazy, shirked his duties, and generally neglected recognized social obligations. A "slacker" lacked the essentials of Progressive manhood. As gendered ridicule, it was meant to shame a man into supporting the war. A "slacker" had chosen to flout the "legitimate" demands of the state and society. Thus, the character flaw that made him less than a man also made him morally suspect. Although throughout the war women were constantly enjoined to do their part to support the war, people rarely used the term "slacker" to refer to a woman who failed to do her part. It was a term reserved for men.

The Duties of White Women

White women's role in guaranteeing a successful war effort was discussed at length in the pages of the *Herald*. The paper urged women to join the Red Cross, to get involved in programs to provide food and clothing to the soldiers, and most of all, to purchase Liberty Bonds. It was, however, always through the men with whom they were connected that women would find meaning in assisting with wartime mobilization. "Perhaps your boy, your brother, your sweetheart, some one you hold dear to your heart, will be called to the war zone to risk his life," it said. If women fulfilled their duties they would "reduce the danger [to their men] to a minimum, strengthen their spirits, and encourage them to victory." The *Herald* concluded with the admonition to women not to "just sit around and wish for victory, peace and the safe return of the one you love."[35]

White women's prescribed role in the war underlined the popular belief that their activities should always be consistent with the nurturing behavior expected of mothers. A poem published in the *Herald* delineated the contrasts between the proper spheres of men and women. In "The Mothers of Men," an anonymous poet defined men's duties as outward, public, and aggressive. They ruled in the marketplace of both goods and ideas; they held civic offices; and they were expected to participate in the ritualized violent aggressions of war. But the analogous roles for women (whom it explicitly defined as white in this instance) were rooted in the duties of motherhood. Women participated in the production of goods and ideas, they worked for the betterment of society, and they made it possible for men to fight. But they should not do these things in public. "Not with eloquent words of thought from the mouths of wonderful men / but deep in the walled-up woman's heart / . . . the bravest battle that was ever fought / tis fought [sic] by the mothers of men," wrote the poet. And although her battles brought her pain, her bravery was in silent suffering. Her glory was in her "faithfulness." Fighting "in her walled-up town / [she] fights on and on in endless wars / then silent, unseen, goes down." Unlike a man, the woman needs "no marshalling troop, no bivouac song / no banner to gleam and wave. / Oh, spotless woman in a world of shame, / with splendid and silent scorn / go back to God as white as you came."[36] The proper southern white woman would be tainted neither by the violence of man's world nor by the stain of racial impurity. The poem thus also excluded African American women from true womanhood. The white woman needs no external forces to guide her. Within her "walled-up heart" she discovers how to live. There she finds her counterpart to man's "marshalling troop," "bivouac song," or "waving banner." Men's guides are external, not intrinsic to him. Women need only look within.

The elite white women in Coweta County, as in many other parts of the country, supported the war in a variety of ways that seemed to be simply extensions of women's duties inside the home. These included canning, food conservation, and Red Cross work. But more importantly, they participated in the direct enforcement of the Selective Service Act by working through the Women's Committee of the Coweta County Council of National Defense. The Selective Service System relied on County Councils of Defense, and particularly the women's committees, across the nation to assist draft boards in carrying out their work. In particular, they maintained surveillance of draft-age men to make sure all registered and that those called responded. Thus, on the first of August, 1917, the wives of several wealthy Coweta white men had met at the County Club in Newnan to establish a local chapter of the Women's Committee of the Council of National Defense. They elected Mrs. Mike Powell chairman. The Powell family had large rural landholdings that were undoubtedly farmed by tenant farmers and sharecroppers. Mr. Powell owned 1,138 acres of land in Coweta and Mrs. Powell held another 135 acres in her name. But the Powells also lived in the town of Newnan on property listed in Mrs. Powell's name. As wealthy town residents it is likely that they shared the values expressed by the *Herald*. The other officers of the committee also lived in Newnan and were married to men who were either professionals or merchants. They thus came from the same social class as the local draft officials.[37]

The Coweta Women's Committee of the Council of National Defense consisted of representatives from a host of local women's organizations. Mrs. Powell represented the Crochet Club. Others represented the Mothers' Club, the Civic League, the United Daughters of the Confederacy, the Daughters of the American Revolution, the Women's Christian Temperance Union, the Reading Circle, the Sewing Club, the Ladies' Benevolent Society of the Presbyterian Church, and local Woman's Missionary Societies affiliated with the Methodist and Baptist Churches. The Women's Committee did attempt to enlarge its representation to include the rural communities in Coweta

County by asking prominent white women in each militia district to help coordinate the work of the committee. In addition, it named Miss Olivia Young to represent the mill district. Young taught at a school that had been established for mill children in the village of Sargent about ten miles northwest of Newnan. Thus, she would probably not have been well known to the mill workers in Newnan where most of the county's mills existed.[38]

Mobilizing the Black Community

Despite white domination of important positions and the exclusion of African American males from the "manly" things according to community standards, a few prominent African Americans supported the community mobilization effort. Some black churches took up offerings for the Red Cross, passed resolutions urging their members to cooperate with the draft, and supported the Liberty Bond drives. In this, perhaps they were influenced by the advice of national black leaders such as W. E. B. Du Bois and Booker T. Washington, who urged black communities to support the war. The *Herald* usually noted these efforts in brief reports that acknowledged and thanked the churches for their support, but in so doing also recognized that the African American people were not part of the collective effort of the white community to support the war. For example, the newspaper reported with no fanfare that "Rev. J. J. Griswold, colored, pastor of Jehovah Baptist church at Grantville took up a collection Sunday for the Red Cross fund and raised $11.63. . . . The donation is hereby publicly acknowledged, with the thanks of the chapter."[39]

But the *Herald* ran few such notices. Whether this indicates lukewarm African American support or disinterest on the part of the *Herald* in recognizing efforts in the black community is difficult to determine. The Council of National Defense had advised local Women's Councils, such as the one formed by white women in Coweta, to organize sub-councils of "Negro women." But there is no evidence this happened in Coweta County. Very likely, the absence of significant evidence of black leadership in mobilization within the black community is due to several factors. First, any mobilization efforts among African Americans simply reaffirmed their political subordination to whites. Second, organizations such as the Council of Defense were primarily surveillance groups designed to identify and shame individuals who they thought did not sufficiently support the war effort. African Americans in Coweta County, according to Willie Lynch, always sought to avoid inviting anyone linked to white authority into their communities.[40] Thus, it is not likely they would have welcomed a Negro Women's Council of Defense that was supervised by the white Women's Council. Third, mobilization programs such as Liberty Bond drives asked for financial support from a community that had little money. It seems that financial support from blacks came mainly from members of the tiny black middle class in Newnan. Finally, it is not unreasonable to assume that the black middle class in Newnan had ties to the larger black middle class in Atlanta, only forty-five miles away. And as we will see later in this chapter, black leaders in Atlanta became disillusioned with the war early in 1918. They, along with other black leaders around the state began to demand restored political rights in exchange for their support of the war, which of course, white Georgia would not agree to.

The Draft Call

Once the draft board completed registration and began its long summer of processing registrants, the local theaters joined the *Herald* in keeping up the enthusiasm for the war. Beginning in July the Halcyon Theatre announced that it would be running a weekly series of "war pictures . . . giving graphic scenes of the operations in the great war." Later in the war so-called Four-Minute Men might deliver patriotic speeches at the beginning of such films.[41]

During the three months between registration and the first inductions, the local draft board processed and numbered the registration cards, keying the order of registration according to the numbers drawn in the national lottery held in July. Then in the first week of August the board began to call men in large groups to appear at the local board offices for physical examinations and to hear their arguments for exemption. It called 506 men to appear on August 7, 8, and 9. Out of these it hoped to certify 253 for military service. Dr. Woodroof, the physician member of the local board, and six other local doctors who volunteered to assist him screened each man for physical defects. Those who passed the physical then went before the other two members of the board if they wished to claim exemption.[42]

In three days the board examined the 454 men who responded to the call and heard their claims, allowing ten to fifteen minutes for each man. One third (152) failed the physical examination. Of the remaining registrants, two-thirds (205) requested exemption from military service. Only eighty-seven made no claim for exemption. After making their claims in person to the local board, the claimants had ten days in which to gather affidavits in support of their case and present them to the board.[43]

The *Herald* met the approaching day when the first Coweta men would be conscripted with constant reminders that participation in this war would mark one as a man of the highest order. Those chosen would be "the fortunate ones [who would face] the armies of autocracy and oppression." Promising that they would be counted as the best men the county had to offer, the *Herald* characterized the men to be drafted as "our chosen ones; the pick and flower of our manhood, whole of body, sound in mind and spirit." They should not go "as reluctant victims of misfortune or a fatal chance, [for] you are to fight in the noblest cause in which man ever took up arms." And the nation, symbolized by the universal female, was now always referred to by the feminine pronoun. The nation stood for the mother, the wife, the girlfriend, the purity of white American womanhood. The nation was "the most generous in all the world to her soldier sons. . . . She trusts you; . . . and whether you return or not she will hold your names in honor and grateful memory until the end of time."[44] Yet the large number of white men who sought to be excused from going to war suggests this rhetoric failed to convince many men to try to prove their manhood in Germany or seek comfort in the bosom of a collective woman.

The local town leaders, therefore, worked hard to make heroes of the first men drafted and to remove any stigma that some might attach to being a conscript. By September 6, 1917, when the Coweta County draft board was ready to send its first draftees to camp, twelve men gathered at the Newnan Court House at nine o'clock in the morning expecting to be put on a train for Camp Gordon, Georgia.

Instead, to honor their first draftees, the local board had arranged to provide these men a "sumptuous" dinner at a local hotel. Then, with bells ringing and whistles blowing, the fire department led a procession of twenty automobiles around the town square. Following the festivities the caravan carried the men fifty miles to Camp Gordon. Each car displayed a banner that proclaimed "Coweta is with her boys." They were the only Coweta draftees so honored.[45]

The collective and individual identities of these men symbolized the contradictions of a society based upon rigid observance of racial segregation. For these men, and all of the men in the first three draft calls from Coweta County, were white. Local as well as regional customs forbade placing white and black men on the same train cars. The federal government, sensitive to the concerns of white southerners, arranged to have African American men transported and trained separately. It issued special draft calls for them as well. Local draft boards throughout the South which had large numbers of African American registrants assumed (correctly) that the War Department was mostly interested in the rapid induction of a large army of white men. Some would probably have announced their "Negro" calls (as they referred to their "colored quotas") in September if there had been no problem negotiating schedules with the railroads for transporting racially segregated draftees. Provost Marshal General Enoch Crowder therefore ordered Georgia local boards to send forty percent of their white quota in the September calls and thirteen percent of their "Negro" quota in one group at the beginning of October. Roughly following these instructions, the Coweta local draft board sent one hundred forty white men to camp in September and sixty-three African American men on October 5, 1917.[46]

The timing of this policy could benefit cotton planters in the county who were otherwise in danger of losing valuable laborers at the peak of the harvest season. It gave them time to adjust their schedules and look for replacements. Many men in the fall drafts of both 1917 and 1918 were not essential to the cotton harvest. In addition, the local board liberally exempted men who had dependents, greatly reducing the number of men who might appeal to the District Board for agricultural exemptions.

Yet, for several reasons Coweta County's white male leaders were not as concerned with preserving the rural labor force as many cotton belt counties were. First, even though cotton prices reached record highs in 1917 and 1918, many of Coweta's largest planters had begun to focus their economic efforts more on the cotton textile industry, merchandising, and banking. Thus, they could stand to lose laborers and income from cotton cultivation better than planters deeper into the cotton belt whose enterprises were less diversified. Second, boll weevil infestation and severe drought in 1917 reduced the cotton harvest in many parts of the county. Third, unlike some neighboring counties, Coweta had experienced little if any exodus of African Americans either to other southern areas or to the North. But finally, the most important reason may be that the District Appeal Board for Northern Georgia established a policy in the fall of 1917 that granted temporary "discharges" (deferments) to farmers to enable them to complete gathering the harvest. While most of the cotton belt fell within the jurisdiction of the District Appeal Board for Southern Georgia, Coweta was in the Northern District. This board took action tailored to the peculiar conditions of cotton growing in northern Georgia when it set December 1, 1917 as the end of the temporary discharges for farmers. When the state Adjutant

General, Joel B. Mallet, questioned the Board about this late date, the chairman responded that the farmers in northern Georgia "cannot possibly finish gathering their crops before December first . . . on account of the late opening of the cotton."[47]

By December, military training camps overflowed with draftees. Selective Service officials ordered inductions halted until the bottlenecks could be cleared. They took advantage of this lull to revise procedures and devise a new classification system. This interlude came only two weeks after most temporary farm discharges had expired. Those who managed to avoid the draft for those two weeks, therefore, had about two months before they again would have to worry about being called. In December, January, and February the local draft board sent a new and detailed classification questionnaire to all registrants. On the basis of this it created new records for each of its registrants who had not been drafted and declared delinquent any who failed to return the questionnaire. It then began again the procedures of hearing claims and examining registrants. The first calls under the new classification system were issued for February 23, 1918. Most of the 1917 registrants thus experienced both systems, but those with extensions should have been the first contacted in 1918.[48]

The cases of two African American men caught up in both the 1917 and 1918 Selective Service systems show how the two systems functioned, and illustrate how the Coweta County local board regarded African American men. These cases show first that neither the local board nor national Selective Service officials saw the drafting of black men into the army as a high priority. They show further that the Coweta County local board members did not regard "negroes" as having agency, or the ability to make decisions and take action on their own cases. And finally, they suggest that the local board regarded "negroes" who worked outside the immediate production of cotton as irrelevant, or inconsequential—so much so that it really did not matter whether or not they cooperated with the Selective Service System.

Marvin Kirk was a twenty-one-year-old African American man with no wife or children. He worked as a farm laborer and lived in accommodations rented from the farm's owner. Neither at the time of registration nor at the time of his physical examination did he seek exemption. The local board certified him available for service on August 11, 1917, and had he been white there is no doubt that he would have been among the first of Coweta's draftees sent to Camp Gordon. In the draft lottery Kirk's serial number drew a lower order number than most of the men drafted from Coweta County in 1917. Yet they never drafted him. Although Kirk had an order number of 395, the Coweta draft board reached all the way to order number 1283 to fill its 1917 quota. This was simply a result of racial quotas. In order to fill its white quota, the board nearly had to exhaust its entire pool of available white registrants. But the highest order number reached in meeting its 1917 "colored" quota was 364. Under the new classification system established in December, 1917, the local board classified him III-A, as "a man with dependent children (not his own), but toward whom he stands in relation of parent." Accordingly, Kirk could not have been drafted until all men in classes I and II had been called. Since class I-A was never exhausted, he was in no danger of being conscripted.[49]

Johnnie Poach, another African American, age twenty-one, worked for Benjamin L. Redwine, the uncle of draft board member Lynch Turner's wife. Poach was single and gave his occupation as "laborer." Unlike Kirk, Poach could not read or write.

The disadvantage of illiteracy when faced with a bureaucratic system such as the Selective Service would be hard to overstate. Poach was certainly dependent upon his employer and other literate persons around him for information and advice as to his rights and the legal demands the draft would make upon him. Like Kirk, Poach escaped the draft in 1917. But once the new classification system was put into effect the local board quickly classified him I-A, or the highest level of liability to the draft. The board mailed him an order to report for induction in February, 1918, with the first contingent of African American men drafted from Coweta under the new system. He did not report to the local board as ordered until seven weeks later, yet the board never reported him as delinquent. Board members surely knew Poach as an employee of Lynch Turner's uncle and they likely already knew Poach's family condition and work situation. According to the 1910 census, B. L. Redwine employed both Poach and his father in "home crafts." At that time, the Poach family of six rented a home, possibly from Redwine, but they were not farmers. Whatever the "home crafts" were, they were not likely either seasonal in the sense that farming was or essential to the financial well-being of Redwine in the way that a tenant farmer, sharecropper, or farm laborer might be. Like other white men of his class, Redwine did believe that he had a right to control the lives of his employees. For example, in April, 1917, he had placed a notice in the newspaper warning the public "not to harbor or give employment to one Smith Price, colored, as said Price is under contract to work for me the present year."[50]

Facing the draft without the benefit of a white patron, and unable to read instructions on the draft forms, Poach never appealed the board's denial of his dependency claim. It may well have been that there was no validity to his claim, or that, as in other cases, the board told the registrant that he had no chance of success and he accepted their judgment. But without support from his employer Poach had little chance of successfully challenging whatever decision the board made. The district board rarely overturned the decision of a local board to deny a dependency claim. The local board treated Johnnie Poach as simply a "non-essential Negro." But, on the other hand, the army was not pressing the Selective Service System for more black soldiers. To some southern boards, probably including the Coweta board, large numbers of African American registrants seemed only to be clogging up the system and delaying inductions of needed white men. The board thus was not likely to be concerned when an African American man whom it knew well did not appear the first time he was called. Quite simply, it was not worth Redwine's effort to help Poach avoid induction, but neither was it terribly important to the draft board when he was drafted. The only reason the board did not draft him earlier was that it had not reached his number, 379, in filling its "Colored" quota. Those with power to make decisions affecting Poach's life were arrayed against his efforts to secure exemption, but in the end it did not matter very much to any of them.

In the next section we turn to the broader, and more complex picture of the statewide operations of the Selective Service System. It is still, for the most part, made up of local stories, but ones that also tell us something about the whole state structure of the draft. More importantly, they offer telling insights into the power of white manhood and ways in which people challenged that power in Georgia in the early twentieth century.

The State Selective Service System in Georgia

In the spring of 1918, the States Division of the Council of National Defense in Washington, D.C., received a pessimistic report on mobilization efforts in Georgia. The federal investigator bemoaned "the darkness in Georgia," where few of the wartime programs seemed to be functioning as intended by Washington officials. Among rural white men in some parts there was outspoken resistance to both the war and the Selective Service System, especially on the part of the renegade antiwar and antidraft Democratic leader, Tom Watson and his followers. There was cynical manipulation of wartime programs by the most powerful white men in the state. There were high rates of apparently unintentional noncompliance with the draft by African American men, and apparently fraudulent drafting of physically unfit African American men by the white men who sat on the local draft boards.[51]

A system that assumes, as the Selective Service did, both literacy and geographic stability among its constituents, and that depends upon the mail to disseminate and receive information, easily runs aground in regions where illiteracy and mobility are both common and mail delivery can be controlled by employers. Draft boards in Georgia frequently had to rely on planters not only to deliver draft notices to the men who worked for them, but to read the contents to them as well. Even then, many addressees would have moved without notifying the draft board. It did not take planters long to realize what advantages these conditions offered them. Planters who controlled the mail of their sharecroppers or wage hands could also control when and if those men would be drafted. If they withheld notices until the men were declared delinquent, planters could also receive a reward for turning them in to the authorities. This system reaffirmed paternalism and enhanced the planters' existing leverage over the draft-age men working for them. For their part, sharecroppers continued their frequent moves in search of the best possible situations.

Reports of delinquency ran high in Georgia and other southern states.[52] It was highest among African American men, and officials in Atlanta and Washington soon thought they had an explanation. In a letter to the Provost Marshal General, Georgia's officer in charge of Selective Service, Joel B. Mallet, stated it baldly, at first blaming the frequent moves of "negro" men:

> The farming industry is largely carried by the white farm owners who employ ignorant negroes, by the year. It is customary for these negroes to move from farm to farm each year. . . . They are very ignorant, and seldom receiving mail never think of leaving their forwarding addresses with the postal authorities. As a consequence, many of these negroes have not received their Questionnaires or orders to appear for physical examination, and are, therefore, classed as delinquents.

But Mallet went on to blame planters as well. He complained that appeals to employers to assist local draft boards in spreading information had "not received the response that [they] should have. . . ." To correct this situation he urged legal sanctions against employers who failed to cooperate with Selective Service officials.[53] Mallet's second point would be confirmed later that year by an investigation at Camp Wheeler, Georgia. But even as he appeared to challenge planters' rights to control African American men, Mallet constructed his own claim to power through reference to the undifferentiated and volatile other of "ignorant negroes" whose custom was to move "each year." That custom, which might be viewed from the "negro" perspective as a struggle for self-improvement, becomes in the hands of government officials a confirmation of black male inferiority and the need for closer white male supervision of "negroes." His memo appropriately signified a conflict among privileged white males, one group in the metropolis in direct control of state mechanisms, the other in the countryside, but the ideological ground of battle was a mass of dark male humanity constructed by state discourse as ignorant, unsteady, careless, and perhaps carefree—male, but unmanly. Yet, Mallet's memo is edged with a paternalistic tone, calling into question whether or not the farm owners are genuinely concerned for the well-being of their dependents. It thus not only denies the manhood of black men, it implies manly failure on the part of the suspected planters.

This racialized and gendered struggle for power is further revealed in a series of investigative reports on African American men charged with Selective Service violations. The conflict was expressly about state action to achieve fairness for African American men. But its true meaning is belied by the arena in which it was fought (one officially closed to African Americans), the terms and categories that defined its parameters, and the men who imposed these conditions on the process. Again, white men in the metropolis benefitted initially by the locus of the discourse in Atlanta and the ability to define the terms and categories. Planters, however, won in the long run because they were located geographically at the actual site where power was constructed in relation to black males. Eleven African American males from the cotton belt had been accused of delinquency and brought before the commanding officer at Camp Wheeler, Georgia. The inspector general concluded that in every case the delinquency "was attributable to the ignorance, isolation and conditions prevailing in out of the way locations." He found evidence that the local boards had been "careless" in their attempts to reach all draftable men in their jurisdictions.[54] Equally important, each defendant testified that he relied upon a planter not only to bring him his mail, but to read it to him as well. Thomas Johnson described his experience with the draft as follows:

> On Saturday, the man whom I worked for, Mr. E. D. Stubbs, of Hahira, Ga., came to me and said "you had better go to the court house, they sent you a card and are talking about coming after you." I immediately went to the court house in Valdosta, walking all of the way, except being given a lift enroute by a wagon. I, immediately upon arrival at the court house, went into sheriff Passmore's office and asked him if he had sent me a card, and he said yes, and told me to sit right there until after dinner. After dinner the deputy sheriff carried me down to the jail, and on Monday Morning he brought me to Camp Wheeler, with hand-cuffs on. As a matter of fact, I never received any notice to report for military duty. . . . [55]

In a Lowndes County case, Charlie Hawkins reported his unsuccessful attempt to secure the assistance of his employer in answering the draft call. When Hawkins received his draft notice his boss agreed to take him to town the next morning. But when Hawkins arrived at the appointed time, his employer refused to see him and had his wife tell Hawkins that he would be unable to go. Lacking money for railroad fare, Hawkins told the investigator "I did not know anything else to do, except let them come after me." Three days later the sheriff arrested him on charges of delinquency and delivered him to Camp Wheeler as a deserter. Similarly, after the sheriff arrested William Lester of Telfair County and took him to camp as a draft evader, Lester swore that he only received mail through his employer and that he had never received any mail from the draft board.[56]

The testimony given by these men suggests that planters conspired with local draft boards and county sheriffs to control the release of black sharecroppers to the army according to their own convenience. Then planters would have the men arrested and delivered to the army camps as "slackers," for which the army provided a fifty-dollar reward. In each of these cases the draft board notified the sheriff that a man was delinquent within a day or two after he received his first notice. The sheriff then arrested the delinquent and delivered him to the closest military camp and collected the $50.00 reward from the camp commander. This delinquent reward system encouraged sheriffs to participate in the planters' scam.

Federal officials in Georgia concluded that sheriffs, planters, and local board members cooperated in the process and split the rewards. Consequently, the U.S. attorney in Savannah declined to prosecute any of the accused draftees. Since there were virtually no such cases involving white draftees, the commanding general at Camp Wheeler called on the government to investigate the possibility "that negro drafted men are being deliberately exploited in some sections." The general suspected that most of the charges had been manufactured to enable the sheriff to collect the reward. "If this be the case," he wrote, "the negro is being greatly imposed upon and the government defrauded."[57] This paternalistic expression of concern for "negroes" under his charge had little effect, for after further consideration, both state and federal officials, chose not to confront the planters' manipulation of the system. After all, in at least half of Georgia's counties, planter cooperation was essential to the drafting of white men.

Under the influence of planters, then, the Selective Service System operated with little effective legal oversight. In some of Georgia's cotton belt counties, local boards simply refused to draft farm laborers until the harvest was over. Boards openly defied the demands of the state and national Selective Service officials that they meet preset quotas in September, October, and November. Several boards pointed out that the 1917 harvest was not only especially large, but that in some areas it might not be completed before December. Many provided only partial "colored" quotas. Some tried to fill them with men who had obvious physical defects or who were social outcasts. The Provost Marshal General complained in December, 1917, that Georgia draft boards sent more physically unfit men to military camps than did any other state. A memo to Mallet indicated that most of these men were "negroes," and implied that many boards resisted sending healthy and hard-working African American men.[58]

Nevertheless, in Georgia as a whole, the number of African American men requested in the first draft was only a small fraction of the total call. In fact, as noted above, in October Washington ordered the boards to call forty percent of their quota of white men and only thirteen percent of their quota of African American men. Most boards should have had little trouble meeting the latter call since African American men were less likely to have been exempted or deferred.[59] In counties with a large number of African American men, the larger quota for whites meant that some boards would have to call all available white men. The experience of the local board in Coweta County, which sent its full "colored" quota on schedule, illustrates the extra burdens placed on white men by the federal policy. Although fifty-six percent of its registrants were African American and nearly all of these were certified available in August and September, 1917, the board called only forty African American men in 1917, while calling 110 white men.[60] Still, some local boards regularly failed to meet their "colored" quotas while filling their white requirement. By December 1917, Camp Gordon, which received most of Georgia's "colored quota" reported that "more than six thousand colored men," out of nine thousand total due in the fall drafts had "not been called to date."[61]

In some parts of the cotton belt planter fears of a shortage of African American workers were shared by the moderately well-off yeomanry to whom a cheap reserve labor force was also important. Many enthusiastically offered their sons to the draft with the understanding that African American labor would remain available. Military service, they believed, as well as patriotic behavior in general, was a sure mark of true southern manhood and should be reserved for whites.[62] Thomas Lee, of Forest Park, complained about the absence of his son only after he perceived that the large African American farm labor force in his area was depleted. There is "no one here but me to gather [the cotton crop]," Lee wrote to the Georgia Council of Defense. "All the Negroes have gone to the army and to public works."[63]

Lee was only partly correct. The army made an insignificant dent in the supply of African American males available for rural labor. Furthermore, African Americans had little hope of increasing their presence in Georgia's homegrown industries such as textiles.[64] But if they were willing to endure the close scrutiny of their social activities that the police in Georgia's towns and cities were sure to impose, the newly opened armaments manufacturers, which lacked the racial traditions present in older Georgia industries, offered to some an escape from the perpetual dependency of sharecropping. This became a serious concern on which elite white males were unified. Planters and statewide officials in Atlanta believed that a flood of African Americans to wartime industrial jobs would pose a serious threat to the southern caste system. Even if African American men were offered little more than hope that such industrial opportunities would open up for them, social relations in rural communities would be altered and the racial caste system of the state threatened. Hope itself was thought to be subversive.[65]

Georgia's political leaders feared that once African American males had experienced the higher pay and greater freedom associated with work in war industries, or the self-respect that might accompany military service, they would also demand greater social and political freedoms. Price Gilbert, chairman of the Georgia Council of Defense, fumed early in the war that even respectable "negroes" were more interested in taking advantage of the flush of prosperity to press for social equality and political rights than in winning the war.[66] The only solutions immediately obvious to Gilbert lay either in higher returns to African Americans for farming, or the imposition of social controls. The first solution carried the same danger that well-paying jobs in industry offered—better living conditions that would give African American men a greater sense of their importance, and thus threaten planter dominance.

The white men who served on the Georgia Council of Defense hoped to find a solution to this dilemma while ensuring that the draft law would be enforced throughout the state.[67] They would have been skeptical of economist Gavin Wright's argument that racial segregation in southern industries can be explained by market dynamics. They firmly believed that without government assistance in controlling the labor of black males, market forces would erode the racial caste system. This system provided both a process through which elite white males gained a sense of their own manhood and as a structure to divide and control laborers. Wright asserts "that racial practices of employers were almost completely unregulated by law in the southern states. Explicitly racial laws enforced segregation in public conveyances, marriage, schools, places of public accommodations, amusement, and burial, but not employment."[68] But the Labor Committee of the Georgia Council of Defense made it clear that one goal of racially specific laws was labor control. And they were particularly concerned with black males, whose leisure time and geographic mobility had to be restricted in order to preserve their dependent status and compel them to labor full time.

Addressing the question of higher pay for what it characterized as "common labor," the State Council of Defense complained to Washington that something had to be done to contain the cost of farm labor or Georgia's social fabric would be jeopardized. This was mostly framed as a problem of race—or more precisely, of "negroes," meaning African American men—although the Council in a sense racialized and gendered some white men as both less than white and less than men because they acted in ways generally attributed to "negroes." According to the Council, many able-bodied males, both black and white, chose not to work full time, or worked in nonessential occupations, creating a shortage of workers for war-related work. In April 1918, the Committee on Labor of the Georgia Council of Defense asserted that "a portion of the common labor of the State is shirking and we have a great many slackers among them." Committee Chairman H. M. Stanley, who was also the State Commissioner of Commerce and Labor, estimated that employers had on hand up to fifty percent more laborers than they would need if there were some way to compel full-time labor of all help. He advocated strengthening the existing vagrancy laws, not in order to put people to work "on the rock pile," as he put it, but in order to place them "where their labor is most needed." In what can only be interpreted as approval of existing peonage practices, he sent letters to local judges throughout Georgia advising them to parole men arrested as vagrants to work for farmers in the surrounding countryside. Stanley argued that the "most serious question with respect to Georgia is to get the common labor that we have to make a crop, work in fertilizer factories, etc., and even to work on municipal and government contracts." In a tone consistent with the condescension implied in the common practice of referring to black males as "boys," he added that the exodus of labor was hurting the state, because "a free ride to Hadley's Bend, Tenn.," appeals to the common laborer. "Getting away into a new country, jumping his debts., etc., also appeal to him." Other committee members agreed. "The skilled laborers of the State give very little trouble," said Sam J. Slate, the State Game and Fish Commissioner. "It is the ordinary laborers who are delighted with and seize the opportunity to be drifting from place to place."[69] He had drawn a portrait of the "common laborer" as childlike, immature, unstable, and unreliable—a "boy," and most decidedly in deliberate contrast to himself as a responsible white man.[70]

Member Ross Copeland suggested a plan that was reportedly being tried in his home town of Augusta. The situation there was serious, said Copeland because "two-thirds of the population are laborers and 33 1/3 per cent of that population is idle." To correct this the Mayor was requiring that each laborer carry a card signed by his employer "certifying that he is regularly employed." The card had to be punched weekly to show that the worker remained employed. Slate agreed that other towns in the state ought to take similar action. But to increase the effectiveness of the plan all Georgia towns should "close up the pool rooms. . . . There are many idlers and loiterers," he said, "who waste their time in playing pool and loafing around pool rooms during work hours. This is true of both negro and white laborers." Committee members from Rome and Toccoa said that such programs were in effect in their towns and had been found useful in keeping men from loafing during the daytime. All agreed with Slate that the Georgia vagrancy law was inadequate and that additional measures to keep men working fulltime were required. The Commissioner of Agriculture, J. J. Brown, repeated the commonplace assertion that Georgia's idlers were immune to monetary inducements, making state coercion necessary. The committee agreed and passed a resolution, which was sent to all Georgia municipalities, urging them to pass ordinances that would require any person found loafing, idling, or loitering around hotels, pool rooms, or other public places to provide proof "that he is regularly employed during the customary work hours."[71] They had constructed an "other" that was lazy, nonproductive, prone to frivolity and playfulness while a world war raged on. Such an image was foundational to their claim of superiority as men who were themselves none of those things. They were deadly serious about working and fighting, and making important decisions for other persons who were presumed inherently inferior and permanently childlike.

Farm Furloughs for "Negro" Soldiers

Two auxiliary programs of the Selective Service System took some of the burden off of the Council of Defense Labor Committee and seemed to promise even more effective solutions to the supposed labor crisis. At the same time, they would expand the channels through which elite white men could impose their will on a subordinate population. The first was a system of Farm Furloughs; the second was essentially a work draft known as "work or fight." These combined easily with the existing traditions of labor coercion and social control.

In March 1918, Congress amended the Selective Service Law to permit army camp commanders to furlough drafted men to farms for short periods during planting and harvest time. Like many wartime programs, the farm furlough program had an informal beginning, and an irregular operation. Selective Service officials in 1917 had temporarily released some farm men to complete their harvests.[72] In Georgia, camp commanders were formally granting furloughs under the new program as early as April 1918. Selective Service headquarters in Washington, D.C., had announced the program that month and established quotas for each state.[73] Although policy-makers in Washington said they had set up the program to relieve individual cases of hardship rather than to correct the rural labor shortage, state and local officials seized upon it as a way to maintain the farm labor supply while adding yet another vehicle for controlling African American men. In addition, commanders at some army training camps, where African American draftees were more likely to be considered excess baggage than soldier material, may also have welcomed the program. In fact, a report carried in 1917 by the *New York Age*, a northern black newspaper, lends credence to suspicions that the furlough program received its first impetus from the concerns of federal officials in Washington about what to do with drafted black men. In August 1917, the *Age* reported that Major General Leonard Wood proposed creating farms of 120–150 acres at each southern cantonment to be cultivated by troops thought to be "especially fitted" for that work. The newspaper assumed this meant "negro conscripts."[74]

From April 1918, when formal procedures were announced, until the end of the War, the Council of Defense, local draft boards, and the state Selective Service Office processed hundreds of furlough requests. Some local boards enthusiastically adopted the program while others ignored, or perhaps were ignorant of, it. The Floyd County local board in the upper piedmont was typical of many. In late summer it sent a frantic note to Atlanta reporting that it was entirely out of farm furlough applications and requesting a new supply at once.[75] The local board for Jones County in the cotton belt sent word "that practically every drafted man from this county both white and black, being about 90% farmers and farm hands, are asking for farm furloughs." The board commented, "We appreciate the need for soldiers and also the need for farm production."[76] Still, some communities remained unaware of the program. In mid-August, for example, the chairman of a county council of defense in Sylvania, Georgia, wrote to the Georgia Council of Defense asking if such a program existed.[77] Georgia Selective Service officials did not establish regular procedures for applying to the program until August 2, 1918, but there is little evidence that this made much of a difference.

When the Bureau of Farm Furloughs, established in August under the umbrella of the Georgia Council of Defense, began to coordinate the application procedure it promised to provide expert guidance and efficient management of the labor supply for the fall harvest. The bureau sent local draft boards standardized application forms. It asked applicants to complete the form and secure affidavits from at least "two men not related to [the] applicant or soldier." They then had to secure the endorsement of their local board before sending this material to the Bureau of Farm Furloughs in Atlanta. The presumption was that [male] neighbors and the local board would be familiar enough with local conditions to spot fraudulent claims and stop them before they could be sent to Atlanta. In reality, this meant that traditional community controls on farm labor were strengthened. Those who relied heaviest on farm laborers often were, of course, the political and economic patrons of the local draft board members.[78]

But by September the program was left primarily to the discretion of camp commanders, and it became even more arbitrary. Since their primary interest was in providing men to fight, commanders were not always concerned with needs of the communities around them. Their responses to furlough requests thus turned as much on military considerations as on local labor situations. Still, it appears they sought to appease influential local white men. Most camps cooperated enthusiastically while a few shunned the program. Camps Gordon, near Norcross, and Greenleaf, at Chicamauga Park, granted furloughs readily on the basis of recommendations either from local boards or the Bureau of Farm Furloughs. However, Camp Wheeler, near Macon, at first flatly denied all requests for furloughs. It would later furlough men upon the request of several large planters, but it bypassed the Bureau. The Commander of Fort Screven, near Savannah wrote to the Bureau in August, 1918, that "the country is now engaged in a great war which must take precedence over crops and all other matters. . . . The furloughing of a single soldier at this time for more than a few days is out of the question."[79]

Racial considerations may account for policy variations among commanders. In practical terms a racially weighted policy would benefit large-scale white planters at the expense of the white yeomanry. At the beginning of the war Camp Gordon was designated to receive the bulk of Georgia's African American draftees. Although by the summer of 1918 most of the other camps were also receiving African American soldiers, they received far fewer than Camp Gordon. But the army's demand for African American soldiers was never urgent because of official reluctance to use them in actual combat. More than fifty percent of Georgia's draftees were now African American, yet a segregated army had little use for them. In addition, throughout 1918 Fort Screven's white soldiers were preparing for imminent shipment overseas. It is not clear why Camp Wheeler remained unwilling to cooperate with the Bureau of Farm Furloughs, even when it had an excess of African American draftees, but its position is consistent with its adversarial-style relationship with Georgia's local draft officials on other issues as well.[80] One would be tempted to credit this commander with principled opposition to such an exploitative program had he not later chosen to supply African American draftees directly to several planters, circumventing the prescribed procedures.

Although most furloughs seem to have been granted to African American draftees at the request of planters, the majority of surviving applications came from white farmers. The application records provide a glimpse of Georgia's poorer white farmers and ways in which they constructed themselves relative to the wartime state in racially gendered terms. They reflect the burdens of manhood felt by white farming men for whom support and protection of the family was paramount. In their correspondence with Selective Service officials they focused very narrowly on the practical concerns of preserving an existing family-centered way of life. At the center of these concerns was a constant, palpable awareness on the one hand of their own inferior status relative to the white men to whom they were writing, and on the other, to the presence of "negroes" as a category of other males to whom their own well-being was somehow connected and whom many of them feared or resented. They understood the terms by which government officials defined manhood, and many phrased their appeals in those terms. Many recognized their duty as white men to offer their sons to the nation, frequently combining pleas for the release of their sons with statements that they did not want them to be "slackers."[81]

Most applications seem to have come from relatively poor white farmers who either owned a small amount of land or rented their farms. Their correspondence depicts a rural wartime population consisting of several groups: white fathers deprived of the essential labor of their sons; white women forced to do the work of men and deprived of the support and protection of their husbands, sons and fathers; and black men who were essential to the rural economy but viewed as an increasing threat in the face of the declining presence of white males. Black women and their children are largely invisible. The letters were often written on scraps of paper, many in pencil. The English is awkward and the spelling often phonetic. Appealing for the return of a son, John H. Ferguson of Talbotton described the hardships caused by his son's absence:

> Me and his mama are both old and in bad health, and no one to see after us at all,,[sic] and he left a big two horse farm to see after, and no one to see after it for me and one hand to gather it. . . . The farm is two miles from home and his crop is going to waste,,[sic] Wish you would find out where they sent him,,[sic] wish you would do everything you can to get his furlough.

A woman from Fayetteville pleaded with Governor Dorsey to help secure a furlough for a man who had "a farm and two little motherless children."[82] R. C. White, from Suwanee, said that because of his illness and advanced age he could not work for more than half a day, yet the draft board took his only son and "they carried him to camps just the same. Now we are just poor renters and [k]now only farming. Now what are we to do with our only plow hand gone?"[83] A farmer from Coolidge felt torn between economic necessity and the possibility that social scorn would follow early release from the military. He "didn't wish for his boy to be a slacker nor shirk his duty as a citizen," but having him home for the harvest would certainly also help the country "in this trying time."[84]

There was often a sense of distance between these farmers and authorities that is missing from the letters of middle-class people.[85] Despite having three sons in the army, R. W. Grow of Colquitt gave the local draft board a letter addressed to "His Excellency, Hugh M. Dorsey." Grow desired a furlough for his son James, who was stationed at Camp Wheeler, Georgia. Two of his sons had volunteered, one of whom died in training. A third had been drafted, forcing Grow to take "my two sons under 15 from school to fill the place of regular field hands." He had

> released all men subject to the service, filling in women where possible. The Boll Weevil, causing an exodus of labor, the Military Draft striking the rural districts much heavier than the towns, and taking that age of men who do the most and best agricultural work, has left this section in a crying need of labor.

He had tried selling products other than his primary cash crop of peanuts, such as lard, meat, and corn, on the local market, but had no success because the merchants "were also farmers and had these things on their own farms."[86]

But the issues were not solely economic. White women who lived in rural areas often feared being left alone without a white man to protect them from the dangers they imagined African American men posed. Mrs. E. R. Griner of Daisy, Georgia, said that she needed to have her son returned to her "as I am needing him both for protection and dependence I am here with three girls and no protection surrounded with negroes no whites nearer than one and half mile I am afraid to stay home at night. . . . I can't get anyone to work at two dollars per day."[87] R. O. Moore of LaGrange voiced a similar concern for his brother's wife; he wrote that she was living two miles away, had no one to gather the crop, "an [*sic*] she cant stay there at night alone. . . ."[88] Since the voices of African American men are scarce in these records, and those of African American women virtually mute, we are left to wonder to what extent black women whose male relatives had left felt vulnerable to impositions, sexual and otherwise, from the white men remaining in the countryside. For a century after the Civil War, southern white men's sexual access to black women was virtually assured by the legal system. Between emancipation and 1969, not a single southern white male was ever convicted of raping, or attempting to rape, a black woman.[89] Just as the absence in the court records of black women's complaints against white men for sexual violence will not sustain a claim that white men did not rape black women, the absence of their voices in the furlough records should be seen as little more than an acknowledgment on their part that the system did not exist to respond to their needs. In all likelihood, most blacks stoically recognized that state institutions, as instruments of wealthy white men, were implicated in organized violence against them. By contrast, many poor white men signified a perhaps naive belief that state institutions would protect their interests. They failed to recognize that in the eyes of those who ruled, their poverty and relative dependency diminished their manhood, called into question their whiteness, and consequently limited their enjoyment of the full advantages of citizenship. It suggested something akin to the presumed natural status of the "negro."[90]

Thus, the most successful furlough applicants were wealthy white male planters whose full citizenship status as independent men conferred upon them both legal and extralegal privileges denied to most Georgians. They submitted applications, not for themselves or their sons, but for the replacement or return of sharecroppers and laborers, almost always black men, who had been drafted. They usually requested more than one man. On several occasions, groups of planters submitted requests along with predictions of dire consequences if they did not get their laborers. One of the earliest such requests was made by four farmers in Screven County, even before Congress had authorized farm furloughs. The drafting of single African American men with no dependents caused special hardships, the planters said. It took away their most productive workers—what they called their "wages hands." These were more valuable than either tenants or "croppers," who were usually married and thus worked less and required more.[91]

Echoing the views of the Georgia Council of Defense, these planters argued that it was foolish to expect a "negro" to behave according to the standards of white manhood. "You must be aware," they wrote, "that the negro only labors to gain a livelihood, and when he has made enough to exist on his efforts cease. . . . By no stretch of reasoning or imagination can he be induced to exert himself from patriotic motives." Lacking the internal discipline essential to manhood in Progressive Era America, the "negro" surely could not be expected to reach the fullest expression of manhood—that which was achieved by white men only through willing service to the nation. Reading similar complaints made by British colonial officials against native workers, Edward Said has pointed out that such observations "commodified [the workers] and their labor and glossed over the actual historical conditions, spiriting away the facts of drudgery and resistance." But beyond obscuring the workers' reality, such accounts also "spirited away, occluded, and elided the real power of the observer, who . . . could pronounce on the reality of native peoples as from an invisible point of super-objective perspective."[92] Similarly, members of the planter class claimed superior, objective, insights into the being of "Negroes." Such planters included the Anderson women, who grounded their rights to, and responsibility for, dependent "negroes" in a common history in a [colonized] place. And their own being was constructed out of what the "negro" objectively was not. For planters and colonizers the function of objectivity has been to name and scrutinize at arms' length that which is genuinely other. What could be identified as most unlike the observer, then, was what might be most objectively "known," and through "knowing," controlled.[93]

"Knowing," then, the uselessness of expecting patriotic service from African American men, planters could imagine no alternatives to using wartime programs to prevent them from leaving agricultural work where they would be under the supervision of white men. But although the argument was couched in terms of patriotic service, these planters had clearly identifiable economic interests that were threatened when the war economy offered new opportunities to African Americans. Thus, the Screven County planters warned that drafting "the single men has a tendency to so diminish the size of our wages farms [sic] as to make their productiveness almost negligible." And the effect would cascade down through the rest of the black labor force. They reported the additional loss of the seasonal labor of "negro women, old men and children. . . . growing out of the giving of pensions to so-called dependent negroes." The Screven County petitioners urged the War Department to furlough their "negroes to enable them to make and harvest their crops." Without such action, they predicted, farm production "would be decreased at least 30%."[94] This amazing document also permits us to imagine the voice of the subordinated population by reading against the grain and by interpreting the silences. Not only do we see African American women, their children, and old men making work choices in violation of the rules of rural Georgia, but we also witness working-age African American men claiming them as dependents. It suggests the existence of a hidden transcript of resistance and desire for collective self-determination. To the planters, it was an untenable situation. Persons whom they claimed as their dependents, according to Georgia traditions of paternalism, now claimed their own dependents. The planters were incredulous.

By mid-1918 such requests were commonplace throughout Georgia. The apparent arrogance of a peanut farmer in Mitchell County who in September "urgently" demanded "a detachment of colored soldiers for a period of thirty days to assist in saving this crop," makes perfect sense if we understand him as a white man who believed that his right to citizenship partly rested on his duty to care for, control, and secure production from dependent individuals, and on his ability to translate performance of this duty into economic independence. Many others like him circumvented the bureaucracy. In the late summer of 1918, for example, a committee of planters from Bibb County, in the cotton belt, arranged a meeting with the commander at Camp Wheeler near Macon. They demanded that he furlough large groups of African American soldiers to help pick their cotton. As a result, Camp Wheeler reversed its previous refusal to grant furloughs. As one newspaper reported, "one hundred Negro soldiers from Camp Wheeler [Georgia]" were furloughed "to pick cotton around Macon in Bibb Co."[95]

Many planters requested that specific African American draftees be furloughed, and in so doing, claimed proprietary rights to them. In August, Pink Anderson, who had already lost four tenants to the draft, wrote: "Another one of [my] negroes was called to war and left this morning for Camp Wheeler." Anderson added that she had arranged for the local board to recommend a furlough for this particular man. As was the case in her attempts to secure agricultural exemptions for her four workers drafted previously, there is no indication that this draftee had any involvement in the process, or that he wished to be furloughed.[96] The case of Solomon Lee, an African American sharecropper from Statesboro, was similar. The day after he was drafted, the owner of the land Lee was farming applied for "a farm furlough for Solomon Lee, Col., [sic, colored] who was carried off yesterday with the Bullock quota in present call. He was working a share crop for me, and I have no one to put in his place."[97] Local officials defended such practices on the grounds that African American laborers were incapable of applying on their own behalf. The sheriff of Mitchell County reported to the United States Department of Agriculture that the serious shortage in farm labor in his region was due to the fact that the draft had taken a disproportionately large number of African American men. "Now—a majority of these laborers drafted are ignorant negroes and cannot go about getting out themselves—they cannot file applications—someone will have to do it for them," he asserted.[98]

The many complaints about the farm furlough program came mostly from the white yeomanry, who perceived the large number of African American furloughs as preferential treatment. Many thought this was the reason that they or their sons had been denied a furlough. They had heard about the cases in which large planters received groups of African American men on furlough. Criticism, however, focused on the furloughed African American soldiers rather than the favorable treatment afforded the planters. Relying on a report he had read in the local newspaper, R. W. Grow, who had lost three sons to the draft and had been denied a furlough for one, found an outlet for his frustrations in an attack on the African American male population of the state. Focusing on the two things he possessed, which he believed qualified him to claim the full privileges of citizenship, Grow emphasized his whiteness and his contribution of three sons to the army. His maleness was not mentioned, but it was surely as a male that he assumed paternal responsibility for his wife and children. And in defending the rights of his sons to special considerations by the state, Grow conflated whiteness and manhood. He was less able to identify what it was to be white (Anglo Saxon) than to state how it was unlike being a negro. He had read that furloughs were being granted "mostly for negroes, who came home wearing the uniform, [and who] believing themselves free from arrest, shot, murdered and committed Larceny." Grow proposed to "grant furloughs to men of character, and thus supersede the necessity of such complications." Unlike negroes, by implication such men would understand the limits of freedom, be law-abiding, and not have the urge to murder and steal. They would be white. "Any one knows," he insisted, "that the Anglo Saxon as a race is superior in character to the Mongolian [sic]." He predicted that without the help of his drafted sons he would "not be able to harvest one half of the [peanut] crop which is made."[99]

Grow's basic charges had some validity. While most applications were from white farmers most of the men being furloughed were "negroes." On the other hand, this was hardly a favor to them. Few of the furloughed African American men had any reason to desire a release from military service. Army pay combined with allowances for dependents exceeded what they could hope to earn picking cotton, and the army withheld pay from soldiers on furlough, depending upon planters to pay the going wage.[100] Regardless of the preferences of either black or white draftees, the racial policies of the army itself would have made it easier for a commander to release African American than white soldiers. According to the furlough regulations, commanders could not release men who were in training, or about to be in training, for immediate overseas duty.[101] Because southern Congressmen had objected to ordering white and African American men into combat together, the army placed all African American combat troops in one division, the 92nd, and when they were sent to France, brigaded them with the French army. This severely limited the demands of the army for African American soldiers while increasing the need for white soldiers. Compounding this was that white draft age men were fifty-nine percent more likely to be given an exempt or deferred status than were African American men. As Emmett J. Scott, the African American Special Assistant to the Secretary of War reported, "proportionately more Negroes were drafted than was true of whites."[102] Under such conditions camp commanders would not have felt that the African American soldiers under their command were important to the war effort. In addition, most of the recent African American draftees were held at southern camps where the potential for racial conflict with white residents was real. Violent confrontations between white residents and black soldiers had left seventeen white people dead in the streets of Houston, Texas, and resulted in the execution of thirteen black draftees and life imprisonment for forty-one others.[103] Commanders of southern camps, therefore, must have welcomed the chance to limit the number of African American soldiers under their jurisdiction by furloughing them to pick cotton.

"Work or Fight"

But the furlough system only reached a small number of men and did little to address the issues of social control that concerned white men such as those on the Labor Committee of the State Council of Defense. Georgia's political elites, therefore, enthusiastically endorsed a 1918 amendment to the Selective Service regulations that gave local draft boards the authority to induct immediately any draft age men in their jurisdictions who were not working at jobs judged essential to the war effort. This provision, called "work or fight," also permitted local draft boards to order men to work in specific jobs or face immediate induction. Some boards that had experienced difficulty meeting their quotas now simply issued induction orders to men pursuing unsanctioned occupations. But it appears that "work or fight" served primarily as a labor draft. Nationwide, according the Provost Marshal General, it "was in large measure self-executing, the prompting of conscience and the pressure of public opinion causing thousands of men to seek productive employment without awaiting notice from their local boards." Local boards ordered an additional 118,541 men to change jobs.[104] In Georgia draft officials used the "work or fight" law to assist in the coercion and control of African American labor.

The federal law inspired Georgia's politicians to enact their own version. The governor and the labor committee of the Georgia Council of Defense drafted a proposal that the legislature approved. The result was a law that looked much like a

Georgia vagrancy law. In many jurisdictions the Georgia "work or fight" law was used interchangeably with vagrancy laws to assert greater control over black labor, male and female. With high wages available in the war industries around the state and the farm labor shortage improving the potential economic leverage of rural laborers, many middle- and upper-class white Georgians echoed the Council's complaint that laborers, especially African American laborers, were spending less time at work. Domestic workers in particular became scarce in areas close to war production plants. Many African American women whose husbands now earned enough to support them dropped out of the wage labor force. The chairman of the Mitchell County Council of Defense complained that "the allotment for support allowed by the government to the wives, sisters and other dependents of the negro soldiers has made it well nigh impossible to get the negro women to do anything of value on the farms." But he predicted that the situation would improve with the "work or fight" law.[105]

The Georgia leglislation went significantly beyond the federal law. It applied to all male residents of Georgia between the ages of sixteen and fifty-five. Failure to be "regularly engaged in some lawful, useful and recognized business, profession, occupation, trade or employment" was declared a misdemeanor, and made a person liable, not for induction, but for arrest and possible imprisonment. In addition, enforcement of this law would be local and according to the judgment, or perhaps whim, of the local sheriff or police department or the political patrons who controlled them. Having sufficient income or independent means to support oneself was no defense. Any law enforcement official who failed to enforce this law would be guilty of a misdemeanor.[106]

African American leaders in Georgia were quick to express distaste for the law. "This bill has stirred up the colored people throughout the state," wrote a minister in Atlanta. "Already large numbers of people are speaking of leaving Georgia," he added.[107] The African American community in Atlanta was credited with persuading state legislators not to include women within the provisions of the law. But the same group lacked the clout to prevent the bill from passing. It was also powerless to block the local "work or fight" ordinances passed in many Georgia counties. Many of these did permit the arrest of women who either were not working or worked at jobs sheriffs and local draft boards found unacceptable for black women. The stresses that the war had placed on social relations brought the state into the business of overt control of the labor of African American women. As historian Tera W. Hunter has pointed out, leading white men and women in Georgia justified use of "work or fight" ordinances as a way to force more black women to take on domestic work on the grounds that it "facilitated the entry of white women into war production."[108]

Walter F. White, who toured Georgia for the National Association for the Advancement of Colored People (NAACP) in 1918, reported that both the state law and local ordinances were being enforced only against African American men and women. He told of an African American woman in Macon who was charged with not working. Her argument that her husband made enough to permit her to stay at home with the children did not impress the court, which fined her $25.75 and ordered her to either find a job suitable for a "Negro woman" or leave Macon. The town marshal in Pelham ordered an African American life insurance salesman to find another job, as he did not think that selling insurance was a proper occupation for a

Negro. A part-time laborer at the fertilizer plant in the same town was ordered by the marshal to stop selling life insurance on the side and go to work full-time at the plant. In Wrightsville and Bainbridge local "work or fight" ordinances applied to women as well as to men. In Columbia County the ordinance forbade one "Negro" to work for another. White concluded that "many employers of Negro labor in the South utilized the national emergency to force Negroes into a condition which bordered virtually on peonage."[109]

As a result of White's investigation, the NAACP began a campaign across the South to abolish state and local "work or fight" laws. An NAACP member in Bainbridge, Georgia warned the city council that attempts to use the "work or fight" ordinance to force black women to work "would bring about a race riot." According to Hunter, the issue invigorated the NAACP, "bolstered black resistance and increased the NAACP's southern membership."[110]

The Georgia "work or fight" law demonstrates several characteristics of government in Georgia. It shows, first, the informal nature of government there. Second, it illustrates ways that law functioned to support personal relationships of domination and subordination. And third, it suggests ways in which race-specific laws could alter the social functions of gender. Technically, this law should never have been enforced. The state attorney general ruled it was unenforceable because the governor had failed to issue a proclamation establishing which employment was "necessary and essential," and because the legislature had not appropriated money to enforce it. Yet, throughout the state officials did enforce the law. It did not matter that in a technical sense the law did not exist. It existed *de facto* because local officials said it did and because they personally had the power to act upon that basis.[111]

"Negro Man Rights" and The Duties Of Citizenship

Illegal enforcement of the "Work or Fight" law was apparently still not enough for the Georgia Council of Defense, whose primary concern had been with preserving a stable, obedient, and dependent labor force in cotton cultivation. The state chairman, Judge Price Gilbert, continued to fear that expanded job opportunities in Georgia as a result of the war would lead to a loosening of the social and economic restraints on the African American population. Finally, seeking assistance from black leaders against such dangers, the council organized a Negro Workers' Advisory Committee made up of "respectable" African American men from across the state. In a letter to Clark Howell of the Atlanta *Constitution*, Gilbert explained that the purpose of the advisory committee was to make sure that the flush economic times did not result in less work from rural African Americans:

> We hope to get more and a better quality of labor from the negro. . . . He is not simply to labor until he has acquired enough money to last him two or three days and then knock off until he spends it, but he is to labor six days in the week regardless of whether he needs the money, because the Government needs his services in useful labor. Equally important with this is to teach him the value and sanctity on his contract which he has made with his employer to labor. . . .[112]

When Gilbert wrote this letter, he was fresh from a stormy meeting with one hundred of those white-approved African American leaders called together to help create the

Negro Workers' Advisory Committee. The constitution adopted by this committee declared that it would secure "from Negro laborers greater production in industry and agriculture for winning the war. . . ."[113] President Wilson's Director of Negro Economics, George E. Haynes, who was a Booker T. Washington protegé, presided. Haynes warned Georgia officials to keep word of the conference from spreading beyond those invited to participate. "We do not care for a great deal of agitation about this conference," Haynes wrote to the Georgia Commissioner of Labor.[114] Judge Gilbert was the featured speaker. He lectured the gathering on the importance of keeping the Negro labor force in its place as a patriotic duty to the nation in time of war. "Every man who makes a contract to labor six days and then works only three, is a slacker in just the same class as a deserter from the army," Gilbert told them. It was the duty of "Negro leaders" to see that there were no slackers among their people. Holding forth the promise of better conditions after the war, Gilbert said that better relations between the races "depends upon how [Negroes] measure up to their duty during the present crisis. . . ," adding that "the present is no time for a race or faction to get its feelings hurt."[115]

But some of those in attendance apparently were unimpressed. Gilbert complained in a report to the Secretary of Labor that they were interested "in calling for benefits accruing to them, but were somewhat negligent in making any promise, or even favoring improvement on the part of labor."[116] In another letter he reported that "this meeting had seized upon the occasion for negro laudation and the furtherance of self-ish interests. The attention paid to them by the Government seems to impress them with the idea that now is the time to strike for individual betterment."[117] In virtually all of his voluminous correspondence regarding this meeting, Gilbert repeatedly returned to this theme. Better relations between the races, he advised patronizingly, depended upon African Americans recognizing "the binding force of contracts" and "improving the condition of the morals of their race," developments that Gilbert and his allies, based upon what they "knew" about "negroes," were confident would never occur.[118]

A few African American men in Georgia were willing to promote Gilbert's agenda. E. W. Garner wrote Gilbert that "I hold myself at your orders as a representative of the Negro people of Jeff Davis Co. Should there be any orders to hand down to my people I shall be glad to do so."[119] H. M. Hubbard, principal of the Forsyth Normal and Industrial School, County Training School for Colored Youth, responded to Gilbert's invitation to attend the meeting by saying "the Negro is patriotic and must contribute valuably [to the war effort]."[120] These few individuals were not sufficient to ease Gilbert's racial fears. In fact, he appears to have ignored all such correspondence. Those African American correspondents to whom he did respond frightened him. G. W. Uphshaw, for example wanted to know "how long we must do all you say for us to do educatively, industrially, morally, etc.," before regaining the right to vote? Upshaw, a black farmer from Cartersville, then laid forth why "negroes" had earned the rights of citizenship:

We are giving our sons and money to help save this country for democracy. We are doing all in our power, and all you ask on all lines. What do the government ask the Negro to do that he fails. Look at our boys, under arms, look at every demand that you make of us don't we fill it, yes but can't vote for bailiff. Some of us went North. You folk don't like that, but we want better treatment. Is it fair for us to pay every tax emposed upon us, meet every requirement of law for the protection and safety of this country and then not allow to express our desire as to who shall rule. We Negroes don't think its fair.

Gilbert's curt response that "we are not much concerned with matters of this kind at present," drew a lengthy discourse from Upshaw enumerating the qualities that should confer upon him the status of manhood and therefore citizenship: Payment of taxes, service in war, financial contribution to the war effort, and contributions to the general economic well-being of the state. Despite all this, wrote Upshaw, "we . . . are deprived of our man rights." "Restore to us our citizenship," he demanded. Acknowledging the legitimacy of maleness as one requirement for full citizenship, he went on to deny that race was a valid criteria for exclusion: "We want to vote as men. . . . Men of a race that cannot vote can't seemingly get his justice in law against the voting race no matter his claim."[121] Gilbert did not respond to the second letter, but he was obviously alarmed at the prospect that there were others like Upshaw in Georgia.

Haunted by the specter of black male masses in Georgia escaping from the bonds that held them in perpetual dependency, Gilbert and the Georgia Council of Defense emphasized that the Negro Workers' Advisory Committee had no authority to act on its own. The white-only county councils of defense were to supervise closely the Advisory Committee chapters in their communities. The councils should stress to the African American population the primacy of cotton production. On September 4, 1918, Gilbert asked Hooper Alexander, the U.S. attorney in Atlanta, to investigate "a negro that is giving lectures to the colored population tending to promote undue race ambitions." Alexander responded that he had previously investigated the negroes of Georgia and found "no disloyal purposes . . . , but rather a purpose to insist upon certain rights to which they conceived they were entitled under the laws of Georgia, and of which they claim they are deprived." Gilbert demanded specifics as to "the rights to which they conceived themselves entitled," but Alexander dodged the question and told Gilbert that the Bureau of Investigation would make further inquiry.[122]

There was a role for white women, as well, but it was not to be as participants in legal and regulatory activities as the Anderson women had hoped. Instead, according to the Council, "white women [could] accomplish much individual work . . . with Negro women who work for them."[123]In other words, white women should use whatever influence they had with black women to persuade them to remain at work in those jobs the white male elite deemed appropriate for their race and sex. By entering the fray over the draft status and labor of black men, the Anderson women had gone beyond the role envisioned for them by Georgia's wartime leaders. These wealthy white women and their southern white sisters would shortly achieve legal, if not necessarily effective, political equality with white men through the Nineteenth Amendment. But the disfranchising laws that had applied to African American men kept African American women from making similar political gains. The increased independence achieved by many African American women in Georgia during the war also inspired them to demand suffrage in 1920, but that right would be brutally denied them.[124]

Conclusion

The end of the war in the fall of 1918 would relieve neither Georgia's rural labor crisis nor the racial fears of whites like Price Gilbert. So, as Georgia's elite white men had modified the programs of the Selective Service System to make them consistent with existing social relations, after the war they continued to seek solutions to their labor problems through traditional coercive measures.[125] By January 1919 the nationwide war-related labor shortage had turned to a surplus in twelve states. But throughout the South, a shortage of "common labor" continued.[126] The Georgia Council of Defense planned a meeting in 1919 to consider the problems of demobilization. Its leaders thought the rural labor crisis was the most important issue facing the state. S. J. Slate summarized the situation: The military had taken 50,000 men from Georgia's rural areas; in the years immediately preceding the war the state had lost more than one hundred thousand farm laborers due to boll weevil infestation. Uncounted others had been drawn off the farms "by the high price paid by the government for common labor." Finally, he claimed that "negro women, wives of soldiers, practically have ceased to be of any help" in producing crops because of the $30.00 monthly allowance they received from the government. The most important consequence was that the war had changed the expectations of many African Americans in Georgia, and the state would have to move to contain these expectations quickly if it were to avoid serious conflict. "The negro in my opinion," wrote Slate, "will have to be taught firmly and kindly his position and our citizens will have to realize also that in the general prosperity of farming the negro will have to have a share."[127] To continue to view "Negroes" as distinct from "citizens," despite their participation in the war effort, and still to consider them in need of careful guidance from white men, was, in reality, an important way for Slate and his fellow elite white men to construct their own manhood.

But the prosperity did not much outlast the war, and Georgia's farm economy sank into depression long before the rest of the nation did so in 1929. In the 1920s, many more white farmers fell into sharecropping and peonage. Under such conditions hope dimmed for African American men and women that their wartime expectations might be met. If some of the coercive labor mechanisms in rural Georgia seemed to weaken under the pressures of wartime exigencies and the greater competition for labor, in general they survived the crisis. Many oppressive institutions emerged strengthened from the war years, in part because the wartime state affirmed the legitimacy of manhood as a system of domination constructed not only by sex, but by race and class as well. Despite the highly publicized migration of African Americans to the North, only a few Georgia counties experienced a decline in farm labor as great as one percent. Lynchings, chain gangs, peonage, and other means of controlling the South's dependent men remained important elements of southern society in the 1920s.[128]

This history suggests that there was little distinction between private power and public, or state, authority in Progressive Era Georgia. The apparatus of the state there did not exist apart from the private social and economic interests of elite white men. Especially in rural Georgia, the state was an extension of the informal social relations by which dominant white males justified their exercise of power. White men who controlled government institutions could ignore white women, such as the Andersons, who tried to exercise political power. In vain, poorer white men, relatively feminized by both poverty and political disempowerment, like R. W. Grow, held tightly to whiteness and their status as potential soldiers as primary signifiers of manly status. G. W. Upshaw had all the requirements for manhood except whiteness, and was therefore denied citizenship rights. White men and women of all classes shared a belief that "negroes" represented the traits of non-manliness: subservience, dependence, malleability. They were thus ambivalent about conscripting African American men for military service. On the one hand, they believed it necessary to coerce "negroes." On the other, the manly performance of military service should be reserved for white men. As a result, when Georgia turned the draft into a system to coerce the civilian labor of African American males it reinforced the dependent position of African American men, it confirmed the exclusion of women from the realm of the state, it preserved some white men's sense of manhood, and it got the cotton picked.

CHAPTER TWO

ILLINOIS: "A MAN IS NO MAN
THAT IS NOT WILLING TO FIGHT"

In the spring of 1918 Mrs. Marie Barbee of Hillsboro, Illinois, sent a letter to Selective Service officials in Washington, D.C., demanding they draft her son, send him to France, and put him in the trenches. Mrs. Barbee was a widow with one daughter in addition to her draft-age son. She lived in a rural village in the middle of the south-central Illinois corn-belt. In her appeal to draft officials, she called on the values that defined Progressive white manhood. A man must do something productive and useful, like working or fighting. But that alone was insufficient according to Mrs. Barbee. A man must support the women, children, or elderly in his family. Her version of "work or fight" was something like "work to support your family or fight to support your nation." Mrs. Barbee's primary goal was to get economic support from her son, and she would apply the twin prods of white Progressive gender ideology and the Selective Service System to force it out of him. She wrote:

> To the War Department in regard to Lewis Barbee not taking care of his mother and little sister which he fill out questionnaire papers to do. He is working at Okla working in Schram glass factory and making $30.00 a week and wont sent me a cent to live on. He did not want to go to the war. So he put exemption that he had to take care of me his mother and his sister but he is not doing it so see what you can do about it. I think that a son wont take care of his poor old mother when she is not able to work they should be taken to France and put in the trenches. A man is no man that is not willing to fight for his own country. I only wished that I could go but I past that age. This is all. Let me know.[1]

An investigation revealed that his local board had placed Lewis Barbee, a white man, in Class I. He was therefore subject to be called when the board reached his number. Authorities notified his mother that after he was inducted the army would send her an allowance from his military pay. One wonders if this mother might just as soon not have her son sent to the trenches if he had been sending her some of those thirty dollars a week. Perhaps his unwillingness to fight for his country would not then have made him any less a man in her eyes.[2] "A man is no man that will not fight for his own country" was a phrase written with a very specific audience in mind— white male government officials. But the fact that a poor white woman wielded the language to her own immediate benefit suggests how deeply embedded these values were. It does not, however, tell us whether or not Mrs. Barbee and other working class women and men in Illinois actually internalized them, or just understood their usefulness.

White women generally agreed that men owed them protection in exchange for their nurturing, but if the Selective Service records for Illinois are any indication, many insisted on setting the terms of the exchange themselves. The most common interaction between white women and draft officials involved women's demand for economic support from men. They were especially quick to identify men who had gotten deferments under the guise of having women dependent on them but who then failed to provide sufficient support. In short, what they said about proper gender roles depended on who they were addressing, and whether or not those officials held the authority to make the men in these women's lives support them.

The ideology of manhood as white male officials expressed it was far more abstract, but it was derived from a fundamental agreement with Mrs. Barbee's view that the chief function of men should be to support and protect women and children.[3] White manhood, however, was also linked to the role of women in times of war. The Governor of Illinois, Frank Lowden, was quite explicit about this. War would require women to make sacrifices, and at times to step out of their assigned sphere in the home and fill in for the men who had gone to war or to higher paying jobs in the munitions industries. White men in Illinois also gave considerable support to women's suffrage, and white Illinois women frequently participated in political events. But men like Lowden meant to control carefully such reforms by making sure that they reinscribed on the public consciousness nineteenth-century ideals that made domesticity, or matters associated with the home, the primary sphere of white womanhood.

Child welfare and women's labor laws proposed by the governor in 1917 were based on beliefs that women must first be society's nurturers and mothers. It was a fitting symbol on the day before the young men of America were asked to affirm their manhood by registering for the draft, that Governor Lowden presented a bill to the state legislature to limit the number of hours women could work for wages in industry. At a time when the demand for labor was rising and the male labor supply was contracting such a bill seemed wrong. But the governor said it was made more necessary by war. He appealed to current ideals of racial purity, notions of women's proper function in society, and the expectation that war would reduce the population of men. The future of the United States was at stake, the governor argued. This law would guarantee "the quality of succeeding generations. What the men and women of the next generation will be depends upon what the mothers of this generation are." Illinois should demand "that our women shall not work under such conditions, or during such part of the day, as to impair their vitality or prevent them from becoming the mothers of a hardy race," by which he surely meant the white race. The English experience had shown, said Lowden, that both the efficiency and the health of working women suffered when they were allowed to work for more than eight hours a day. "Over-time should be abolished and an eight-hour day established for them." War provided no justification for increasing the workload of women in industry. Women are the future of the nation because they bear its children and nurture them through childhood. The nation could not afford any significant decline in the number of mothers. A decline in mothers threatened the survival of "the race," but the loss of even tens of thousands of men in battle would have only a minor impact. "The purpose is to safe-guard the future of the nation. War must of necessity impair the fatherhood of future generations. Doubly important it is then that we take every precaution to protect the mothers of the next generation."[4]

As Illinois mobilized for World War I, then, and set the wheels of the Selective Service System turning, officials in the state capital espoused a remarkably consistent view of gender relations. However gender was complicated by race. The values to which Mrs. Barbee and Governor Lowden appealed defined white manhood, and white womanhood. To be less than a proper man or woman, was also to be less than white—an early-twentieth-century version of what later came to be called "white trash." We have already seen how Germans in Coweta County, Georgia, were easily racialized as inferior, dangerous, or subversive. A white man, whether of German, or some other European ancestry, who became publicly marked as subversive, for example, suffered emasculation as a man, but was also racialized as an inferior form of whiteness. In Illinois during World War I many Germans experienced nearly as extreme a form of racialized disadvantage as African Americans did in Georgia. In particular, they might be lynched merely for having a German surname.

Many gave up speaking the German language or eating foods such as sour kraut that were identified with German culture. Perhaps more significant, the war caused many Germans to reconsider their religious practices. Rural Illinois was home to many members of the Amish, Mennonite, and Church of the Brethren sects of German origin who stood out not only for their unique religious garb, but for the fact that they did not believe that Christians should participate in war. Their German ancestry could make their opposition to war seem like a pro-German stance and heighten antagonism against them.

In addition, German socialists, although few in number, were particularly visible in places such as Chicago and Rockford and suffered persecution for their outspoken opposition to the war and the draft on ideological grounds. Non-German radicals, especially members of labor organizations such as the Industrial Workers of the World, were treated similarly. Both groups would become prime targets of police, local councils of defense, and a private superpatriotic vigilante organization that called itself the American Protective League.

Nevertheless, in their interactions with the Selective Service System men and women from each of the competing ethnic and political groups in Illinois appealed to a common set of values and principles that defined Progressive white manhood. They did so in ways that promoted the particular interests of their own group, but it was always the potential or lack of it for a common white racial identity that made their claims of manhood plausible or implausible. And this, ultimately, as in Georgia, was literally grounded in the potential to command or control the economically productive capacities of the land, or more broadly, the material world.

Adams County: The Community and the Draft

Adams County, Illinois, is a beautiful land with gently rolling hills of woods and fields, broken occasionally by small streams. Western parts of the County lie in the flood plain of the Mississippi River. At places along the river the land rises to a series of bluffs that can become islands cut off from the rest of the county during extreme floods. This is where European American settlers in the nineteenth century built the town of Quincy, named after President John Quincy Adams, as was the County. Although the river naturally floods annually, periodic extreme flooding occurred during the twentieth century as a result of commercial agricultural practices introduced by Europeans and the denuding of forested slopes throughout the Mississippi watershed. It is partly to centuries of periodic flooding that the land owes its fertility, but it is to less than two centuries of capitalist exploitation of the land that people in Adams County now owe the precariousness of their very existence along the river.

Racist images of the earliest people to live on this land appeared frequently in the early-twentieth-century stories white people in Adams County told themselves about the place they now claimed as home. They knew it had once sustained a large and complex civilization whose people participated in long distance trade networks and built massive structures. Adams County historians in 1919 thought the "numerous and impressive remains of the civilization" were left by a people too advanced to have belonged to the "red man."[5]

According to a 1905 history, the land was "thinly populated by tribes of savages" at the time two French fur traders arrived in the eighteenth century. In 1813, according to this history, "mounted rangers from Illinois and Missouri . . . found remnants of some rough stone chimneys and a few wigwam poles" near the present city of Quincy. "The legendary stories of the existence of this savage village of the Sauk tribe . . . relate that its uncivilized inhabitants fled from their homes and left the village to the tender mercies of the palefaces. [The] rangers burned the village and passed on."[6] This matter-of-fact account, with a small attempt at humor in the use of the term "palefaces," tells us that white people in Adams County in 1905 marked the vanished Sauk in absentia as a racially inferior people. Racial inferiority, especially when attributed to savagery and lack of civilization, led to the assumption that white men (i.e., "palefaces") were entitled to occupy and exploit the land taken from the Sauk in military conquest.

The 1813 burning of the Sauk village occurred in the midst of the War of 1812, a war that wrenched twenty-two million acres of land away from American Indians in the Southeast, including the Creeks of Coweta County. The U.S. government offered land of the Sauk, including half of what became Adams County, Illinois, as a bounty to the white male veterans of the War of 1812. It opened the rest to other white men for homesteading.[7] In 1831–1832 Sauk warriors under the leadership of Black Hawk tried to retake this land. A young Abraham Lincoln fought in the ensuing war that historians call the "Black Hawk War." It disrupted white commerce and slowed settlement in western and northern Illinois and parts of Wisconsin. Whites in Adams County used this war as a point of reference and local identity seventy years later. For example, in 1901, banker Lorenzo Hull of Quincy told the Illinois Bankers Association that his bank owed its success to the defeat of Black Hawk in 1832.[8]

Since the earliest permanent settlements of white people who arrived in the 1820s, commercial farming and river commerce have shaped people's relations to this landscape. In the process, white invaders replaced not only native peoples, but native species of animals and plants. Corn was, of course, a nonnative plant hybridized in Mexico centuries earlier that the Sauk later cultivated. But the dramatic impacts that whites had on the natural environment in Adams County were unprecedented in scope and speed. Extensive cultivation of corn in the late nineteenth century, not for human consumption, but to feed hogs and cattle, and the existence of the hogs and cattle themselves, radically disrupted the ecological balance the Sauk had maintained for centuries in their interactions with the natural environment. By 1905, at least four species of birds indigenous to the area had vanished. It had taken less than seventy-five years to drive them away or to extinction. The County's historians, William H. Collins and Cicero F. Perry, saw the vanishing of birds and Indians as part of the same inevitable process by which civilization must advance. With reference to one particular species of bird, Collins and Perry wrote: "It would seem that they passed away with the Indians, as they were still here when the red men passed through the town, going and coming for the annuities they received from the government at that time, about 1848."[9] More plausible evidence to explain the disappearance of birds is described in a 1919 history of Adams County. According to that account, to make the land suitable for white men's agriculture required government assistance in draining wetlands and taking control of the river so as to prevent its annual floods. "Under Congressional laws the swamp lands . . . commenced to come into the market and be systematically drained, while the county took up the matter, in behalf of the farms, in that and other tracts naturally subject to overflow, and lands formerly considered worthless were transformed into valuable farms."[10] What these two accounts of the changes wrought on the landscape by white men's activities have in common is a sense that the changes were preordained. In the first account, white men have no culpability in either the disappearance of the Indians or the extinction of birds. These things appear to have happened in the normal course of events. In the second account, although draining wetlands and protecting floodplains required government actions, the passive voice of the passage credits no one in particular for these "improvements." Swamplands "commenced to be drained," and "lands considered worthless were transformed." By telling their history in this way white men in Adams County constructed a myth of white innocence even as they vanquished the Indians and conquered the land. These histories also made it possible in later years to portray white farmers along the Mississippi River as innocent victims of an angry river during the devastating floods of the 1920s, 1930s, and 1990s. The theme of man against nature in Adams County, whether expressed in 1919 or in 1993, was deeply rooted in the soil of white supremacy.

In taking possession of this land and writing their own stories across the landscape, white men erased the voices of the removed or vanquished indigenous people.[11] The stories that remain of the Indians on this land are the white man's stories. To be white in early twentieth century Adams County was, in part, to be alien to the remnants of the indigenous people they had replaced. But white supremacy there also was justified by white men's claim to "know" the now-absent Indians, so that they could simultaneously refer to them as "savage," or "uncivilized," and speak with sorrow of their tragic disappearance. To live and prosper there after the Indians had been vanquished, the land surveyed and mapped, and deeds of private ownership issued, meant to enjoy the privileges secured in the violence of white male conquest. No doubt, a man of Indian ancestry could have passed as white in Adams County in 1910 by purchasing land, making a farm, joining a Christian church, and participating in the manly rituals of the state, such as voting or performing military service. But he would have had to do so at the expense of all that made a man an Indian. He would have had to undergo a process of deracination—a process that was, in fact, prescribed by the U.S. Congress in 1887. Indian men, said the Dawes Act of that year, could become civilized and therefore citizens of the United States if they claimed private ownership of land and "adopted the habits of civilized life." According to Senator Henry Dawes, this meant that they would "wear civilized clothes . . . cultivate the ground, live in houses, ride in Studebaker wagons, send children to school, drink whiskey [and] own property."[12]

The "civilized" ways of the white man in Adams County were based on patriarchy and rooted in private ownership of land that was, in turn, cultivated to produce goods for capitalist markets. Consistent with national policies, Selective Service officials in Adams County made sure that drafting men into the army would not disrupt either the white patriarchal system or the production of agricultural goods for market. They would not only protect this system but strengthen it by using their power to classify men on the bases of their role in white patriarchy and their relationship to the land.

This may be illustrated by the story of one family. It is the family of the man who would be the first called by the Adams County draft board in 1917. Fred Heberlein was born in 1893 into a German American farm family in Hannibal, Missouri, across the Mississippi River from Adams County. In 1898, when Fred was five years old, his father Louis purchased a farm of eighty-four acres near the Adams County community of Liberty and moved his family across the river. Louis Heberlein and his wife Ida had two more sons and two daughters, to complete a family of five children, a relatively small family for rural Adams County at the turn of the century. Over the years the family prospered, increasing the number of acres it farmed by renting an additional forty acres of land, and by 1918, Louis Heberlein's farm was exactly the average size of an Adams County farm.[13]

Like most other farmers in Adams County, Louis Heberlein probably relied primarily on his sons to help him work the land. Like other German Americans, his wife and daughters probably did some of the farm work, as well as managing work in and around the farm house.[14] But sometime before June 1917, Fred Heberlein moved off of his family's farm and into the city of Quincy, where he enrolled in the Gem City Business College. When he registered for the draft, Fred gave his occupation as "student." Fred's father had been left to farm his one hundred twenty-four acres with his two remaining sons, two daughters, and his wife. Although many farmers in Adams County had by this time purchased labor-saving technology, such as tractors and threshing machines, the Heberlein family owned neither. Nevertheless, Fred's move to the city to study business probably served his family well. He and his brothers were old enough to start their own families, but the Heberlein farm would not support more than one family. Fred's decision was typical of many farm sons in the prairie Midwest, and represented a process that preserved a patriarchal system of land control.

Patriarchs—white married males with children—owned most of the land. They determined who would own it after them, and when they would transfer that ownership to the next generation. To farm the land successfully, they needed sons, but not all sons could inherit the land, since dividing it among three or four would make it unlikely than any one of them would have enough for a viable farm. Most sons and daughters eventually had to leave the patriarch's household and the farm that sustained it. The one or two sons who remained in expectation of eventually inheriting the land might be well into the process of creating their own families by the time the patriarch would either pass away or transfer title of the land to them. When there were daughters, but no sons, a son-in-law might receive a promise of inheritance in exchange for managing the farm and caring for his wife's parents until their deaths. By giving up the family farm to his brothers, Fred Heberlein got out from under the patriarchal control of his father. Provided he was successful in business, Fred could be fully in charge of his own household almost immediately. If his two younger brothers were typical, they stayed on the family farm working for their father, even after marrying and establishing their own households. Not until Louis Heberlein transferred the land to them, or they inherited it at his death could they become independent patriarchs in their own right.

Fred was twenty-four years old when the first draft call went out. But he clearly was not an essential farm laborer, and neither his parents nor minor siblings relied upon him for support. He had two younger brothers and two younger sisters living at home to help his parents run the farm. In fact, he demonstrated willingness to be drafted when he registered with the Quincy City Clerk twelve days before official registration day.[15] And so, having drawn a low number in the draft lottery, Fred Heberlein became the first man drafted by the Adams County local board. His case perfectly illustrated how propertied, married white men who wrote and administered the Selective Service Act hoped it would work. He was a healthy man in the prime of life who was essential to no white family or economic enterprise.

Setting up the Local Draft System

As in rural Georgia, in Adams County middle-class-white men who were not farmers, but who were economically linked to the farm economy administered the Selective Service System. They did so in ways that preserved the social system in the countryside through which white patriarchs exercised mastery over the land, over women, over young landless men, and over children. The local draft board excused young men, whether German or Anglo, largely on the basis of their conformity to heterosexual marriage, patriarchal values, and the extent to which they successfully exploited the land.

Political leaders organized registration day with minimal fanfare. Unlike registration day in Newnan, Georgia, there were no parades, no patriotic speeches by politicians, no public ridicule of slackers. On June 5, 1917, 2,056 rural Adams County men between the ages of twenty-one and thirty registered for the draft.[16] As in Coweta County, volunteer registrars positioned in the various communities signed up those who could not make it either to Liberty or Quincy. Adams County registrars were more representative of the county population than were those of Coweta. Two-thirds of the 1917 registrars in Adams County were farmers. But more significantly, their farms were generally of average size. None of them owned enough farm land to place them among the farming elite. In addition, a few were women, and several were young single men who still lived with their parents. The social status of these registrars not only suggested official equanimity about the success of Selective Service operations in Adams County, but suggested political leaders were hesitant to engage in heavy-handed enforcement of the draft law.

Although the registrars were more representative of their constituents than those in Coweta County, the three Adams County draft board members had social and economic relationships to their constituents that were similar to those of the Coweta County draft board to its constituents. In this farming community, none of the board members was a farmer. On the other hand, unlike the Coweta County local board members, the members of the Adams County board did not own any local farm-land. Thus, their connection to farm interests was less direct. But since the economy of the county rested upon a foundation of commercial family farms, no one with business or political interests there could afford to ignore the farmers. In addition, all three board members lived in the rural surroundings of very small towns, none of which bore much resemblance to the town of Newnan, where all of Coweta County's local board members lived. The chairman of the board, J. A. Ausmus, was a county supervisor who also had a law practice in the small village of Loraine. Steven G. Lawless, the secretary of the board ran a small bank in the town of Liberty and served on the board of directors for the Liberty High School. A. D. Bates, the board's examining physician, had a medical practice in Camp Point.[17] These board members, then, were small-town civic leaders and petit bourgeois who assumed the job of managing the wartime activities of young farming men.

The process of selecting draftees for the first call demonstrated both the sensitivity of the local board to the concerns of farmers at harvest time and the ambivalent attitude of most draft-age men toward the war. In order to get eleven men for their first call the local board had to reach all the way to order number 395. For a variety of reasons, the lowest number available was six. The men with numbers one and two failed to show up when called. The local board had exempted men with numbers three and four because they had family members dependent upon them. It had declared the man with number five available for induction, but he had appealed the board's denial of his claim for exemption. This effectively removed him from being called until the District Board acted on the appeal. Nineteen men with numbers below 395 failed to appear for their physical examination. The board reported these men as delinquent, but later discovered that thirteen of them had enlisted before the board sent out its orders.[18] The remaining six delinquents were eventually inducted, but their failure to appear delayed processing of their Selective Service files until after the new classification system was installed at the end of the year. The delay enabled them to escape induction for at least six months.

As in Coweta County, it appears that the local board readily granted dependency exemptions and temporary extensions to protect essential farm labor at a crucial time in the agricultural year. The season for corn harvests in Adams County was virtually the same as that for cotton in Coweta County. Harvest began in early to mid-October and continued through most of November.[19] As in Coweta County, the first call issued by the Adams County local board affected few, if any, men who were actually farming. Among the eleven men called on September 4, only two came from farm families. One of those two, Fred Heberlein, had already left the farm for the city at the time he was called. In total calls between September and December, 1917, the local board ordered ninety-two men to camp. Only twenty-seven of them came from farm families, and only two did not have brothers living at home to help with the fall harvest. The farm men drafted from Adams County in 1917 came from smaller than average farms and from families that the board judged had more men on hand than necessary.[20]

The largest group of draft registrants unavailable for military induction, therefore, consisted of men who either failed the physical or were exempted by the board on the grounds that they had family members directly dependent upon them. Sixty-two percent (246) fell within this category. The District Board, with original jurisdiction to issue exemptions for men considered "essential to a necessary agricultural or industrial enterprise," only exempted four percent (17) of the first 395 men from Adams County. But this figure is misleading. By instituting a liberal policy of dependency exemptions the local board blocked the district board from hearing many claims for agricultural exemption. The local board, in effect, used dependency exemptions to keep men on the farms during the peak harvest months of September and October.[21]

As the demands of the War Department for more soldiers intensified in the spring of 1918 and the new classification system increasingly located power in district rather than local boards the draft board was forced to call more men who were actually engaged in farming. Farmers had constituted a minority of the men called in the first drafts of 1917. But between April and October 1918 seventy percent of the men conscripted from Adams County were either farmers or farm laborers. Although this shift was inevitable given any military engagement of more than a few months, both the local and district boards continued to favor farmers with a disproportionate share of exemptions and deferments until the end of the war. The farm population of the county exceeded eighty percent, yet nonfarmers made up thirty percent of Adams County draftees. Eighteen percent were engaged in manual wage labor and seven percent could be called nonfarm middle class. These included artisans, small businessmen, merchants, and white collar workers in jobs requiring some specialized training. The remaining draftees were either students or men whose occupations could not be determined. Statistics published by the Provost Marshal General at the end of the war suggest that draft-age farming men in Adams County received preferential treatment. The local board, which was not empowered to grant agricultural or industrial exemptions, excused 991 men on the grounds that they had family dependent upon them. The district board, with original jurisdiction over all occupational exemptions awarded 153 agricultural deferments and one industrial deferment. To put it more graphically, the ratio of exempted to drafted men among industrial workers was about 1 : 100 while among farmers it was 1: 2: 5. The contrast would be even greater if we could account for the dependency deferments given in lieu of agricultural exemptions.[22]

When the local board in June 1918 asked federal draft officials for permission to delay inductions for thirty days it gave further evidence that it wanted to preserve the farm labor supply. It wired the Provost Marshal General: "The harvest in Adams County, Illinois, is unusually heavy, [and] the call for June 24th will take one hundred fifty men all very actively engaged in farming, leaving lots of harvest in the field with no one to harvest it." The requested delay would "enable this county to save wheat and oats harvest and complete the cultivation of corn," said the telegram.[23] The files contain no reply from the Provost Marshal General, but the local board apparently found a way to deal with the problem. It sent only two men to camp between the date of the telegram and July 29, 1918, a span of more than thirty days. One of those men was a minister. The other, who listed farming as his occupation, failed the physical examination at the Kansas City, Missouri, training camp. The army discharged him.[24]

The local board's attempts to protect the farm labor population seemed to satisfy most county residents. The complaints were few. However, one farmer who had lost his sons, at least temporarily, to the army and navy took out his frustrations on the draft board. George L. Anderson, who owned a larger-than-average farm near the community of Clayton, demanded that the Provost Marshal General order an investigation of alleged irregularities in the granting of exemptions in Adams County. Neither of Anderson's sons had been drafted but both had enlisted in 1917. Now he felt at a disadvantage competing for farm labor against men whose sons had been excused from the draft. "I need my boys just as bad as my neighbors need their boys," he wrote.

> I run a farm of 340 acres besides what my boys run, they left everything and went to the war there are single men right now in my neighborhood that . . . ought to be gone . . . and one single man about the age of my boys that is in class 3 that ought to be in class 1. His father is a good deal better able to hire help than I am and besides that he has two younger boys to help him do his work.

Anderson then proceeded to name persons whom he believed had been given preferential treatment by the draft board. In addition, he thought that the chairman of the board, Steven G. Lawless, ought to be investigated separately. According to "a woman that lives right by Liberty," wrote Anderson, ". . . he was not 31 at the time the first draft came out but he claimed he was and he is still at home he has two younger brothers that I am told are in Class 2 or 3 and they have an older brother at home to do the work."[25]

Anderson's status as a white patriarch was linked to his ability to exercise mastery over the land he owned, which, in turn, depended upon his ability to compete for labor with other patriarchs. He thus focused his ire on young, single men and the local Selective Service officials who were failing in their duty to select first those men who had no wives, children, or elderly parents dependent upon them. In essence, his letter agreed with Enoch Crowder's views that the Selective Service System should function not only to win the war, but equally to protect white families and to organize the productive activities of the nation's manpower in ways that did not upset existing social relations. In the context of rural Illinois, where social and economic stability required most single young men to leave the community, Anderson's complaint seems perfectly consistent with national policy.

Conscientious Objectors

When the propertied white men in Adams County, Illinois, first began to organize the various governmental and volunteer agencies that would oversee wartime mobilization, Reverend G. O. Stutzman, pastor of a small pacifist Church of the Brethren congregation in the town of Liberty, volunteered to serve as an official Selective Service advisor to draft registrants. The Church of the Brethren held a doctrine that they called "nonresistance," which forbade Christians to participate in the use of force by any means. Holding positions of civil authority, participating in war, and for some, even voting, violated Christ's command to "resist not evil." Such people could not in good conscience either resist conscription or take up arms. They were not anti-war activists, but religious objectors who seemed embarrassed and apologetic for the trouble their convictions seemed to cause.[26]

The Selective Service Law permitted members of recognized "peace churches," such as the Church of the Brethren, Mennonites, Quakers, and others, to receive exemptions from combatant duty in the armed forces. The law identified as a "conscientious objector" anyone who was a "member of a well-recognized religious sect or organization . . . whose creed or principles forbid its members to participate in war in any form and whose religious convictions are against war or participation therein." But the first 1917 draft forms contained no reference to this choice, and only those who learned of it from some other source had the opportunity to request the exemption.[27] It was therefore initially up to the ministers of local congregations of peace churches to inform the men of draft age in their churches of it. With the institution of the classification system in December 1917, the Selective Service System gave men the opportunity to declare their conscientious objection to war on the standard questionnaire.

Because it provided the option of conscientious objection, the draft had a mixed impact on the Liberty Church of the Brethren. The Selective Service System helped to alter both the civil and ethnic relations between the Church of the Brethren and other Adams County residents. The Brethren saw their local pastor's status and authority enhanced by the draft. And because they were also mostly of German ancestry, they feared that their reputation as pacifists would imply they sympathized with the German cause. Their response to the U.S. declaration of war against Germany was consistent with the national Brethren leadership. It was ambiguous. On the one hand, many members sincerely believed in the original pacifist doctrines of the church. On the other hand, they had only recently begun to shed some of the practices that marked them as strange to other Americans. To insist on exemption from the draft as conscientious objectors would further identify them as a group whose place in American society was marginal. Many members still spoke German. Some churches conducted services in German; they baptized members by immersion, or dunking. But some of the women were beginning to reject their traditional clothing and the distinctive prayer veil that made them look much like the Mennonites and Amish.[28] This process of "Americanization" parallels the acculturation that other European ethnic groups underwent. Noel Ignatiev and Karen Brodkin, writing about Irish immigrants and Jews, respectively, have defined this as a process of becoming white. Similarly, as the case of California (discussed in chapter four) will show, federal policies relating to American Indians explicitly linked behaving like white men with becoming American citizens. For many groups, central to this process was the adoption of the English language, shedding distinctive forms of dress, and altering religious practices to conform to mainstream American Protestantism.[29]

As suggested earlier, being white but outside the mainstream of American culture has the effect of racializing whites as inferior forms of whiteness—people who don't quite fulfill the requirements of the race. Discomfort about being perceived as being different, and perhaps not "100% American," led the Church of the Brethren as a denomination to downplay its pacifist teachings during World War I. Reverend G. O. Stutzman, acted in harmony with the official position of the denomination when he became Selective Service advisor to draft registrants, and legally became an official of the Selective Service System. The local board relied upon his recommendation in all claims for conscientious objector status. His supporting affidavit was a necessary precondition for a successful claim. Stutzman, thus, had placed himself between the draft registrants from his church and the local board, meaning that anyone not on good terms with him had little chance of being recognized as a conscientious objector. By assuming a position of civil authority, the minister violated basic doctrines of the Brethren, but he also enhanced his authority over his congregation.[30]

Reverend Stutzman completed affidavits in support of seven conscientious objectors in Adams County in 1917 and 1918. The congregation had between one hundred and two hundred members. (A membership of about two hundred in 1882 had dwindled to ninety-four by 1950.) If half the members were men, and forty percent of the men were of draft age, then about twenty members of the local Church of the Brethren should have been liable for the draft. Why a dozen or more Brethren men did not claim to be conscientious objectors is not clear. The draft board may have excused them on other grounds, in which case consideration of their claim of conscientious objection would have been superfluous. Some, however, were drafted as combatants. Helen Ogle, a small child at the time, remembers that some Brethren men fought in the war. And there is other evidence that, as the U.S. role in the actual fighting increased, the denomination as a whole softened its opposition to participation in war. The District Conference for the Northern Illinois Churches passed a resolution in August, 1917, that avoided taking any position for or against conscientious objection. It called on local congregations to assist "our young Brethren of draft age," by providing them with information and helping them "to secure proper treatment before exemption boards." The resolution urged congregations "to keep in touch with the brother pressed into army service . . . [and] to give moral support to the home from which a brother has been called into service. . . ." The Brethren Conference for the Southern District of Illinois, to which the Liberty congregation belonged, did "encourage our young brethren, who have been or may be drafted, to stand loyally for our nonresistant principles. . . ." But it took an apologetic stance for its "nonresistant" doctrine when it stated that "we gratefully recognize and appreciate the privileges granted us by the civil authorities of our government in exemption from combatant military service. . . ."[31]

The first conscientious objector claim considered by the Adams County local board was that of Lucas C. Akers, a member of Stutzman's congregation. Akers had a low enough order number that he could reasonably expect to be called before December. Thus, on August 9, 1917, as required by Selective Service regulations, he submitted an affidavit affirming his membership in a church "whose creed forbids participation in war." On the same date, Reverend Stutzman filed an affidavit stating that Akers "is personally known to me and is a member of the Liberty Church of the Brethren." The local board approved the claim and attached a statement to his file that Akers "shall not be required to serve except as a non-combatant." Then, as in all other cases, Akers's case was forwarded to the district board for final approval of the local board's action. Despite having jurisdiction over a large population of Illinois Mennonites, this was apparently the first case of a conscientious objector that the district board for southern Illinois had seen. It did not know what to do with the file, sending a note back to the local board stating, "Akers seems to be . . . exempted and not exempted. Which is correct and what should be done with this case?" Steven G. Lawless, clerk of the local board wrote back that Akers was "exempted on religious grounds only. He has been accepted as a noncombatant soldier."[32]

Akers had asked to be deferred from induction claiming that his parents were dependent upon him. Had the board agreed it would have classified him III-A, meaning that the likelihood of his ever being called would have been remote. At age twenty-two, Akers was the only son of Justin K. and Christena Akers who rented a one hundred eighty acre farm in the Payson Township. But the local board evidently did not think that Akers's parents were dependent upon him. The district board similarly disagreed with his claim that he was an essential agricultural laborer. Akers only worked full-time on his father's farm during the late spring and summer months. He reported that during that time his father paid him wages for an average of ninety-six hours a week. For the rest of the year, including the labor-intensive harvest season, Akers worked forty hours a week as a school teacher and twenty hours, mainly on weekends for his father. Nevertheless, he argued that since he was an only son the board should have deferred him. Both parents as well as a neighbor signed affidavits stating that Lucas Akers was needed on the farm since his father had been injured in a fall from a telephone pole.[33]

It is difficult to imagine how one man in his late forties could maintain production on a farm as large as that operated by Justin Akers and his family. In 1917–18 they had one hundred sixty acres under cultivation in corn, wheat, oats, and hay. Typically for Adams County, the corn mostly went to feed twenty-six hogs, ten cows, and eight horses. Compared to a cotton farm of comparable size this farm would have required minimal labor. But owning no tractor or thresher, the elder Akers would have had no choice but to hire nonfamily help. In similar cases, the local board had recommended agricultural deferments and the district board had usually agreed. Approval of noncombatant status should not have deprived a draft registrant of his rights to any deferments or exemptions for which he might also have qualified. One is tempted to speculate that prejudice against Lucas Akers for his religious objection to war may have lessened the local board's sympathy for his father's economic well-being. On the other hand, by Akers's own report, his father only used him as a full-time worker four months out of the year. Both the local and district boards might reasonably have wondered how the elder Akers managed during the most labor intensive months of the farm year with only part-time help from his son.[34]

Local boards inducted conscientious objectors such as Akers, who were not otherwise exempted, and put them on trains to military camps. Once in camp, such men were not to be required to train with arms. Most training camp commanders reportedly respected this right, but there were few official attempts to protect conscientious objectors from the hostile treatment of both officers and enlisted men in the camps. Secretary of War Newton D. Baker initially ordered that camp commanders segregate conscientious objectors from combatant draftees. Later in the war authorities kept them with the rest of the draftees in hopes of pressuring them to join the combatant soldiers. As a result of these policies and the minimal oversight of local commanders, many conscientious objectors suffered from extremely harsh treatment in the camps. As John W. Chambers II has written, there were "at least forty cases of brutal punishment in the first seven months of the draft. Military authorities starved the objectors on bread and water, hanged them by their wrists, forced them to exercise and then drenched them in icy showers, and beat them with belts and broom handles." As a result of harsh treatment two Mennonite conscientious objectors died in military custody. Authorities dressed their bodies in the uniforms they had refused to wear and sent them back to their families.[35]

By the summer of 1918 such reports led Baker to appoint a board of inquiry to interview conscientious objectors in military camps and make recommendations for handling them. In effect, the board of inquiry was to second-guess the decisions of local draft boards by questioning the sincerity of the conscientious objectors in camps. The board recommended that those judged insincere as well as those who would not obey any military orders be court-martialed and imprisoned. If judged sincere, a conscientious objector either would be placed on active duty noncombatant military duty or furloughed to do farm work as a civilian. The board found virtually all members of traditional peace churches, such as Quakers, Mennonites, and Brethren, to be sincere. But it ruled most other objectors insincere, often because they were unable to answer correctly trick questions designed to show that their objections were based on political considerations rather than personal beliefs. Military courts tried these men for a variety of offenses, sentencing seventeen to death, 142 to life imprisonment, and 345 to long sentences at hard labor. None was actually executed, and between 1919 and the end of 1923 the administrations of Presidents Warren Harding and Calvin Coolidge freed all World War I objectors from prison.[36]

Lucas Akers arrived in camp just one week before Newton Baker appointed the board of inquiry and at precisely the moment that the War Department's revised policies toward conscientious objectors took effect. As a member of a recognized "peace church" the board of inquiry likely gave Akers the option of entering into noncombatant military service or being furloughed to agricultural work.[37] If he was typical of most "peace-church" conscientious objectors, Akers would have chosen the furlough and been sent either to a private farm or to one of the model government farms established to raise food crops during the war. As a furloughed conscientious objector, Akers would not have been allowed to earn more than a private in the army. Any additional money that he earned would have been taken away and given to the American Red Cross. A government investigation found that some farmers in the Midwest would have been unable to harvest their 1918 corn crop without conscientious objectors. "Certainly they proved a godsend to the farmer, and, indirectly, to the country at large," wrote the head of the investigation. In addition, he wrote, "the American Red Cross benefited substantially."[38]

The parallels to the farm furloughs for drafted African Americans in the cotton belt were striking. In both cases the Selective Service System drafted men deemed in their region to be unsuitable as soldiers and returned them to civilian occupations that would benefit white farmers who owned large farms and enhance wartime mobilization. In both cases the federal government regulated the wages paid to the furloughed men, and in both cases the result was ironic. African Americans were forced to labor for the benefit of a society that denied them the most basic rights of citizens. Conscientious objectors were forced to labor in ways that contributed to the prosecution of the war that they believed to be morally wrong. By the end of the war about fifteen hundred conscientious objectors had been furloughed to farms. This amounted to approximately thirty-eight percent of the 3,900 conscientious objectors drafted into the army. The rest were either assigned to noncombatant military duties, sent into combat as insincere, or imprisoned at places like Fort Leavenworth, Kansas, as "general prisoners."[39]

It is difficult to ascertain the attitudes of other Adams County citizens toward the conscientious objectors. But the complete absence of public criticism of them in surviving records suggests that the official position of the Church of the Brethren on war was known to many people and they recognized it as a legitimate religious tenet. The relations between Reverend G. O. Stutzman and the local draft board seem to have been cordial. The fact that Brethren were mostly ethnic Germans does not appear to have incurred accusations that their opposition to participating in the war was inspired by loyalty to the German cause. Conscientious objectors in Adams County came from the same large middle sector of farming families that most rural residents of the county did, and this membership in a common social and economic class outweighed differences in cultural practices and religious doctrine, even when that doctrine kept many of them out of the war. Outrage against Germans or others for failing to support the war found expression in Adams County, but not against conscientious objectors. Unlike blacks, Indians, or Asians, the Brethren had the option of choosing whiteness by taking on the cultural practices and political views of white-middle-class Americans. The Brethren had been careful to affirm their loyalty to the United States and avoided speaking favorably of anything German. Many had stopped speaking the German language. They began conducting church services in English and sent their children to public schools. Even the role of Stutzman as an official advisor to draft registrants confirmed that this tiny minority had been sufficiently neutralized as an antiwar voice.

The experiences of conscientious objectors and members of German peace sects elsewhere in rural Illinois were not always as benign as in Adams County. Sometimes, the combination of German ethnicity and refusal to join the war effort led to complaints about them. The mayor and postmaster of Gridley, Illinois both signed a letter to Crowder charging that, "there is a tendency with the German people in this part of the Country to try and beat the draft by false representation." Many of the "German people" in the Gridley jurisdiction were Mennonites. But the officials making the complaint focused on cultural and religious practices rather than the nonresistant doctrine. Families were the primary culprits. "The young men who were drafted last spring and not yet called are getting married and their fathers and fatherinlaws [sic] are renting them land so they will appear to belong in class 4." But the church was also at fault said the correspondents. "The menonite [sic] Church is allso [sic] making a big drive to get their young men in the Church so they wil [sic] stand better show to be exempted." The letter writers asserted that having "lived and done business at this place from 25 to 40 years [we] are in a position to know the feeling of the public at large . . . and we know there is a strong feeling among the loyal

Americans against any favors being shown the above class of people."[40] Someone in the Office of the Provost Marshal General filed away with no reply this expression of religious, ethnic, and cultural bigotry.

The German American Factor

It seems certain that the presence of a large number of Germans probably muted wartime fervor in Adams County. In late March, 1917, the U.S. representative Edward J. King, whose district included Adams County, believed that at least eighty-five percent of his constituents opposed going to war against Germany and thought that war hysteria was being promoted by "the press of the East and the money interests." King's judgment would be confirmed as the war commenced. The county initially rejected offers from the state and national councils of defense to provide local wartime propaganda. Farmers also turned away offers by the Illinois Council of Defense to help solve the farm labor shortage caused by the war. Both of these responses to the war reflected the important place of Germans in the county. Council of Defense officials interpreted the rejection of propaganda as a sign of German influence in county affairs. They were probably correct, but for different reasons than they thought. Few Germans in Adams County openly criticized American participation in the war once the declaration passed Congress. But Germans did help in small ways to make the draft less disruptive. One example is that the labor shortage caused by the war was mitigated by the willingness of many German women to replace men in the fields and barns of Adams County.[41]

On the other hand, even before the United States entered the war people in Adams County, including German Americans, expressed concern over German attacks on American ships. The war also emboldened people who had silently resented the strong ethnic German presence. Given undercurrents of both pro- and anti-German sentiment among county residents, leaders wisely chose a policy that played down emotional appeals in either direction. Nationally, much wartime propaganda promoted derogatory images of Germans, and its use in Adams County would have introduced divisions in the community that would not have served the interests of any particular group.[42]

The situation in the city of Quincy differed markedly from that in the countryside.[43] As in many other small Illinois cities, Quincy was sharply divided between those who suspected all Germans of disloyalty and those who defended them. The changing editorial positions of one of Quincy's two daily newspapers reflected this division. The *Quincy Journal*, edited by a Civil War veteran, had supported the neutrality advocated by Democrat William Jennings Bryan and Republican Robert M. LaFollette and opposed the preparedness movement until 1917. By spring, 1917, the *Journal* had reversed its position, supporting a large Quincy patriotic celebration attended by 10,000 "flag wavers." The city council ordered all German language publications removed from the public library's reading room. A local National Guard officer headed a chapter of the American Protective League (APL). The APL was a private volunteer organization headquartered in Chicago that with government sanction operated like a vigilante group. With approval from the Provost Marshal General and the Justice Department, it assisted local police and federal marshals in massive "slacker raids" in towns and cities around the country. Its agents spied on draft-age men, carried official-looking badges, and in some cases even "arrested" men they suspected of violating the draft law. By November 1917, the Adams County APL reported that it had two hundred operatives seeking German sympathizers throughout the county. But many resisted these efforts as unfairly impugning the intentions of the large local German population. Such people opposed not only local speeches by the "Four Minute Men" and the investigations of the APL, but spoke out against campaigns to raise funds for the war. Theodore Pape, a prominent Quincy lawyer turned the Liberty Bond people away from his home and publicly encouraged others to do the same. The war would end sooner, he argued, if people did not support it financially.[44]

Some anti-German sentiment appeared in the countryside as well, but its intensity there was muted. Dorothy Baker Jacobson, who was a young girl in 1917, remembered that her father, Lewis Baker, owner of one of several threshing machines other farmers relied upon, received warnings not to thresh the corn of local German farmers. Mr. Baker, believing that Germans "needed to have their gain threshed just like everyone else," ignored the threats. But first, he sent his wife to see a lawyer in Quincy to find out if there was a law against threshing grain for Germans. When someone attempted to sabotage the Baker thresher by placing an iron bar inside a bundle of wheat to be threshed, Baker's brother spotted the bar in time to prevent damage. The Bakers were not deterred by this incident and they continued to thresh wheat for the local German farmers throughout the war. In later years a resident of the Paloma area recalled that "anyone who did not support the war was termed a slacker and had a yellow stripe painted around his house. If he was a farmer, his wheat, worth over $2 a bushel, was left in the field unthreshed." Another clash between the pro- and anti-German factions in rural Adams County would occur in 1918. An APL operative reported that William Altenheim had told a group of people, "I am for the Kaiser and I hope he wins this war." Federal officials had him tried and convicted for violating the Sedition Act, but the conviction was overturned on appeal.[45] Nevertheless, political leaders and the small town press in the countryside never tried to exploit such divisions for political or economic advantage as they did in Quincy, as well as in Newnan, Georgia, and Paterson, New Jersey.

In the final analysis, the moderation with which the men of rural Adams County performed their duties may obscure the reality of the larger systems in which they were participants. The system of conscription existed only because they, and men like them in other communities did their duty. It exploited the labor of conscientious objectors and punished them harshly for their religious convictions. At the same time, it reinforced less visible systems that kept heterosexual white property-owning men in power.

Statewide Selective Service in Illinois

In a very broad sense, politically, economically, socially, Illinois may be divided between Chicago and the rest of the state. It was a division that would also be reflected in the operations of the Selective Service System. Chicago firms controlled banking and industrial interests. National white male leaders related to Chicago as an entity separate from and more significant than the rest of Illinois. Much like New York City, Chicago had outgrown the state to which it belonged so that many in Chicago considered the rest of Illinois as outlying territory. The condescension of Chicago's leaders toward the rest of the state was met with resentment in the countryside. The attention paid to the city by nationally prominent men who visited Chicago during the war to promote patriotism, warn against German influence, and decry opposition to the war or to the draft, fed Chicago's sense of importance and fostered further antagonism toward it among the farming and small town populations.[46] The attitude of Chicago officials toward the rest of the state was demonstrated when the mayor sought to preempt the governor's power as head of the Selective Service System in the state. In addition, the actions of the War Department appeared to undercut the governor when an army judge advocate arrived on the scene claiming authority to administer the Selective Service System in Chicago, bypassing officials in Springfield. Draft officials in Chicago had their own unique problems. As a result, they often left state officials uniformed of their actions and informal local policies. This is not surprising since the population of the city was larger than that of most states.

But almost everywhere in Illinois the question of German Americans in relation to the possibility of war with Germany shaped first debates about the wisdom of going to war, and then over issues of loyalty to the United States. German American men in leadership positions had to carefully divine the attitudes of their constituents before taking a stand. Some Anglo leaders feared that supporting the war might offend citizens of German ancestry. German culture had insinuated itself into many areas of public and private life. The German language was a popular subject in public schools. Many Protestant churches held services in German. Throughout rural Illinois men of German ancestry occupied important civic positions and were leaders in agricultural agencies such as the Farm Bureau. Allies of German Americans in Illinois took pains to distinguish between them and the German nation. Nevertheless, in many areas men with political ambitions sought to take advantage of nativistic wartime paranoia to displace influential German Americans.[47]

The fact that some German American groups had worked in the recent election to elect a President more friendly to German Americans, simply made them easier targets once Woodrow Wilson had been reelected. During the Presidential election campaign of 1916 the Illinois Chapter of the National German American Alliance took a hard line against both Wilson and Roosevelt, the two candidates who criticized ethnic groups that remained culturally distinct from the rest of American society. Just as the eugenics movement in science sought to prevent "race mongrelization," Wilson and Roosevelt ridiculed the "hyphenism" of immigrants who, they said, wanted to enjoy the benefits of American life while maintaining separate cultural identities. Instead, they pushed an ideology of "one hundred percent Americanism." In his State of the Union address in 1915, President Wilson called declared that "hyphenates" were "infinitely malignant . . . creatures of passion . . . and anarchy [who] preach and practice disloyalty." Two months earlier Roosevelt had proclaimed that "there is no room in this country for hyphenated Americans." Both men associated the use of non-English languages with "foreign" ideologies such as socialism and anarchism.

Such attitudes on the part of the two leading politicians in the United States alarmed many German Americans.[48]

The German American Alliance believed that attacks on "hyphenism" were thinly veiled attempts to sow doubt in the public mind about the patriotism of German Americans. As a result, even before the Republican convention the Chicago German American Alliance had endorsed Charles Evans Hughes for President. This decision was based mostly on the fact that Hughes had not spoken publicly against "hyphenism." Roosevelt's well-known desire for war with Germany made him a further anathema to German Americans in Illinois. President Wilson had kept the United States out of the war so far, but by 1916 the President's neutrality was wavering. He had approved the sale of weapons to the Allies on credit. He had finally succumbed to calls to enlarge the armed forces and increase the supply of weapons in the U.S. arsenal. To German American observers in the spring of 1916 it appeared that the likely outcome of either a continued Wilson presidency or the election of Roosevelt would be war with Germany.[49]

Whatever they thought of the Kaiser, German Americans also expected that domestic repercussions would follow an American war declaration. Their fears began to materialize with the series of events in February and March 1917 that led the President and Congress to join the war on the side of the Allies. The chain of events from the German announcement that it would resume submarine attacks on merchant ships, to Wilson's decision to break off diplomatic relations, the torpedoing of four U.S. ships, and the unanimous advice of Wilson's cabinet in March to ask for a declaration of war, left German Americans and others opposed to joining the war in a high state of anxiety.[50]

War Fever

As the United States drew closer to entering the war the pro-war factions in Illinois, quickly gained superior power and influence by virtue of their closer ties to the white men who exercised government authority. The cement that bound these groups to each other was hardened by the greater opportunities the war offered each to enlarge its scope of power and influence. As we have seen in the case of Georgia, war could open the net of government authority and reinforce it. At the same time it would offer opportunities to those previously on the margins of governmental power to expand their personal influence under the umbrella of the state. Such men were often euphoric at the prospect that war might enable them to insinuate themselves into the vortex of national power. In short, to the extent that they acquired advantage in the competition for mastery over other men and women, and over the productive capacities of the earth, these men became the ultimate representations of white manhood in Illinois.

Administrators and professors of the state's major universities seized these opportunities early in 1917. Two months before Congress declared war, Edmund J. James, president of the University of Illinois volunteered the services of his institution "in the event of war." Through Governor Lowden the university president offered "to the President of the United States in case of war the facilities of the scientific and technical laboratories of the University of Illinois."[51] In March the president of the

University of Chicago convened a pro-war committee that produced a series of resolutions calling for Congress to authorize immediately the enlargement of the armed forces and to equip them so that their effectiveness "shall be second to none." The same committee demanded "universal obligatory military training and service, as the only just and democratic method of national defense."[52] Two days before the declaration of war, the dean of the state college of agriculture gushed that the people at his institution had "had gooseflesh ever since the prospect of war looked keen." He proposed a centralized system by which the state would manage all agricultural production. It would create an analog to the Selective Service System with registration of each farm operator, enlistment of farmers to produce food for the war, and training camp farms to train city men to farm.[53] Shailer Mathews, Dean of the University of Chicago Divinity School, declared that anyone who opposed the war was "either a myopic idealist, a fanatic, or a proGerman." He asserted that by joining this war Americans would continue the historic national mission to create "a world so controlled by justice that the social movements which are now checked shall go on to full fruition; . . . that men and nations shall see that it is more blessed to give justice than it is to fight for rights."[54]

Other groups had equally enthusiastic responses. The Springfield Federation of Labor responded to the April declaration of war by calling on "all loyal citizens to show their colors at this time, that they are for America first."[55] The Illinois State Bar Association condemned as "unpatriotic, disloyal, and treasonable," the words of a former U.S. senator who said that the declaration of war was "without just and reasonable cause."[56] The Illinois State Teachers' Association rewrote Abraham Lincoln's "House Divided" speech, proclaiming that the German and American governments "are so antagonistic in purpose that the world cannot continue partly under the one and partly under the other. Either all peoples and all nations shall be free, or all shall bow to the will of the Kaiser." The thirty thousand teachers of the state of Illinois pledged to teach "loyalty to our government, reverence for our flag, and devotion to the principles of liberty, justice and humanity for which our nation stands. We will do all in our power to assist in winning this war."[57]

Leaders of the Military Training Camps Association in Illinois also hoped the threat of war would add to their prestige and influence. The organization had successfully operated camps for young white college, professional and middle-class men on both the East and West coasts since 1913, but the "Central Department" with responsibility for arranging camps in the Midwestern states had been unable to recruit enough volunteers to organize even one camp in 1916. As the chasm between Germany and the United States grew larger during February and March the Association fully expected and pushed for the United States to enter the war. War would heighten the importance of the training camps as a way to prepare white-middle-class men to become military officers.[58] But as the personal animosity between former President Theodore Roosevelt, who supported the camps, and President Wilson, who had been ambivalent, grew bitterer, the President began to oppose virtually any idea associated with Roosevelt. The training camps movement as well as the drive to establish universal military training lost momentum without support from the Administration and in the face of the Selective Service legislation drawn up by Wilson's advisors in March and April.[59]

Perhaps the most important pro-war group in Illinois was the American Protective League (APL) started by a Chicago businessman in March 1917. Certainly, none had a greater impact on the military draft. Initially the APL proposed to spy on enemy aliens, especially German immigrants who had not sought U.S. citizenship. By June, however, APL "secret service" agents had joined with the Committee on Public Information and the Illinois Council of Defense to identify and harass all Illinois residents who dared dissent from the nation's war policy.[60]

In communities throughout Illinois the APL campaign against dissenters often facilitated, and sometimes initiated, nativist attacks on German Americans. The organized German American opposition to Wilson's reelection and the popular association of Germans with the consumption and manufacture of beer were now added to their supposed affection for the German government. This combination brought together the superpatriotic groups and the temperance wing of Progressivism. As social, physical, and mental purity became essential to creating the ideal American soldier, prohibition leaders realized that war would strengthen their efforts to ban alcoholic beverages. AntiGerman, pro-war activists charged that beer-makers, beer distributors, and beer drinkers contaminated the manhood of the United States. With German Americans dominating the brewery industry, it was not difficult to make the connection between Germans and alcohol. Before the end of 1917 another semipublic organization, the National Security League (NSL), joined with local temperance leagues, the APL, and the U.S. marshal in Peoria, Springfield, and Rock Island to promote prohibition initiatives tinged with anti-German nativism.[61]

Pro-war groups also charged that German cultural influence in the schools of Illinois undermined efforts to secure the loyalty of all American residents. Under pressure from the APL and NSL, local school districts throughout the state banned performances of German music and instruction in the German language. The Illinois State Superintendent of Education encouraged school districts to eliminate anything associated with Germany from their curricula. He praised as "altogether desirable this intense and widespread hatred against everything and anyone who manifests the slightest proGerman tendency."[62]

Many Illinois citizens who in the past silently feared or disliked the German Americans in their midst now lashed out in a variety of ways. In dozens of Illinois towns and cities German Americans found themselves under siege. A mob in Collinsville kidnapped a man, tortured him for hours, and finally lynched him primarily because of his German surname. Even with a sworn confession from one of the participants, prosecutors could not persuade a local jury to convict members of the mob. Newspapers in Illinois and nationwide praised the spirit of the mob that tortured and killed Robert Prager. Referring to this case the *Washington Post* editorialized that "enemy propaganda must be stopped even if a few lynchings may occur."[63]

Confusion and Conflict in the System

The first registration for the draft in Illinois went off with few hitches, according to official reports. Authorities in Chicago wired Crowder: "Registration proceeding very quietly in Illinois." They predicted "almost universal compliance," adding that "no deserters or confusion whatever is anticipated." Lowden's telegram to Crowder on the day of registration reported "absolute quietness and satisfactory progress" in all sections of the state. In one area of Chicago, he admitted, "some posters advising persons not to register were put up" opposite a registration site. But "this is the only evidence of any registration propaganda. It would not be mentioned if you did not desire any instance of activity of anti-registration influences however small." It appeared at first that the only serious problem occurred where men in several counties could not get to registration centers because of storms and flooding. The governor wired Crowder on the day after registration expressing euphoria. "Show of splendid spirit by those concerned practically universal in Illinois."[64]

Despite this rosy picture painted by Governor Lowden and Adjutant General F. S. Dickson, the actual administration of the draft would not go smoothly in much of Illinois. Tensions between Chicago and Springfield surfaced early. White men living near large populations of nonresident aliens not subject to the draft complained that the quota system was unfair to them, which of course it was, since quotas were based on census reports of total population, including those exempt from the draft. When men of German ancestry sought and received exemptions the non-German population often accused them of not being patriotic. In addition, the APL did not trust Dickson and attempted to co-opt his office in the handling of delinquents and deserters. And state authorities had trouble persuading some board members to continue after their initial experiences.

The issue of quotas concerned both the state, as a whole, and specific communities. First Dickson sparred with the Provost Marshal General over the credits Illinois would receive for men in the state's National Guard. Then the governor protested that the Illinois quota was inequitable because of the number of exempt aliens in the state. Officials in New Jersey and California made the same complaint. Lowden argued that the number of men drafted from Illinois should be reduced by the number of aliens in the population. Dickson added his objections, characterizing the quotas as "manifestly unjust," and warning Crowder that this issue threatened to undo the good will he thought the Selective Service System enjoyed in most communities. "There is much dissatisfaction in the state with reference to this matter of apportionment," Dickson reported.[65]

Displeasure with Illinois' draft quota extended to local boards. All three members of Board No. 42 in Chicago submitted their resignations to protest the quota rules. In a letter to the president, the Board wrote that in their jurisdiction nearly sixty percent of the registrants were exempt aliens, yet their quota was based on the total number registered rather than the total number that could be drafted. The quota should be based upon the number of citizens registered and not upon total registration. Unless this change was made, they said, "we do hereby and herewith tender our resignation to take effect immediately." Crowder rejected the resignations and threatened to have them prosecuted if they carried out their threat.[66]

Separate racial quotas caused additional confusion. Illinois, like California, had a considerably larger population of dark-skinned immigrants from places such as the Philippines and Mexico than either Georgia or New Jersey. Both local boards and registrants from those groups often wondered by what criteria they were to define men as "colored" or "white." One inquiry identified "a Filipino . . . now a citizen of Litchfield, thirty-nine years of age who will be in the next draft. . . . He would like to know how he will be classified, being neither white nor negro." In another case a board wrote that a Filipino registrant "would like to know if he could be required to report for duty with colored troops." In the latter case the adjutant general ordered the board to send the man to California to help make up a Filipino unit there.[67] For the record, PMG Enoch Crowder had informed Governor Lowden in 1917 that "the word 'White' includes all persons except those of African descent."[68] But this communication apparently did not filter down to Dickson or to local boards. Sending their draftees of indeterminate race to California might be a solution for Chicago, but as we will see, Crowder's definition of "white" made no sense to white men in California either.

The wide variety of ethnic groups in the city, including recent African American arrivals from the South and a large number of men who spoke little or no English, caused additional problems. A letter from the Clerk of Chicago Local Board No. 4 to Crowder, August 9, 1917, succinctly expressed the problem with respect to African American migrants: "In our district there are a lot of colored men who have recently moved here from the South. They have written their local boards asking that their examination be transferred here. In many instances there have not been any answers. It is impossible for these men to return home. We believe they should be given a square deal. Will you investigate?" Crowder replied that he could only give advice regarding this problem on a case-by-case basis.[69]

Many draft-age male citizens of nations having offices in Chicago sought the advice and intercession of their consuls. Dickson's assistant, June C. Smith, complained that the Russian consul general "has become a positive nuisance. This office is swamped with letters and telegrams from this man, and local boards are annoyed beyond endurance." Smith charged that "this man exists on fees he charges to registrants who call at his office," and implied that the man might not be a legitimate diplomat. Crowder was unwilling to get involved in such a controversy and referred the correspondence to the State Department, which apparently ignored it.[70] Chicago attorney Carioli Gigliotti made similar charges against the Italian consul. Gigliotti alleged that for $2.75 men could purchase certificates of Italian citizenship that would, if accepted by their local boards, excuse them from the draft.[71]

Opposition to the War and the Draft

From the beginning, Chicago was the center of an organized white Progressive criticism of the Administration's plans for war. The leading pacifists of the day, who were also some of the most famous Progressive reformers, called an antiwar conference in Chicago in March 1917. Attended by such luminaries as Jane Addams, Stanford University President David Starr Jordan, and William Lloyd Garrison's grandson, Oswald Garrison Villard, the Emergency Peace Federation convention advised the president that his ideals could not be achieved if the United States was a party to the European conflict. The socialists among them in particular insisted that if the United States joined the Allies it would be to protect the investments of Wall Street types.

But these "respectable" voices against the war had little effect. Less organized, more spontaneous, and more radical opposition to both the war and to the draft endlessly complicated attempts by state authorities in Springfield to run a smooth operation. Such random and unfocused opposition generated deep paranoia among supporters of the war. The Industrial Workers of the World (WW), active in both New Jersey and California as well, was a key part of this kind of opposition. They went on the offensive against the draft on registration day. In the northern Illinois city of Rockford two hundred draft-age men under the leadership of James Cully, a local IWW leader, marched to the courthouse and informed the sheriff that they were refusing to register. In accordance with their request the sheriff jailed the men. But then, according to the sheriff, the men began to vandalize the jail. In order to save the jail he divided the men into three groups, taking one group to the jail at Freeport and another group to the jail at Belvedere.[72]

The U.S. attorney general appointed a special assistant U.S. attorney to investigate and prosecute those involved. When this man, Charles F. Clyne, arrived at Rockford on June 8 he found fifty men remaining in the Rockford jail. He persuaded forty-three to register for the draft but kept them all incarcerated. "The parties regardless of whether or not they registered are being held in custody," Clyne wrote the attorney general. "The seriousness of the situation has apparently rendered this imperative. It was anticipated another riot would occur in Rockford last night."

Attorney General Gregory agreed with Clyne that the government should make an example of these men. Clyne wired the Justice Department that in his judgment "Grave consequences will attend attempted enforcement of the draft if leniency is shown now." Gregory wired back instructions to prosecute Cully and the other leaders "to the limit of the law." But he thought those who had registered in jail should be released on their own recognizance. When the trials were held at Freeport, 112 men were convicted. For some reason these men, who were convicted of federal crimes, were sentenced to prison at the Chicago House of Correction. But because authorities feared popular attempts to free these men if they were taken through the streets of Chicago they decided to carry them right into the center of the prison by sealed railroad car. To accomplish this the Justice Department paid the Illinois Central Railroad to lay a temporary spur line from a nearby permanent line to inside the prison walls. The government then transported the draft resisters by train from Freeport directly into the Chicago House of Correction, avoiding the need to carry them in buses through the city streets.

Prison, however, could not keep them out of the army. Six of the men convicted in the Rockford antidraft demonstration completed their prison sentences by the following May. Acting on instructions from Crowder, the Rockford Local Board assigned them low order numbers, inducted them, and sent them to training camp.[73] Whether these men followed the advice of IWW leaders and carried their radical agitation into the military is unknown.

A less militant antiwar gathering met in Chicago as the September draft calls were going out. The governor's decision to send the National Guard to stop it once again demonstrated the tensions between the state's largest city and its capital. The People's Council of America for Peace and Democracy under the leadership of Milwaukee socialist Louis Lochner had attempted to hold its national convention in three other Midwestern cities before arriving in Chicago. The governors of Wisconsin and Minnesota had closed them down in Milwaukee and Minneapolis, and a Minneapolis mob forced them out of the neighboring town of Hudson, Wisconsin. Chicago's

Mayor, William Hale Thompson, permitted the People's Council to meet in a hall in that city. Governor Lowden, already upset at Thompson for his attempt to interject himself into the administration of the draft in Chicago, dispatched four companies of the Illinois National Guard to Chicago to evict the pacifists. By the time they reached Chicago the People's Council had completed its convention, and according to historian Frederick C. Luebke, "the troops descended upon a Polish wedding festival which had taken over the hall."[74]

The German American Problem

Despite the Rockford incident and the peace conference in Chicago, concern about the large German American population in the state overshadowed fears of other ethnic groups and IWW radicals. From every part of the state both the governor and Selective Service officials received reports of suspected German plots to sabotage or otherwise thwart conscription. Some folks even distrusted these officials and sent their accusations either to President Wilson or to national periodicals for publication.

Unlike most of the other opponents of the war or the draft, German Americans were not confined to urban environments. They were spread across the state in towns, cities, and on farms. While Germans had traditionally been considered "good" immigrants, with the nation now at war against Germany many among the Anglo-Saxon middle class now thought German American culture undermined American (meaning white) values. Anthropologist, Karen Brodkin, refers to groups like these who held on to non-Anglo cultural traditions as "not quite white."[75] At a time when middle-class reformers were rapidly succeeding in imposing local prohibitions against alcohol across the nation the Germans were identified as the primary brewers in America. And when "One Hundred Percent Americanism" rejected "hyphenism," German Americans seemed inordinately attached to their own language, music, food, political ideology, and religion. Many believed the Germans were the source of radical political thought in America. In addition, people in Illinois knew that three German religious sects with significant numbers in Illinois condemned all war. These three groups, the Church of the Brethren (also known as Dunkards), Mennonites, and Amish Mennonites, also held most strongly to German language and food. These factors all helped to instill fear of German Americans and stimulate fantasies of German intrigue across the state.

A woman from southern Illinois wrote the *Literary Digest* that her family doctor, Herman T. Bechtold, who was also the examining physician for the local draft board, was "entirely pro-German." She alleged that "on his office table is to be seen 'Faderland.'" Furthermore, the doctor was openly sympathetic to a neighbor who had proclaimed that his son "would die on this side before he would cross the ocean and fight." Equally serious was the behavior of the principal of a local school. "Mr Ferdinand Reuss will not allow the U.S. flag on the school house here," she declared. When a teacher put one up anyway, "Mr Reuss's sister and wife waited on him and the flag has not been seen since." The editor of the *Literary Digest* agreed with the correspondent that "these two men ought not to hold influential positions." He forwarded the letter to the Secretary of War with the comment that "it reveals a state of affairs which should have official attention and correction at once."[76]

An unexpected event, nonconformity with community norms, or innocent behavior that was out of the ordinary could generate suspicion. The local board secretary in Williamson County suspected a Western Union telegraph operator of disloyalty when messages received in the evening were not delivered until the next day. Other boards denied exemptions to registrants on the grounds that they or their families opposed the war. When a district board for the Southern District of Illinois acted against a local board recommendation and exempted one of its registrants on agricultural grounds, the members of the latter board struck back with charges that the registrant was disloyal. According to the local board for Rock Island County the man's uncle had a picture of the Kaiser on his wall, and "the father was a radical pro-German, bitter and very pronounced in his denunciation of the draft law, the United States Government and the President."[77]

But the response to German Americans was hardly uniform throughout Illinois. When a U.S. attorney sought the dismissal of an entire board for treating its registrants of German ancestry with too much consideration Governor Lowden ordered an investigation. The local board for Monroe County "and their henchmen," according to U.S. attorney Charles Karch, had pursued "a persistent course of nagging and contentiousness . . . against factions in the county who have been more or less active in surveiling the loyalty of the local population and demanding rigid fairness and a blind justice in the draft procedure." The Illinois Military and Naval Department carried out one investigation of this complaint. It concluded that the local board had mistakenly classified a group of men who had been physically examined and disqualified under the original Selective Service regulations. In the process of converting to the new system of classification established for the 1918 draft calls this board had been confused but not fraudulent, said the investigator.[78]

The board apparently had been at odds with some elements of the community before the mistaken classifications were discovered. The large German population there was suspected of favoring the Kaiser, and when the board began granting agricultural and dependency exemptions to German American men of draft age other people in the community began to complain. The conflict intensified when someone discovered that the son of a board member had been exempted. The governor declined to ask for the board's dismissal, accepting the investigator's judgment that "it might tend to inflame the community against the Selective Service Law. The County is very largely German and originally there were no doubt many pro-German citizens in the county." But he predicted that if left alone this condition would change. The Military Investigative Bureau of the United States War Department also sent an investigator to Monroe County. He concluded that the charges against the draft board were "due to personal and political animosities and persons there using issues of the war and draft to promote their own interests."[79] In this case, a community was deeply divided between German Americans or immigrants and citizens of non-German ancestry with xenophobic inclinations. The latter group saw the operations of the Selective Service System in this community as an opportunity to express their resentment against the German influence in their community. Illinois officials wisely decided that it would be counterproductive to humor the anti-German sentiment in Monroe County.

Sometimes the charges that draft board members were pro-German had roots in social relations of long standing that may have caused resentment to build for years against particular members. Class and ethnic antagonisms often combined. One accusation zeroed in on a board member at Blue Island who was also "President of the biggest bank here." As in Monroe County the controversy was sparked when the son of the board member in question received a deferment. Then local dissidents added other charges and BI chief Bruce Bielaski sent an agent to look into the matter. His report concluded that the bank president/board member and his family "were rabidly proGerman before the United States declared war on Germany." There were intimations from local people that this board member had secured his appointment through illegitimate backroom political dealings. The agent thought it appeared that the board had favored German American registrants with a liberal deferment policy. He gave an example in which the local board recommended an agricultural exemption to a man farming twenty-five acres behind his house.[80]

A possible, and in fact probable, explanation for this board's behavior is less incriminating. It is likely that the board was concerned that by pressing too hard on registrants who had ambivalent feelings about the war it would offend the large German American population, of which it was a part. Thus, in order to deflect discontent from that quarter the board simply freely recommended agricultural deferments for most who claimed them. But the decision to grant or deny such claims lay with the district board. That board apparently did not shrink from ruling against local board recommendations. As a result, those men were returned to the local board to be included in the call when their number came up. If the local board had really desired to keep such men out of the draft it could have acted as most rural Georgia boards did and offer dependency deferments in lieu of agricultural ones. The board at Blue Island thus was able to appear to favor the German American population by leaving final decisions up to the district board.[81]

In the face of such confusion Dickson and Governor Lowden, sought to downplay the coercive aspects of the Selective Service System. They urged local officials and newspapers to encourage cooperation with the draft by appealing first to the "patriotism and loyalty" of Illinois men. Then mayors and local boards should ask the newspapers in their communities to place a short notice on the front page of their Sunday editions the week of registration that would state briefly what acts would be punishable under the Selective Service Law and indicate the penalty for committing them. "The harsher side of the law must be put plainly before the people . . . in a way to get before everybody on the same day and without any preliminaries," wrote Dickson. He hoped this would be sufficient notice to the men of Illinois.[82]

Apparently it was not enough, for many draft-age immigrant men in Illinois did not register as required. But equally important, local law enforcement officials were sometimes enthusiastic about carrying "the harsher side of the law" to its farthest conclusion. In one of the most egregious examples, the local police in Chicago saw non-English-speaking immigrants as easy targets for arrest under the Selective Service Law. For example, within two months of the 1917 registration dozens of Mexican immigrant men had been jailed for not registering. The Mexican consul in Chicago wrote Secretary of State Lansing to report that "various Mexican citizens of the peon class, who because of their ignorance of the language and laws, excusable in view of their conditions, failed to live up to the requirements of the draft registration." These men were taken from jobs and imprisoned. State and federal officials saw these men as essential labor in the wartime economy and quickly agreed to Lansing's request for their release, but not before they had suffered substantial humiliation and economic loss.[83]

Government-Sanctioned Vigilantism: The APL

In many parts of Illinois the American Protective League (APL) took on the primary function of enforcing the Selective Service Act. Like officials in Chicago, the APL openly questioned the ability of state authorities in Springfield to oversee properly all aspects of the draft. APL "secret service" agents enthusiastically stepped into the enforcement vacuum they thought existed. Such men assumed the cloak of governmental authority yet no institution of the government oversaw or supervised their activities. This was an extreme arrogation of state authority through which APL agents often constructed their own sense of manly purpose by denying legitimate free agency to other men. Those other men might even be government officials who in the judgment of the APL wielded power weakly or ineffectively. APL agents advised local boards to forward their reports of delinquents and deserters to the APL offices in Chicago rather than to the adjutant general in Springfield. One board did not discover until spring of 1918 that it should send these reports to the adjutant general.

Dickson, in the dark about the legal status of the APL with respect to investigating Selective Service violations, requested clarification from Crowder. The Provost Marshal General's reply left no doubt that this privately organized group operating under no formal government oversight had been given virtual governmental authority. "The American Protective League is working in conjunction with the Department of Justice in the investigation and rounding up of delinquents," wrote Crowder's assistant, C. A. Hope. Yet there was evidence in Illinois and elsewhere that the APL's investigations and "arrests" occurred unevenly. The "secret service" agents were free to pick and choose their investigations. As a result, they "rounded up" large numbers in some regions and none in many others. Despite their heavy presence in Chicago, however, one local board complained that the APL "have been unable to report to our Board the result of the investigations on delinquents who failed to file their questionnaire." This was four months after the questionnaire system had been instituted.[84]

Slacker Raids and "Work or Fight"

By the summer of 1918 the national "work or fight" policies were in place, and officials at all levels in Illinois in collaboration with the APL made no secret of the fact that they would use the draft to discourage young men from any activities that did not directly aid the war effort. Chicago police, as well as those in Peoria, East St. Louis, Rock Island, and Danville, would have state and federal sanction to make dragnet sweeps of places where idle young men were likely to hang out.[85]

The Chicago event, characterized as a "slacker raid," took place during four days in July 1918. There, as elsewhere, APL agents outnumbered the local police, and private citizens made most of the arrests. The raid began on a Thursday afternoon with five thousand APL "operatives" and "all available police officers." They swept through Chicago's ball parks, theaters, bars, pool rooms, elevated and railway stations, parks, the docks, and "in fact all places where young men congregate," Dickson reported to Governor Lowden. The raids continued until midnight on Thursday, Friday, Saturday, and Sunday. The city's local draft boards remained open until midnight each day of the raids in order to substantiate charges or clear men unjustly detained.

No accounting of the total number of men arrested during this operation appears in Selective Service records. One report, however, said that APL members alone interrogated 150,000 men. Forty thousand of these were said to be "non-willful delinquents," twelve hundred "evaders," and 265 "deserters." Officials delivered men who had failed to respond to induction orders to nearby army camps as deserters. There they could collect fifty dollars from the army for each deserter. Most of those rounded up, however, were men who had either failed to register or had not completed the required classification questionnaire. These men were delivered to their local draft boards where they were forced to register and complete the questionnaire.[86]

Unlike the New Jersey raids in which a local prosecutor and private detectives sought deserters and delinquents at factory gates, the Illinois raiders made a point of arresting only men found gathered at spots where upstanding middle-class-white men would not be found. This selectiveness guaranteed that few workers essential to the wartime economy would be taken from their jobs. In addition, since the raids were conducted on a weekend, those few detainees who did have legitimate employment could be processed and freed without losing work time.

The enthusiasm of Selective Service officials for such raids inadvertently encouraged some police and APL agents to indiscriminately stop draft-age males and demand proof of their compliance with the "work or fight" demands of Selective Service. This caused considerable inconvenience to men such as those in the National Guard who did not have to register for the draft. But state Selective Service officials were unable to get the cooperation of either federal or local authorities in their attempts to halt the practice. Dickson complained to Washington that local police as well as the APL secret service men frequently detained Illinois National Guardsmen who were not wearing the federal uniform. But Crowder and others apparently had more pressing concerns and did not reply to Dickson's plea for help with this "considerable annoyance."[87]

Ironically, the groups that most fanatically supported both the war and conscription at the same time frustrated many of the efforts of the Illinois adjutant general. They weakened the legitimacy of state authority by confusing it with the acts of ambitious white men who acted as state-sanctioned vigilantes. The adjutant general's office virtually lost control of the Chicago boards. Rumors spread that draft officials in Springfield were ineffective and easily swayed by private local interests. By the end of the war local boards outside of Chicago also sought to bypass Dickson, often appealing directly to the Provost Marshal General, who nevertheless referred them back to Dickson.

Women and the Draft

As the story of Mrs. Barbee that opens this chapter suggests, "work or fight" often served women's interests quite nicely. Women's communications with draft officials nearly always made explicit the connections between ideals of manhood, productive labor, serving the nation and supporting white families. Nearly all the surviving letters from wives, mothers and sisters of draft-age men are from white women. They made little attempt to hide the fact that they would use the stick of military conscription and whatever insults to manhood were necessary to get protection from abusive men or the economic support they believed the men of Illinois owed them.

For some wives, the draft offered hope that perhaps an abusive husband might be removed from the home without jeopardizing their economic survival. Mrs. Charley McNeely asked the Committee on Public Information for guidance in getting her husband of eight years drafted. "He is very mean to me," she wrote, and "it seems like the longer we stay together the meaner he gets." She said that she had left him twice, "and both times he coaxed me back. I was in hopes he would haft to go to some training camp and Baby and I would be happy." To her dismay the local board for Cumberland County recommended that he be deferred on occupational grounds and the district board agreed. The solution, thought Mrs. McNeely would be to find a way to put him in class I and get him drafted. This would both take him away from home and guarantee her an income. "Now I could live without him if I had a common salery," she said. She was almost, but not quite, resigned to having him remain at home. "I don't suppose he will haft to go to war at all, al though [sic] he is strong + healthy never was sick much in his life."[88]

In addition to claims of nonsupport and abuse, women used the draft to wage battles against social ills in general that they believed made it difficult for them to live without support from their husbands. Local boards looked askance at such women. Myrtle Williams of Salem addressed her concerns to "Mr. Wilson" [the President]. Her husband had deserted her and the children after being deferred as their sole support. "He has not done but two days work in the last month he gambles all the time." Her letter then described the difficulties a woman faced trying to support herself in the wartime economy. "I do all I can to make a liven but everything is so high I just can pay rent and buy fuel and grocerys by my self." Mrs. Williams's social commentary left the local board less than sympathetic to her complaints about her husband. The board secretary wrote to the adjutant general that "from personal conversation with the wife it appears that it would be impossible for any body [sic] to live with this woman." The board decided that she was an unfit mother. Far exceeding its authority, it attempted to remove the children from her home and place them with a guardian who would then receive the husband's military allowance if he were drafted.[89] As long as white men's wives met white-middle-class males standards for women in wartime they could expect sympathetic assistance. But sympathy for women like Mrs. Williams quickly vanished.

Some women saw themselves in a kind of partnership with the government in making men act according to accepted standards. A wife from Montgomery County who had left her husband because "he got so bad and mean to live with," informed the War Department that "from last year sometime and from August he has been at large" as a deserter from the Canadian army. "Could we not put him in the United States Army," she inquired. He was currently living in Nokomis, Illinois, with his mother and had her two children. The wife was expecting another child in five months and thought if her husband were drafted she would get the other two children back along with an allowance from his military pay on which she could live. She hoped the War Department would "make it hot for him he is a Scotchman and reports he deserted 4 times so fix him if you can and oblige Mrs. John Reid." She got her wish two and a half months later when authorities informed her that her husband would be immediately inducted into the military service provided she signed a waiver as his dependent. "When Reid is eventually inducted," she was told, "the Treasury Department Bureau of War Risk Insurance will furnish you information relative to the allotment and allowance due soldiers' wives."[90]

At least one African American woman from the South appealed to similar values and used the same strategy as these white women as a way of tracking down her husband who had gone to Illinois.[91] Melba Darensbourg White, a black woman, wrote to the War Department alleging that her husband William "has been skipping and dodging from one place to another," trying to avoid the draft. She gave an address in Galesburg, Illinois, where authorities could expect to find him. But a review of draft registration files revealed that William White, officially designated "colored" by draft officials, and originally from Louisiana, had registered for the draft at the Knox County Local Board in Galesburg. White had submitted his classification questionnaire, waiving any deferment claims, but was rejected by the board physician because of blindness in one eye.[92] This case is, however, highly exceptional. Given the movement of tens of thousands of African Americans from the South to Illinois during this period, it may be more remarkable that there were not more such letters in the Selective Service records for Illinois.

In response to women's inquiries Selective Service officials prepared a form letter that was sent to the adjutant general of the state for each such complaint.[93] The decision to investigate a particular complaint appears to have been either random or subject to the whim of state officials. In the vast majority of cases there is no record of an investigation.

Delivering Men to Training Camp

The final stage in a draftee's relationship with his local draft board was known as "entrainment." Those men called up and declared fit were put on a train to a designated army training camp where an army physician would once again examine them. As we have seen, many local draft boards in Georgia entrained African American men who were rejected by army physicians on arrival. Investigators concluded that local boards were trying to meet their "colored" quotas without sending healthy and valuable farm workers.

In Illinois there was no widespread pattern of local boards routinely using the draft to rid their communities of men they considered "useless" or troublemakers as there was in Georgia. Nevertheless, training camp commanders did criticize and even ridicule the performances of local board doctors in Illinois. Some boards sent men to camp whose physical condition even the most casual observer could see would prevent them from becoming effective soldiers. The motives of local board physicians, army medical personnel, and military commanders were complex, and no single explanation for their acts in regard to physical examinations will suffice.

But the commander at Camp Logan reported so many examples of physically "defective" draftees from particular boards that Crowder asked Bruce Bielaski of the

Bureau of Investigation to investigate. "These reports indicate that some of the boards proceeded upon the principle that certain persons undesirable in civil life should be sent to the army to be cured of the maladies from which they suffer," Crowder wrote. He asked Bielaski to "please have these cases investigated with the view of prosecuting criminally the guilty parties whether they be medical examiners or entire boards."[94]

Some board examiners undoubtedly knew that such men would not be cured in the army. However, pressure to meet quotas, requests for exemptions, and the shortage of male labor made some physicians send men to camp who clearly would be rejected. Crowder was correct in more ways than he knew when he noted the desire to rid communities of "undesirable" men. Not only might undesirable mean someone who could not or would not contribute manly labor to the community, or someone whose social behavior invited scorn: it also could mean a man whose physical features contravened dominant standards for men.[95]

In some instances the examining physicians on the local boards may have believed they were doing the men a favor by drafting them. Perhaps the army doctors could correct the malady even though it obviously demanded rejection under the Selective Service regulations. The Decatur Local Board sent a man who, according to Army physicians, had obvious symptoms of syphilis. The investigation revealed that his draft registration card contained the notation, "chronic syphilis." The man told the BI agent that his local board said that he would "be cured in the Army without cost to himself."[96]

Sometimes examining physicians both on local boards and at army camps amused themselves, perhaps hiding embarrassment, at the expense of men with tragic conditions that most certainly made them social pariahs. The board physician at Lewiston "laughed and made no comment," when a draftee told him that he could not control his urination. The army reported: "soldier has wet bed since childhood. Also lacks control during the day. Since coming to Camp Logan has wet bed every night, and has wet clothing on drill field several times during day."[97] One can only imagine the humiliation this man was made to feel. Without a doubt, such a condition, associated in the minds of adults with childhood, called into question his manhood in the eyes of other soldiers.

An even more extreme case involved an individual said to have both male and female secondary sex characteristics. This person became the object of curiosity first at his local board in Monmouth, then at Camp Dodge, and finally at Camp Logan. Because of his physical oddities the local board physician asked permission to photograph him. He told an investigator that the doctors at Camp Dodge said they were sending him to Camp Logan because they sent all "defective" draftees there, although this was not an official army policy. Those who described him were at the same time inadvertently listing physical characteristics that they believed to be inconsistent with white manhood. And they exhibited a mixture of curiosity, amusement and pity, but also confusion regarding what should be done with him. The Camp Logan report depicted him as having "very characteristic feminine build,—no beard, large well-developed breasts, prominent abdomen, feminine pelvis, small male genitals, testicles size of beans, large hips, thin tapering legs, high pitched voice, scanty hair over public [sic] region and no hair on body, poor muscular development. States has never had an erection. He lives on a farm but has never been able to do heavy work."[98] In a time when an intrinsically masculine institution—the state—was engaging in its most explicitly manly activity—war—which it justified in terms of protecting a symbolically universal woman—the nation or liberty—no one knew what to do with an individual who was neither manly nor womanly. Such a person was reduced to the status of a sideshow curiosity.

This unusual, certainly atypical case thus threw into sharp relief the social meaning of physical characteristics. The report carefully avoided suggesting that this person was woman, or even part woman. He was, rather, of "feminine build," could not do heavy work, had little body hair, wide hips and thin legs. Many of the features that interested the examiners had nothing to do with sexual function, either male or female. Instead, they were attributes that had taken on gendered meaning in the context of a society that held up male and female physical archetypes that were unrealizable for most. Yet many American men and women measured their own manliness and womanliness by such archetypes. The attention paid to a hermaphrodite, if that is what he was, must have reflected more than simple curiosity. Perhaps those men who viewed and photographed him derived some comfort in noting how much closer their bodies adhered to the desired type.[99] But in the final analysis, men in charge of a system whose purpose was to select some "men" for war and others for civilian pursuits by means of a system of classification, were thrown into a state of confusion by a person who could not be classified according to the most essential of categories—that of sex.

Conclusion

At the end of the war as draft boards and other wartime groups demobilized, Samuel Insull, Chairman of the Illinois State Council of Defense reflected on what the wartime home front had told us about Progressive manhood and citizenship. Progressive men, he said, were "shareholders" in the nation's civic life, investing in the nation their talents and money. The Progressive man has "undivided loyalty and unfaltering devotion to the cause of America," He could thus be neither a pacifist nor a "hyphenate." He would spurn partisan politics, but would "not conceal his convictions nor camouflage his attitude for political purposes." If foreign-born, he must give up his foreign language and alien ideologies, become assimilated, and exhibit "a sound and enduring patriotism."[100] Excluded from Insull's definition of a Progressive American man are the conscientious objectors, the imprisoned IWW resisters and socialists, the German Americans who kept their language and their religious beliefs, and especially the women who manipulated the male state for their own purposes. Each refused to bow to Insull's emasculating language, and in so doing they exercised the kind of agency that Theodore Roosevelt believed was essential to whiteness and manhood.

CHAPTER THREE

NEW JERSEY: "HE'S HIS MOTHER'S BOY; GO AND GET HIM"

In March 1916, about a year before the United States declared war on Germany, a commission created by the New Jersey State Legislature announced its opposition to military training for boys in New Jersey's public high schools. It thus took a stand against the growing military "preparedness" movement sweeping the nation under the leadership of men such as former President Theodore Roosevelt and his friend, General Leonard Wood. Preparedness leaders advocated military training for high school boys as well as summer military camps for middle class and professional white men whose lack of physical fitness or experience of hardship Roosevelt and Wood thought undermined the virility of the nation.[1] The commissioners directly engaged this debate over manhood, focusing on the relationship between age and military training. "Those who urge the military training of pupils of the high schools," wrote the commissioners, "urge it mainly as a preparation for manhood service in time of war." But military training of high school boys could have no beneficial effect at this stage of their lives, and furthermore, might hinder the boys' natural development. Being yet boys, they could not use "manhood training." "Juvenile training must, at some time, be followed by manhood training and service," agreed the commissioners, but manhood and juvenile training could not be simultaneous nor could manhood profitably precede juvenile training.[2]

As good Progressives, the commissioners feared blurring the lines between the categories of man, boy, soldier, and citizen, and between military training and education. "Military training and service, if they are necessary, are an obligation of citizenship, not of education," they maintained. Boys were not yet citizens—a status reserved for men. They noted that there was not yet a "sufficiently comprehensive plan of the service of adults." To institute such a plan for boys would be to threaten the meaning that men found in differentiating themselves from boys. They quoted General Baden-Powell, British founder of the Boy Scouts, in opposition to military drill: "Drill a boy and spoil a soldier." Truncating the period that was naturally part of boyhood, these men thought, would blur the lines between the two identities (those of boyhood and manhood) and in so doing threaten to limit boys' eventual full realization of manhood.[3]

The commissioners feared that military training in the public schools would weaken the boundaries between men and non-men. It would make boys think that they were men before they possessed the emotional maturity and the physical stature, strength, and stamina required of men. In addition, the commissioners thought it telling that in Wyoming military training in high schools had weakened gender lines to the extent that girls were incorporated in ways not appropriate to their sex. "In one school," the commission reported, "both boys and girls were required to wear uniforms." Even more alarming was the finding that "girls were not instructed in first aid, bandaging, and other duties commonly considered appropriate to girls, but were expected to attend the drills and other exercises for the purpose of influencing the personal demeanor of the cadets and stimulating them in their work."[4] A consequence of blurring the line between boys and men was thus a more egregious blurring of the line between male and female.

The New Jersey Commission Report demonstrates a salient aspect of gender construction among white men who were involved in politics and government during the Progressive era, and especially during World War I. It shows that men who differed in the ways they constructed their manhood nevertheless did so with reference to a common set of values and assumptions. Both military preparedness advocates and the Progressive New Jersey politicians who opposed them thought that in order to enter fully into manhood American males needed to develop their "powers of muscular and mental coordination" by subjecting themselves to "unusual and trying circumstances." Both groups thought that manhood required self-discipline, obedience to authority, internalization of accepted rules of society, participation in the political life of the nation, and recognition that they had military obligations. The New Jersey Commissioners tried to protect what they saw as natural delineations between men and non-men from forces that threatened self-evidently correct manhood. But preparedness leaders such as Roosevelt said men had to create their own manhood through strenuous effort. According to Donna Haraway, Roosevelt had an all-encompassing vision of manhood—that "[a]ny human being, regardless of race, class, and gender, could spiritually participate in the moral status of healthy manhood in democracy, even if only a few (anglo-saxon, male, heterosexual, Protestant, physically robust, and economically comfortable) could express manhood's highest forms."[5]

The commissioners disagreed with Roosevelt over the nature of military training. While they believed that the armed forces required people who were fully men, they did not believe that military training was essential to the development of manhood. Military training provides "nothing of value" to men. "Obedience to military authority is generally unthinking. It is often blind and superficial, not real." It is "actual war," according to the commissioners, for which men would "willingly undergo training, . . . because the work is definitely motivated." Under peacetime conditions, military training "is obedience under restraint." They denied that "those who have had military training, or been subject to military discipline, are superior to other citizens in the possession of [the] qualities" that made a good man. These qualities they identified as "alertness, promptness, industry, truthfulness, . . . obedience, patriotism, [and] orderly behavior." "Military forms and observances," according to the commissioners, "may furnish opportunities for the manifestation" of such traits, but they could not be expected to produce them. Every "upright, useful citizen" possesses these characteristics, but not every one will choose military service. "Military training must aim at military service" and nothing more.

This view of manhood, citizenship and military training and service was the most fundamental principle of Selective Service. Manhood could not be dependent on military service if only some men were selected. There had to be room in the concept of manhood for those who performed their duties in other ways. Yet this left enough room to shame men who worked ineffectively or did nothing to assist in the war effort by calling their manhood into question. In this view a citizen was a particular kind of man. He was one who had self-discipline, was well-trained and thus effective, and who retained agency in the affairs of his own life. He could be the conscript who President Wilson would call the one selected "from a nation which has volunteered in mass [*sic*]."[6]

White middle class concepts of manhood, although not uniform, existed within a fairly narrow range of similar alternatives. Even many feminists, labor radicals, and leaders of the movement against militarization, accepted the terms through which the discourse on manhood took place. The American Union Against Militarism (AUAM), which included many women activists as well as leading socialists, reproduced and distributed the commission's report. The AUAM viewed it as a victory for the opponents of the ideals that fed the preparedness movement. But as their enthusiasm for the report reveals, they also unwittingly accepted the gender values that underlay preparedness ideology. Some opponents of militarization were thus trapped a gender paradigm whose principles linked manhood to individual self mastery, mastery of the earth and other people, and the assertion of state power both through law and through war. But those like labor radical Emma Goldman and IWW leader Elizabeth Gurley Flynn who seemed to reject the dominant discourse on manhood were particularly susceptible to social and political marginalization, and by the end of 1916 did not constitute a serious challenge to the hegemony of traditional white manhood. Kathleen Kennedy discovered that not only did the state label such women "disorderly," but their radical male allies continued to define them as the " 'other' through which the male citizen defined himself." The AUAM disintegrated in the Spring of 1917 when many influential members decided to support American entry into the war. The left wing of the former AUAM abandoned any fundamental challenge to the social order. Under the leadership of Roger Baldwin, it would later establish the Civil Liberties Bureau to defend the legal rights of individuals who opposed the war. After the war this organization became the American Civil Liberties Union.[7]

When the United States entered World War I, then, New Jersey opponents and supporters of militarization and the war shared a common ideology of gender and race. This seriously compromised antiwar organizations, leaving most truly radical opposition in the hands of random individuals acting alone. Selective Service System officials were intensely aware of this and sought to capitalize on it by emphasizing the individual white man's relationship to the state and duty to the nation. Men, in the words of President Wilson, would become part of a "team." But teamwork emphasized the duty of each individual, as an individual, to internalize the rules and values of the team. Thus, particular men who could not or would not conform would be singled out as odd. Each man would be judged individually in a process of categorization that would legitimate his place in American society.[8]

Paterson: The Community and Its Local Draft Board

Paterson, New Jersey, in 1917 seemed in many ways the epitome of an industrial town. Yet, as in rural Georgia and Illinois, and borderlands California, white men performed their whiteness and manhood through the exercise of state power that gave them property rights over the labor of women and other men and over the productive resources of the earth. Even after a century of industrial enterprise had been imposed upon this parcel of earth, propertied white men still battled to defeat the forces of nature, and propertied white men still struggled to claim manhood by dominating propertyless white men, women, immigrants, and children, not as non-white, or non-men, but as inferior forms of whiteness or manhood. This required strict governmental and social regulation until, if ever, they should acquire the qualities of whiteness and manhood. As Paterson prepared for entry into the European War, this was reflected in its physical contours no less than in its political organizations and economic relations.

Alexander Hamilton and William Paterson chose to build the first industrial city in the United States at the Great Falls of the Passaic River in what is now New Jersey. Here water that has seeped from springs in the Kittatinny Mountains of western New Jersey and has flowed into hundreds of small streams that feed the Passaic, tumbles over a seventy-seven-foot wall of rock. From there it makes a semicircle, inside which the city of Paterson would be built, and slowly winds its way south across a low-lying plain to Newark Bay just east of Staten Island. One way or the other around Staten Island, the water eventually reaches New York Bay. Below the falls land is mostly flat, sloping gradually toward Newark to the South and the Hudson to the east. Above the falls the landscape that justifies New Jersey's nickname, "The Garden State," offers a countryside of hills and valleys carved out by small creeks and rivers. The soil is fertile but rocky.[9] But fatefully, the power potential of the Great Falls coupled with its proximity to what was already in 1790 the nation's major commerce center inspired Hamilton and Paterson to build their city there.

Paterson's first hundred years paralleled the rise of the United States as a major industrial capitalist power. Founded in the 1790s to be a manufacturing center, it had become an important industrial town by 1840. Its geographic location was ideal in several ways: It was close to the greatest commercial center in the nation; it was not too distant from coal and iron mines of Pennsylvania; and a major river reached its fall line there. Paterson's founders harnessed the force of the Great Falls of the Passaic River to power factories built there during the nineteenth century. Cotton textile mills transformed slave-grown cotton from southern plantations into yarn and cloth. Then iron mills supplied locomotive and tool manufacturers. The more than five thousand locomotives built in Paterson between 1837 and 1879 helped drive the "transportation revolution." Other heavy machinery manufactured in Paterson during the nineteenth century was used on transoceanic steamships and in factories in England, Russia, and Latin America.[10]

The peculiar advantages of location and history made the capitalists who built Paterson unique among industrial capitalists of their time. Unlike most major industrial capitalists in the nineteenth-century United States, the men who founded Paterson's factories nearly all began as workers themselves.[11] By mid-century many such men headed large successful enterprises and enjoyed great wealth. This was, no less than in Coweta or Adams Counties, a white patriarchal system based in both public and private heterosexuality. These men were virtually all married. Their wives managed their households, even if they paid poor women to do the housework; their wives raised their children; and their wives, like those in rural Georgia and Illinois, engaged in civic activities and social networking that helped make the system of patriarchal industrial capitalism function more smoothly. Without the various labors of women in both paid and unpaid support of the households of white men who directed industrial enterprises in Paterson, it is fair to say that industry would have ground to a halt.

During the second half of the century silk and textile manufacturing replaced the earlier iron industries in Paterson. The white men who brought silk to Paterson converted it from a city of small iron workshops that hired only men to a multiple-industry city offering jobs to women and children as well. In twenty-four years near the end of the nineteenth century the population tripled as both immigrants and native-born workers arrived to take jobs in the new silk factories. This growth in turn stimulated an expansion of the white male middle class, consisting mainly of professionals and small entrepreneurs, and the women married to them who kept their homes and raised their children.[12]

In the 1890s the middle-class-white men of Paterson became increasingly estranged from the working class. Factory workers no longer looked or acted like good Anglo-Saxon Americans. The flood of immigrants who began coming from southern and Eastern Europe at that time brought social patterns and cultural practices that seemed alien to the older residents of Paterson. Immigrants were not new to them, but earlier immigrants to Paterson had come mostly from the British Isles. The Irish and the English, about equal in number, were the two largest groups until shortly before the turn of the century. By the early twentieth century Italian immigrants had become the largest ethnic group in Paterson, and by 1915 they were more numerous than the Irish and English combined.[13] In 1910 old-time residents would recognize little of what had been nineteenth-century Paterson. Fewer of the factory workers spoke English or attended Protestant churches.[14]

Two events in early-twentieth-century Paterson are important for understanding how the Selective Service System would function there, and in particular, the ways in which it would build on and reinforce the dominance of propertied heterosexual white males. The first was the creation of a juvenile justice system that applied Progressive principles of gender and scientific racism toward the goal of making Paterson's white boys into men. The second was a radical labor upheaval in the silk industry that taught industrialists important lessons about women and immigrants as workers. They would apply these lessons as they established the Selective Service System in Paterson.

Like Progressive leaders in many American towns and cities during the first decade of the twentieth century, Paterson's authorities instituted a whole system of interrelated programs to control adolescent boys and to guarantee that parents raised them properly.[15] Not only did they create a new category of juvenile crime, but city fathers established a detail of truant officers who visited 2,649 homes in fiscal year 1911–1912, a juvenile court, and a special disciplinary school for adolescent boys who were not considered bad enough to send to reform school. The male focus of the juvenile system was reflected in both the proportion of boys to girls caught in its web and in the fact that the disciplinary school was for boys only.[16]

At the disciplinary school authorities divided the boys into three categories: (1) "Defective," and presumably beyond rescue; (2) Boys "having no respect for law or order and unwilling to learn;" and (3) "The simply unruly, mischievous boy, temporarily out of control," who could be quickly straightened out. They apparently wrote off Category One boys as hopeless. They sent Category Two boys on to longer terms at the reformatory. Those in the third category remained at the disciplinary school until teachers determined that they could be safely reintegrated into the regular public school.[17]

The boys subjected to this new form of government surveillance starting in 1910 would make up the bulk of those required to register for the draft in June 1917. The juvenile justice system would prepare these boys for the intrusion of the federal government into their lives through the Selective Service System. Paterson's adolescent boys during this period were increasingly likely to experience directly the power of the local police. Although males under the age of twenty-one were only 18.5 percent of all men arrested in 1911, by 1919 they were 26.1 percent. Males ages twenty-one and under constituted approximately twenty percent of the city's total population and forty percent of all male residents during this period.[18]

There are startling similarities between the ideology that led to the creation of a juvenile justice system in Paterson and ideology of race specific criminal laws applied to African Americans in Coweta County and to American Indians, Mexicans, Chinese, and Japanese in San Diego. There is an unspoken racial allusion in the application of juvenile law in Paterson and an unspoken age allusion in the application racially specific laws in Coweta and San Diego. Both targeted primarily males. Both treated the targets as noncitizens, economic and political dependents of adult white males, and both were inordinately concerned with imposing standards of public etiquette, often with respect to ways the targeted population interacted with middle-class-white women.

This is simply another side to the scientific racism that pervaded the thinking of the white middle class in the United States at that time. They called it the "theory of recapitulation." It twisted Darwinian thought, holding that "lower races," meaning those considered inferior to the white race, were stuck in various primitive evolutionary stages of humanity. Black children, or American Indian children, according to recapitulation theory, were generally as intelligent and capable as white children until about puberty, at which time their mental capacities stopped developing. Advocates of this theory believed that adult blacks, in particular, were either perpetual children or perpetual adolescents. On the other hand, they believed that white adolescents, especially boys, were like adult black men, at a savage stage, one at which, writes Gail Bederman, "they possessed powerful masculine passions [but] were believed to be unable to wield civilized manly power because they lacked the racial [or manly] capacity for sexual restraint."[19]

Thus, Paterson authorities sought to help those white boys who seemed unable to complete their "savage" stage and move on naturally to become good self-controlled white men. For if they were white boys, as it appears all those placed in the juvenile system were, a certain amount of uncivilized behavior was predictable, yet transitory. It also suggests that those boys placed in category I as hopeless were thereby also racialized as less than fully white, or as unsuccessful at becoming proper white men. Recapitulation theory also justified the lack of any interest on the part of white men in Coweta County in rehabilitating black men who transgressed the boundaries of southern white civilization. Racial evolution, after all, particularly in the case of black men, they believed, would take millennia. Improvement in the behavior of black men in the space of one man's life was impossible under the principles of recapitulation theory. The juvenile justice system not only helped to familiarize teenage boys with government systems of control over their lives, thus preparing them for the coming Selective Service System, it also offered a model of racially gendered classification that Selective Service would mimic.

On the other hand, the dramatic strike by silk workers in 1913 helped future Selective Service officials understand interrelated issues of gender and labor that they would use in administering the draft. In January 1913, weavers at the Henry Doherty Silk Company just outside Paterson precipitated a citywide silk strike when they walked out to protest changes at the plant that amounted to a "speed-up."[20] In the events of the next six weeks the silk workers would discover that they could not depend upon either the support or neutrality of public officials or the white middle class.[21] The police lost little time demonstrating whose interests the Paterson City government represented. On the first day of the strike they arrested two thousand strikers on such charges as "unlawful assembly" and "disorderly conduct." According to one account, "the strikers saw the police offensive as proof that the local authorities . . . had finally become pawns of the manufacturers."[22] Public officials universally condemned the strike. Grocers would not offer credit to the strikers as they had done in the previous century, and the daily newspapers added insult by calling the strikers dupes of outside agitators.

Four years later when the same combination of industrialists, middle-class men, newspapers and elected officials took control of the draft in Paterson their policies reflected assumptions formed during the strike. Based on their experiences during the strike, they believed that the most tractable workers were those who were most "Americanized." They also believed that immigrants were susceptible to foreign ideologies as evidenced by their attraction to the Industrial Workers of the World (IWW), which had provided leadership throughout the strike. In 1913, native-born Americans walked off the job last and went back first, while many foreign-born workers and their children took a hard line against both silk manufacturers and the local police.[23] Local government officials and their allies in manufacturing, banking, and merchandising, therefore, welcomed wartime mobilization as an opportunity to "Americanize," in other words, to whiten, the largely immigrant working class. They took charge of those wartime organizations that held the greatest potential to bring ethnic groups into the American mainstream.[24]

Setting up the Draft in Paterson

Paterson local draft boards began their work in the context of unprecedented economic boom. The war brought new demands for the goods produced by the silk manufacturers. Factories quickly geared up to produce military belts, powder bags, and parachutes. In addition, purchases of ribbons used in patriotic displays rose. The demand for manufactured silk goods eased the pressure that Paterson industry had been feeling from newer mills in Pennsylvania, and, in turn, owners were more willing to offer better wages. Workers saw that during wartime more efficient methods of production would not depress wages and working conditions. Wartime mobilization thus temporarily provided the appearance of the best of all worlds for both workers and factory owners. But in reality new governmental organizations gave industrialists and their allies additional means to control their workers at the same time that economic conditions virtually guaranteed profits. In this environment employers briefly abandoned attempts to control the cost of labor.[25]

Paterson newspapers, the mayor, and owners of the silk factories formed the vanguard of support for the war. They knew that the wartime economy would benefit both workers and manufacturers, yet they were unsure that good conditions alone would make workers loyal. They rallied all their resources to persuade each Paterson man that his peers supported the war. During the first week of April, as the whole nation waited to see if Wilson would choose war, Mayor Radcliffe proclaimed the loyalty of Paterson's men and requested all "to show the flag." The newspapers featured this call prominently. In the *Evening News* a cartoon next to the Mayor's proclamation showed Paterson's boys telling Uncle Sam that they were ready to go. An accompanying editorial urged, "Show your colors! Let Old Glory wave." The same editorial proposed a universal income tax in order to give poor people the opportunity to help pay for the war.[26]

Paterson's white-middle-class men enthusiastically joined the demands for a show of civic solidarity in favor of war. They established new organizations and reoriented the activities of existing ones to promote war. The Employers' Association announced that it favored war and demanded that labor cooperate with management to increase production to meet the expected demand. Industrial efficiency, the Association announced, equals patriotism. "Labor should not be behind on its patriotism," it said. The *Paterson Evening News* presented American Federation of Labor President Samuel Gompers as a fine example of the proper attitude of workingmen toward war and military service. Gompers had not only supported Wilson's decision to go to war against Germany but like Paterson's elites and middle class favored Universal Military Training (UMT). The *Evening News* appealed to the naturalized immigrants of Paterson, "say to Wilson, 'I am an American and a legal citizen.' " It added that "no loyal son of the United States and no good Patersonian can take exception to avowing his Americanism."[27]

The best way for an immigrant to "avow his Americanism," according to the *Evening News* and city leaders, would be to sign a loyalty pledge. To this end a Public Safety Committee formed by the Patriotic League attempted to register every man in Paterson. Hoping to secure signed loyalty oaths from one hundred percent of the men in Paterson, the Patriotic League assigned campaign captains to organize the drive in each ward and district. The League instructed Captains to concentrate especially on "foreign elements." They would demand that immigrant men not only swear allegiance to the United States but "avow Americanism." But with the actions of this same middle class during the silk strike still fresh in their memories immigrant workers greeted the program with indifference and suspicion. Working class immigrants in Paterson knew that the white middle class, the local government, the newspapers, and silk manufacturers had a different concept of what was good for workers than they did. Many thus regarded the Patriotic League's loyalty drive as a plot to trick them into the armed forces.[28] Nor were they particularly impressed when the Paterson papers told workers that the popular evangelist Billy Sunday supported the war, or that ninety-three percent of the newspapers in the United States favored Universal Military Training for American men. The *Evening News* agreed with the advice given by the U.S. attorney general that opponents of the war should "obey the law; keep your mouth shut."[29]

It was becoming clear that war would offer opportunities for the alliance of middle-class-white men and those who controlled industry to consolidate its position in Paterson. It would strengthen the power of manufacturers over workers; of incumbent politicians over challengers; of older men over younger men and boys; of white, AngloSaxon Protestants over nonwhites, the new immigrants, Roman Catholics, and Jews. The subordinated would have to adopt the values and standards of the dominant white middle class or remain subordinate. This realization added a feverish expectancy to official proclamations, newspaper editorials, and public speeches.[30]

If Paterson's newspapers, government authorities, and businessmen thought first about using the war to Americanize the new immigrants, they next thought about ways the war could be used to shape the minds of adolescent white boys. The middle-class-white men who had only recently introduced Boy Scout organizations to Paterson acted quickly to indoctrinate their troops in the righteousness of the war. Through the Boy Scouts these men were able to bring military propaganda directly into the churches of Paterson. All eight Boy Scout troop units in the city met in churches, and it was there that the scouts heard lectures explaining the nation's war plans, received military drill instruction from National Guard officers, and learned of the connection between manhood and patriotism. When antiwar critics charged that the Boy Scouts had become a paramilitary organization, the leading Boy Scout executive for Paterson flatly denied it. He declared that Boy Scouts received only "training for patriotism, courage . . . citizenship."[31] But by June the Boy Scouts in Paterson would be fully incorporated into the mobilization for war by selling Liberty Bonds. One leader reported that "scouting is red hot with Liberty Loan materials."[32]

The publishers of Paterson newspapers would find increasing pleasure in making themselves partners with the War Department in preparing people for war, and they converted mobilization activities into a rallying cry for hometown pride. By the end of April they bragged that ten Paterson men a day were enlisting. Both newspapers prominently displayed the names of these enlistees, and by June the names invariably appeared on page one.[33] The editors saw themselves as partners with the government in the campaign to persuade Paterson men to enlist.

The white men appointed to local Selective Service offices in Paterson were directly tied to manufacturers and entrenched political interests. Nearly every member of the five draft boards in Paterson, as well as other appointed local Selective Service officials, was a business leader, a professional, or someone who already held a prestigious public office. Nearly all were members of the exclusive Hamilton Club. On the other hand, none came from working-class backgrounds, and there were no representatives of organized labor on Paterson's local boards.

The all white Hamilton Club linked Paterson draft officials with each other and other propertied white men. So many public officials, manufacturers, businessmen, and professionals belonged to this organization that it seems likely much of the business of the city was carried out there. The publishers of both the *Morning Call* and the *Evening News* were members, as were most elected officials and the most influential among the local draft board members. These men also saw each other socially at two local country clubs and at meetings of the Elks, the Masons, and the Rotary Club. Without exception, the members of Paterson's five local draft boards were either lawyers, businessmen, or physicians.[34] However, physicians were the only professionals that the law required on each board.

Harris J. Westerhoff, chairman of Paterson's Local Board No. 3 symbolized the close ties that had developed between the silk industry and local government by 1917. An attorney with a private practice, he was close to silk manufacturing through his brother who was president of Westerhoff Brothers Silk Company. Third generation Paterson residents, the Westerhoff brothers descended from an influential nineteenth-century family that had helped to found one of the city's most prestigious white churches. They were members of the Silk Manufacturers' Association and the Paterson Chamber of Commerce. When a newspaper characterized Westerhoff's brother Peter as a "Progressive minded" man it might just as surely have been describing Harris J. Westerhoff. Like the U.S. attorney for New Jersey, Charles F. Lynch, Westerhoff himself became liable for the draft in September 1918 when Congress expanded the age limits. He was thus put in the position of helping to decide his own classification. The potential conflict of interest never became an issue since the board drafted no one from the September 12 registration.[35]

Registration day provided an occasion for the Paterson newspapers to engage in shameless local boosterism of a sort that made explicit their belief that manhood and enthusiasm for the war were inseparable. They announced that on June 5 the "flower of American manhood" would be enrolled for the draft. These would be the "stalwart young men" offering their lives in a "struggle for human liberty." On the day following registration both the *Morning Call* and the *Evening News* suggested that Paterson men were manlier than those elsewhere in the nation where many men apparently did not register. "Paterson Registers Full Quota," announced the *Evening News*. The "best manhood of Paterson responded" to participate in a "great parade" of registrants. They were "the flower of Paterson's young men." Exalting that "there are no Paterson slackers," a newspaper predicted that now the city would become a true "melting pot" for immigrants. "All nations, all tongues, were represented in the homogenous mass of men who will be welded together in the melting pot of national patriotism to stand solidly as a bulwark of strength in the great world war." But the papers' glee in reporting the failures of other communities to respond as patriotically as Paterson belied their true motives. The *Evening News* announced in bold headlines, "**Many States Fall Behind Estimates**" of registrants, and seemed particularly satisfied with the news that one hundred thousand draft-age men in New York City reportedly did not register.[36]

However, it only took a few days for reality to sink in. By June 8 everyone would know that Paterson had its share of "slackers." Furthermore, half of those who did register asked to be exempted. The papers admitted that there were men in Paterson who had not yet complied with the law, and that many of those who had were less enthusiastic about going to war than the newspaper was to have them go. One headline reported: "There Are Still a Number in the City Who Have Not Complied with the Law." It announced that one draft board member "has the names of about twenty-five who failed to comply with the law, and unless these men register at once he will turn their names over to Federal District Attorney Charles F. Lynch for prosecution." Similarly, within a week of the registration, Sheriff William B. Burpo had received so many anonymous letters identifying alleged "slackers" that he issued a public notice that he would ignore all unsigned correspondence.[37]

Enforcement for Profit

Despite Sheriff Burpo's complaint, he and the Paterson police began making arrests of Selective Service delinquents almost as soon as the first registration ended. The *Paterson Evening News*, which had initially denied that Paterson had any "slackers," briefly jumped on the bandwagon against slackers, real or imagined. A front-page headline on June 11, 1917 proclaimed that the sheriff planned to arrest many for failure to register. It reported three arrests on that day, publishing the name of one delinquent. But within another week, Selective Service news had been pushed to page seven where an inconspicuous story noted that despite the fulltime efforts of two Paterson detectives, "no arrests of slackers" had been made since registration week.[38] The reports of these two detectives show how purely personal, economic, or political agendas could determine who came within the dragnet of law enforcement.

The fifty-dollar reward the army paid for each deserter delivered to a base apparently motivated the attempts of these two detectives to round up Selective Service violators. Working sometimes alone but often in concert with other organizations such as the APL, the Bureau of Investigation, or the Military Investigative Branch, they became part of a nationwide net cast by private and public institutions that kept draft-age men under observation in almost every community. Like local police in thousands of other towns across the United States, these Paterson detectives supplemented their income by arresting and delivering deserters to army camps. But in the beginning their inability to grasp the legal distinction between "delinquent" and "deserter" would cost them money. A delinquent was someone who had failed to comply with some aspect of his Selective Service obligation before an induction order had been issued. This included non-registrants, late registrants, men who improperly filled out questionnaires or neglected to complete them at all, and men who moved about the country without informing their local draft board of their whereabouts. If a board declared a man delinquent and he did not respond by correcting the delinquency it could place him ahead of other draft registrants and induct him. At that point he became subject to military law and would be declared a deserter if he did not appear.

These Paterson detectives first decided to take advantage of the reward system in the fall of 1917. They picked up Archie Maskin and took him before a local magistrate who declared him to be "a slacker."[39] The cause of his initial arrest is not known, but the Selective Service charge was a minor one. Maskin was registered with a local board in Michigan and was carrying his draft card with him at the time of his arrest. Nevertheless, the Paterson judge found that he was not keeping in constant touch with his local board and returned him to the detectives. The latter promptly "hired an automobile," presumably with their own funds, and drove Maskin to Camp Merritt, New Jersey, where they demanded fifty dollars for delivering a deserter.

Officials at Camp Merritt refused to pay the reward claiming that Maskin was not technically a deserter. The judge in the case was outraged and wrote to Lynch on behalf of the detectives. As the detectives were assisting in the enforcement of military rather than civil law, the army owed them for their efforts. Maskin "has committed no crime in this district," wrote Judge J. Feeney. "He is a deserter and we can't give him away. I think the officers are entitled to a fee for a deserter."[40] Meanwhile, the detectives decided that Camp Dix might be more cooperative. They were correct. Officials there accepted Maskin and paid the two detectives the fifty-dollar reward the sought.[41]

In a similar case near the end of the war, Paterson detective Adolph Keppler took advantage of a draft registrant whose induction papers had been prepared erroneously. Peter Dolsky was registered with a draft board in Loraine, Ohio, but had come to Paterson during the war to work. Dolsky reported to Paterson Local Board No. 3 on his arrival and the board agreed to notify draft officials in Loraine. But when Dolsky's number came up in the draft, the board in Loraine sent his induction order through Paterson Local Board No. 2, which knew nothing of him and consequently declared him a "wilful" deserter. Keppler apparently got Dolsky's name from Local Board No. 2 and spent fifteen dollars finding him and delivering him to Fort Jay, New York. The army commander there refused to pay Keppler the fifty-dollar reward for deserters because the local board had failed to provide such a recommendation. While Keppler was appealing to the Army Adjutant General Selective Service officials concluded that Dolsky had been wrongly declared a deserter and had charges against him dropped. Keppler thus not only failed to receive his expected reward, but he was out fifteen dollars of personal funds for which the government would not reimburse him.[42]

The inability of these Paterson detectives to collect rewards for deserters exemplifies the internal contests between white men in various government positions for the right to exercise prerogatives as government men. Such contests involved a considerable element of manly posturing. Army officers and federal officials believed that they occupied superior positions, partly because they wrote the rules, and partly because they represented more than merely local concerns. Local draft board members knew who wrote the rules but they demonstrated that the men who wrote them were ineffectual without the cooperation of other men who had the power to impose them on private citizens. The police, lacking the legal authority to do more than the bidding of the dominant classes in Paterson sought opportunities to seize the initiative. During the war, deciding when to enforce "work or fight" policies, and rounding up deserters seemed to offer the police opportunities to become more than simply tools of a particular class. Yet when conflicts arose over such police initiatives, they always lost to the combined power of federal officials and local draft board members. At the bottom of the government hierarchy, the police had the least ability among men of power to choose when and where to act. Other government men circumscribed their volition. As the following case demonstrates, local board members and the semiprivate APL had greater freedom to choose which cases to pursue.

The Subversive German

Both the APL, as the ideological police, and local Selective Service officials used investigations of supposed "subversive elements" in local industries to demonstrate their power and influence. The exercise of such power, in itself, confirmed their white manhood. But in addition, the specific targets revealed a fear of men who boldly asserted other ways to be men. APL agents took inventory of the number of "alien enemies" employed in the silk mills and blacklisted firms owned by foreigners whose loyalty to the United States they questioned.[43] The local draft boards, on the other hand, used the results of APL investigations to harass nonconforming registrants and to defame some of their industrial competitors. One investigation targeted a foreign-owned silk dyeing factory, the second largest in Paterson. Through the combined efforts of the APL, Paterson Local Board No. 3 Chairman Harris Westerhoff, and the military authorities at Camp Dix, three dye foremen were forced out of the Weidmann Silk Dyeing Company. One of them was denied the opportunity to secure employment with the federal government, was inducted at Camp Dix, and put in a position where he would not be able to use his skills as a chemist.

The investigation of the Weidmann Company began with reports that several employees there had expressed sympathy for Germany.[44] Based largely on information gathered about one former employee the Military Investigative Bureau, the American Protective League, commanders at two army training camps, and members of Paterson's draft boards all concluded that, in the words of a Camp Merritt officer, Weidmann "is pro-German from the bottom up." This case thus has two levels: first was the suspicion that local draft officials raised about an entire industrial plant, including both employees and management; second was the focus on a single man as a symbol of the factory. The close ties between Harris Westerhoff and most of the Paterson silk industry suggests either conflict or resentment between the owners of Weidmann Silk Dyeing Company and other silk manufacturers in Paterson.

The actions against the company and its dye-workers began when Westerhoff intervened to stop the government from hiring Ralph Fischer, a Weidmann chemist. On relatively slim evidence Fischer seems to have been singled out by Paterson draft officials as a German subversive. Although Fischer was born in the United States, his parents had emigrated from Germany. In Paterson they became a successful middle-class family. In the twenty years after leaving Germany his now-deceased father had built a thriving medical practice in Paterson. Ralph Fischer attended Dartmouth College where he earned a degree in chemistry in 1914. Upon returning to Paterson, he secured employment at Weidmann, a company owned by a member of the French diplomatic corps in Washington, D.C. By 1917 Fischer lived with his widowed mother in a downtown Paterson apartment.[45]

Ralph Fischer registered for the draft in Paterson on June 5, 1917. The physician for Local Board No. 3 examined him and declared him physically unfit for the army. Several months later Fischer successfully applied for a job with the War Gas Department of the United States Bureau of Mines. It was then, apparently, that Fischer came to the attention of Westerhoff. Fischer's new job coincided with the introduction of the Selective Service classification system at the end of 1917. As a result, Fisher, as well as all other draft registrants, would be classified on the basis of occupation and family status. If not eligible for a deferment he would be called before the local board to have a new physical examination. Following the requirements of the classification regulations Fischer's supervisor at the United States Bureau of Mines wrote Paterson Local Board No. 3 to request that Fischer be classified as exempt from the draft as a necessary war worker. When the local board ignored that request and classified Fisher I-A, available for induction, New Jersey's Adjutant General, Frederick Gilkyson, telephoned Westerhoff to ask that Fischer not be drafted. Demonstrating his independence of both federal and state authorities, Westerhoff responded by immediately ordering Fischer to appear before the local board's physician, William McAlister, for a new physical examination. Fischer complied. This time he was certified fit for induction and put on a train to Camp Dix. But Westerhoff had not finished with Fischer yet. He contacted the American Protective League for information on Fischer's background.[46]

The APL was ready for Westerhoff's request. It already knew about Fischer as a result of its previous investigation of the Weidmann Silk Dyeing Company. From the beginning of the war Fischer was considered suspect on numerous grounds, beginning with the fact of his employment at Weidmann. Although a French citizen owned the company, the APL concluded that it was "strictly operated by Swiss Germans and [was] pro-German to the core." All of the chemists were said to be "bitterly against the US."[47] Fischer's German ancestry and fluency in the German language firmly identified him with the rest of the suspect chemists. By listening to innuendo and constructing a case based solely on circumstantial evidence and hearsay the APL investigator concluded that Fischer and his mother were dangerous enough to warrant "a close observation" until the end of the war. There were two reasons for watching her. The first was that neighbors claimed to have heard Mrs. Fischer speak favorably toward Germany and in opposition to having her son fight against Germany. She had a brother and a sister in Germany, and one neighbor thought the brother was in the German army. Another asserted that Mrs. Fischer had said that if her son were drafted she would shoot him to keep him from going. But her allegedly seditious remarks had all been made before the United States chose to enter the war. By summertime she apparently became silent on the subject of the war.

The second basis for the agent's suspicion was that since the day of the draft registration both Mrs. Fischer and her son apparently had been abandoned by most of their friends. Persons with few friends were suspect. Before the declaration of war, Mrs. Fischer had a club of fourteen women who met regularly at her home. Since then the club had been discontinued and Mrs. Fischer "has not been entertaining for a number of months and appears to have lost practically all her friends," the agent reported. Likewise, Ralph seemed to have lost his friends. By the time of the APL report in December 1917, the agent believed that "his only chum was one John Grimshaw," a local law student. The Fischers' landlord, who lived upstairs from them, apparently disliked his tenants and believed that when they spoke in German with each other they must have been saying disloyal things.[48]

Westerhoff and the APL now thought they had the goods on Fischer. The fact that several of their conclusions were contradictory apparently did not occur to them. They charged that he was a German agent, that he was trying unlawfully to evade the draft, and that he was seeking a government position as a chemist in order to sabotage the nation's war effort. Having finally inducted Fischer into the army on April 1, 1918, Westerhoff and the APL now feared that this would give him the inside opportunity he had sought as a saboteur. But Westerhoff meant to maintain his surveillance through the military authorities at Camp Dix. When the army assigned Fischer to a job as a chemist the APL agent, C. R. Rice frantically notified the head of the Military Investigative Bureau that "they have put him into a good position from my point of view to easily poison food or water." Westerhoff sent copies of previous APL reports on Fischer to the military intelligence officers at both Camps Merritt and Dix. These officers in turn recommended that Fischer "be placed in such a position that he can do no harm."[49]

In addition, the Military Investigative Branch joined the ongoing APL investigation of Fischer's associates and of Weidmann Silk Dyeing Company and continued it past the end of the war. Ten days after the Armistice was signed, the APL and Military Investigative Bureau submitted a report on another of Fischer's associates, a Weidmann foreman said to be "openly pro-German," who had been seen making trips on a motorcycle to Camp Dix. Even with the war over, authorities concluded: "The subject needs watching."[50] The agents suspected another Weidmann employee on the basis of his friendship with Fischer and a German immigrant named Reinhardt Agler. "The man may be O.K.," said one report, "but if he is a friend of Reinhardt's he is in favor of Germany." With this as a starting point, investigators built a highly circumstantial case that Henry Rosen was an agent of Germany. Unnamed witnesses reported often seeing him in the vicinity of army training camps. Another said that Rosen was sitting within three blocks of an explosion that occurred at a Jersey City munitions plant in 1917. This report concludes with a classic example of APL and Army Intelligence reasoning. Referring to the explosion, the agent declared of Rosen: "now he must have known it was coming off as Paterson is 17 to 21 miles from Jersey City. And why he always manages to be some place every Sunday is beyond me."[51] Perhaps the most amazing fact of this case is that despite their claims to have spoken to dozens of (anonymous) citizens who had seen and heard Rosen behaving seditiously, investigators were unable to confront him personally in more than six months of trying.

A Jewish Threat

Westerhoff was also the instigator of another, more public investigation targeting what he thought were attempts by a successful Jewish immigrant factory-owner in Paterson to influence the draft. This led to rather spectacular charges of fraud and to overlapping investigations by the American Protective League, the United States Department of Justice, and the Military Investigative Branch of the Army. The list of accused men eventually included five well-known local businessmen, three of whom were Jewish immigrants, three lawyers, two local politicians who had been voted out of office years before, and a former city judge. Most were men who had some political ambitions that were blocked by some personal characteristic or identity. Ethnic slurs throughout the investigative reports suggest that anti-Semitism pervaded all levels of government. One of the non-Jewish men accused had been charged with election fraud in 1912. Although he was never convicted, according to one investigator, "the newspapers made it so hot for [him] that he left town and did not return until less than a year ago." We should view the fraud, if indeed there was actual fraud, more as a power struggle between competing groups of middle-class men for power than as outright corruption. That some were Jewish simply added anti-Semitism as one more weapon in the battle against them.

In the spring of 1918 Westerhoff called the local APL and asked it to investigate a rumor that Samuel B. Thomson, the owner of a box factory in Paterson, was collecting two hundred and fifty dollars each from draft registrants by promising to get them out of the draft. APL agent E. T. Drew reported back that Thomson had used his friendship with an officer at the Hoboken Port of Embarkation to get his son Abram a job as an army field clerk. This noncombatant army job saved him from induction, perhaps as a combatant. Later, Drew alleged, Thomson began offering to do the same for other draft registrants who would be willing to pay him a fee. These findings were based solely on hearsay evidence, some of it contradictory. According to Drew, "Marion Heath who is a companion of Thompson's [sic] daughter, Miss Lillian Thompson, repeated the story to Mrs. George A. Hilton, who is a daughter of Beekman the informant." The same source reported that Thomson was overheard complaining "that it cost him a lot of money to get his other son Max out of the draft." Drew knew that Max Thomson had been legitimately deferred on the grounds of dependency but that did not make him to question the reliability of other parts of the story.[52]

Westerhoff thought it possible that the fraud involved military authorities at all the army camps in New Jersey and suggested that only someone from Washington, D.C. could carry out the investigation and remain above suspicion. The Military Investigative Branch (MIB) agreed to this. Its agent collected affidavits from a half-dozen witnesses, virtually all of whom recounted only rumors and hearsay. His final report made much of the fact that Thomson was a Jewish immigrant who allegedly "before the war claimed to be [a] German Jew, now claims to be [a] Russian Jew." He "is estimated as a rich man [and] is said to be good for large sums of credit." In a confusing yet clearly ethnically derogatory characterization, it referred to the son Abram as being "of the type of Jew stage comedians." The report also identified several other Jewish businessmen from Paterson who were suspect because of their frequent visits to Thomson's home. Thomson, possibly with the assistance of these conspirators, according to the MIB agent, "placed between thirty and forty men as Field Clerks at Hoboken and most of them were Jews." He suggested a sinister connection between the late registration of a Jewish man because registration day fell on a Jewish holy day and the fact that the man received an appointment to a job as field clerk at Hoboken. Citing Westerhoff's testimony, the agent wrote: "A special provision allowed Jews to register August 26, 1918, as the 24th was a holy day in their sect. On August 26th, Isadore Rabinowitz, appearing to register, presented a letter [from Hoboken] saying that Rabinowitz had been appointed an Army Field Clerk." The evidence that Rabinowitz was part of the alleged fraud consisted of the fact that his appointment letter was signed by the same Hoboken officer suspected of making deals with Thomson, and the fact that both Rabinowitz and Thomson were Jewish. It seemed convincing to the agent.[53]

The investigations finally achieved little more than providing antiSemitic grist for the daily newspapers. The Justice Department concluded that its special agent on the case, Emmett T. Drew, "had been unable to obtain any proof of corruption." Abram Thomson died before the war ended and Drew thought that "with the further need for field clerks no longer apparent it would be quite futile to continue."[54]

Labor and the Paterson Draft Boards

Thomas G. Bailey was a white man whose experience with Local Board No. 3 illustrates how Paterson officials balanced the sometimes conflicting goals of protecting the nuclear family, maintaining labor supply, and building an army. Bailey registered on June 5, 1917, with thousands of other Paterson men. He requested an exemption on the grounds that his widowed mother depended on him for support. Unfortunately for Bailey, he was just the type of man the draft board was seeking. Here was a man who not only did not seem essential to the local economy but who might be made into a man by the army. He is "a single man who lives at home with his mother," a board member noted. As a trolley conductor his labor was expendable, but equally important, Bailey had two sisters both of whom lived at home and held paying jobs. Women held many jobs in the silk industry, and their numbers increased during the war. To draft such a man as Bailey would help to guarantee that his sisters remained in the work force throughout the war. The board voted unanimously to reject his claim.[55]

The large number of silk manufacturing jobs that could be handled by women meant that the draft did not represent much of a threat to the supply of labor. So long as draft boards could use the drafting of particular men to pressure women into entering or remaining in the work force, as they did in the case of Bailey, the mills would be able to meet the increased demand for their products. Despite the important role women played in the 1913 strike, some employers considered women more reliable and less troublesome on the job than men. In addition, women often settled for lower pay. As a result, industry leaders in Paterson hardly worried that a war-induced shortage of male labor might force them to pay higher wages. Paterson factories had a long tradition of hiring women and children when the cost of male labor went too high. In April, therefore, before Congress had passed the Selective Service Act, the Board of Trade had announced that "women and girls" would be hired for traditional men's jobs during the war.[56]

Indeed, comparison of employment and induction statistics from Paterson's Local Board No. 3 indicates that it did not issue exemptions in order to preserve the male labor force in the silk industry. Silk workers drafted by this board were roughly proportional to the silk workers among its total registrant base. In fact, taking into account various other factors, it looks as though Local Board No. 3 was more likely to draft silk workers than men engaged in small businesses, professionals, and white-collar workers.[57]

Still, one must look beyond the numbers to understand the meaning of Selective Service in Paterson. The men who administered conscription there understood both the limitations and the possibilities of the system. The actual number of men taken out of the work force by inductions was minimal. Even if no one knew in the beginning how many men the army would demand, they recognized that the draft would take only a small percentage of the working population of Paterson. A general policy that attempted to preserve a particular class of laborers, such as silk workers, would have very little impact on the industry and would risk charges of fraud. As it happened, even though the war lasted longer than people had originally expected, less than five percent of the male population of Paterson was inducted by local draft boards.

And in a town where women filled many positions in the factories the impact of inductions on labor was further reduced.[58]

But, as Harris Westerhoff showed, the possibilities offered to local officials by the draft were still considerable. And although they were not terribly important in shaping overall conditions in the city they allowed certain white men to exercise this new state power in very personal and thus perhaps more emotionally satisfying ways. First, by choosing their targets carefully, draft board members were able to dominate the lives of specific individuals in very direct ways. Second, the draft board became an ideological platform from which members helped to define and thus narrow the limits of public discourse. The two were connected when board members made instructive examples of specific men like Fischer over whom they exercised control. In the long run, this kind of power was more effective than the power to channel each man into the proper wartime activity as Provost Marshal General Enoch Crowder envisioned it; for those who defined public values and standards exercised an often invisible but potent authority.[59]

Paterson Women and Selective Service

As elsewhere, women in Paterson paid close attention to the Selective Service Law. In particular, they seemed to notice the ways in which local officials used the draft to advance personal agendas. Like white women elsewhere, Paterson women frequently sought to manipulate the Selective Service System to rid themselves of abusive men or to improve their family's financial situation.[60] But their letters suggest they often mistrusted the motives of the officials with whom they lodged their complaints. In the two cases described here, the women assumed that individual draft officials were at least partly culpable in creating the situations of which they complained.

Mrs. John A. Dotterweich used the draft to secure support for herself and her children from Mr. Dotterweich. She lived in Paterson with her two children and was supporting her mother. According to her, she and her husband had been separated for four years, and although a court had ordered him to pay her six dollars a week for child support she received nothing. Despite being a Paterson resident employed at a Paterson Brewery, John Dotterweich registered at a Passaic County draft board and identified himself as a farmer. According to the board his brother swore an affidavit confirming that John was engaged in farming, and on that basis he was deferred. Mrs. Dotterweich saw the draft as an opportunity to assert some control over her estranged husband and to force him to support his family. In a letter to Enoch Crowder setting forth her version of the facts, she would couch her appeal in the terms of the dominant discourse on masculinity.[61]

Collusion between her husband, his employer, and draft officials, according to Mrs. Dotterweich, violated the standards of fair play that were essential to fulfilling President Wilson's call for men to meet the crisis as a "team." They were not playing by the rules of the game.[62] "Through political pull he has evaded it [the draft]," charged Mrs. Dotterweich. Under the mistaken impression that John Dotterweich's employer, a Mr. Katz, was also a member of the draft board she declared that he had used his official position to benefit his business. Mrs. Dotterweich accused the owner of Katz's Brewery of attempting to coerce her into signing a form stating that her husband supported her and the children. Because she had refused to do so, she thought, Mr. Katz had persuaded the board to give her husband a farm exemption. When she went to the board office to complain, a clerk and one of the board members confirmed that Dotterweich had been classified as an essential farmer. She did not think that they were sufficiently sympathetic to her complaints, indicating that they were more inclined to believe Dotterweich and his brother than her. To her it was an "underhanded" business unbecoming good citizens. The board had given "preference" to one man—her husband—over other men in its jurisdiction. "It seems horrible to think that there is a flaw on the board when every American should help there [*sic*] country instead of using there [*sic*] influence to avoid [*sic*] some men from the draft." This violation of the rules of the game had also caused resentment among her friends whose sons and husbands had been sent to France. "Mothers ask me why my husband has not gone yet and they are aware of the fact that he is a brewer." She was bearing an additional social burden because of the failure of some men to be manly in the context of their duties as a team.[63]

In detailing her husband's manly shortcomings, Mrs. Dotterweich's letter defines the standards of both manliness and womanliness that she assumed national leaders such as Crowder embraced. A man had a duty to support his wife and to refrain from physically abusing her. A woman should do whatever she could to help men be manly, from acting as a conscience to facilitating their efforts in war. Even though a court had ordered John Dotterweich to make weekly payments to his wife, "he does not support me at all," she charged. Even worse, "he has already threatened my life several times," wrote Mrs. Dotterweich. It was a shameful moral weakness that "my husband will fight a defenseless woman every time but when it comes to fighting a man he certainly proves to be a coward." With this accusation she linked failure to be a proper man at home and poor citizenship. Their father's failure to do his manly duty as a citizen embarrassed his children. "My daughter, she is always asking me why her dady [*sic*] has not joined the colors yet, I told her prehap [*sic*] he did not want to go, she replied I certainly did think that he at the least would want to be a soldier."[64]

Contrasting her husband's irresponsible behavior with her own patriotic attitudes, Mrs. Dotterweich wrote: "I certainly have no objection to his going, he can go to the colors, any time and I am only glad to think that he will not be a slacker." Although she struggled to support two children and her mother, she reported that she had "taken a liberty bond," and that her "daughter is buying thrift stamps." She concluded, "surely I am doing my bit for the good old U.S.A. . . . I think every man should fight for his country and I can not understand why he should not want to go."[65]

Although Mrs. Dotterweich correctly charged that her husband had fraudulently obtained a draft deferment by lying on his classification questionnaire, it was not true that her husband's employer sat on the draft board. The draft board seized on this mistake to challenge her integrity. They did so in terms that linked her irrational conclusions to the fact that she was a woman. Her "insinuations" with respect to the board were "not worth refuting," wrote board secretary John J. Slater after having just refuted them. "She was in the office this A. M.," Slater reported, "and the bulk of her conversation was 'I thought'—'I was told' 'I guessed.' In her eagerness to have her husband sent to Military Service her imagination has led her to too much guessing and gossip."[66] But the board's victory was purely rhetorical and Mrs. Dotterweich won what was for her the significant battle. The district board revoked her husband's agricultural deferment and ordered him for immediate induction as a draft delinquent. The War Department sent her instructions for applying to receive an allotment of up to one-half of his army pay and an additional government-contributed allowance as a member of a soldier's family. Having won the economic support she sought, Mrs. Dotterweich ceased her rhetorical argument with the draft board over gender.[67]

Other wives placed the entire onus of their problems on Selective Service and other public officials. Mrs. William J. Porter would not believe accusations that her husband had left town to avoid the draft. According to her account, her unemployed husband disappeared after having gone to a neighboring town in search of a job. She then received a letter from him saying that the government had sent him to Charlestown, West Virginia. In a letter to Governor Edge, Mrs. Porter told the story:

> when he got on the corner [in the town of Wayne, New Jersey], the cop ask him if he was working[.] he said no[.] so he sent him with 5 other fellows out to W Virginia and he had no money when he left[.] The Police told him the Government needs all the men so he started to work out there[.] and on July 9th, 18, his card came for him to Report on Friday 12th for Physical Examination[.] So I tried to locate him but could not do so and he failed to appear[.] and I went to the Local Board No. 2. and told them about it and they try to tell me they did not send him that he went of his own free will[.] Now I wish you to look in this matter and see about it. Saturday I Received a letter telling me he was in Charleston Jail and that he was examined and the doctor said if I as his wife could fix this with the Board he would be sent home. Otherwise I don't know what they would do. I went to the Board + Mr Ferrary, one of the members, told me my husband is lieing [sic]. and they know nothing about this. Now I am forced to believe they do know and that they are to Blame[.] now I have two very small children and no means of supporting them as I am unable to work with two Babies and they already know this but do not have any sympathy and have taken my husband away from his family and still say they don't know about it[.] how am I to live and no money to help myself with[.] now I kindly ask you to attend to this and let the Blame fall where it belongs. When it cost $20.00 to go there I am sure he could not go unless he was sent there by them to work. . . . [68]

The villains here, according to Mrs. Porter, were the draft board members and possibly the police. They represented manly authority gone awry. The proof of how far off track it had gotten was the fact that the men wielding governmental authority didn't seem to care that their actions destroyed the proper relationship between a man and a woman. She completely trusted that William Porter wanted to support her and their children, and there is no hint in her letter that she believed his inability to do so diminished his manhood. Yet still the assumption that it was part of a man's duty to provide for women and children underlay her entire argument. On the other hand, Mrs. Porter portrayed herself in the most helpless and dependent terms. But as a woman, she expressed no shame associated with her helplessness. To her the only shame here was in the misuse of governmental authority by the men entrusted with it.

Unlike Mrs. Dotterweich, Mrs. Porter was apparently powerless to affect her husband's draft board. Her letter to Governor Edge got her nowhere. His secretary sent a *pro forma* reply denying that the governor had any jurisdiction in the matter and suggesting that she contact the Passaic County prosecutor.[69] The Secretary of

Local Board No. 2, Anthony M. Ferrary, apparently felt no shame for his part in administering the draft. He became the leader of a movement among Paterson local board members to persuade the War Department to recognize the service they had rendered by issuing them brevet commissions and "a medal to be worn with a uniform." It would recognize "their faithful and untireing [sic] services rendered in this gigantic work," and would entitle them "to become members of Military Officers Clubs, etc., which are bound to spring up."[70]

Selective Service Statewide in New Jersey

In March 1918, Governor Walter Edge of New Jersey received a letter from R. L. Watkins, MD, of New York City. "There is a young man in West Hoboken [New Jersey], in a family of mine who is able bodied, capable but his family are in medium circumstances or worse and the boy won't work, he's his mother's boy. Go and get him," the doctor urged, providing the full name and address of the offending boy. As a "P.S." he added, "It will be the making of the boy and the relief of his family."[71] It was one of thousands of such letters Edge would receive in response to New Jersey's "Work or Fight" law passed to supplement the operation of the Selective Service System. In 1917, before the first draft calls, Maryland and West Virginia had led the way with similar statutes. These laws, as well as New Jersey's, predated the Selective Service "work or fight" regulations. In New Jersey, it seemed a fitting legal application of the principles articulated by the Commission on Military Training and Instruction in High Schools in 1916. It directly addressed the problem of how to make boys into men, and unmanly men into manly men without putting them through military training.

With a far more radical measure than the federal "work or fight" provisions would be, New Jersey, according to the governor, called upon "Sheriffs, Mayors, and Chiefs of Police to immediately apprehend all persons physically able to work without regard to financial status, who were not engaged in some useful employment."[72] As in other states that enacted such legislation, this law was tailored to particular labor conditions. For New Jersey, labor shortages had been created by a combination of the cut off of immigration and the return of many immigrants to their native lands during the war. A statement of purpose at the end of the New Jersey statute read: "Immigration, the employer's reliance hitherto, has almost ceased; thousands of reservists and patriots of all the countries involved have returned home from America to join the colors, . . . our own brave sons are now preparing to take part."[73] But the law also addressed the uneasiness that middle-class citizens felt in the presence of particular kinds of men. Men who lacked acquisitive instincts and thus only worked long enough each week or month to secure sufficient wages for subsistence were targeted by the act. It demanded that all men work at least thirty-six hours a week to avoid prosecution. As the regulations promulgated by the New Jersey Commissioner of Labor expressed it, the law was "an effort to curb vagrancy, uselessness and mendicancy during these times when every red-blooded citizen of our country should be doing his bit. . . ." The law expressly applied only to men, yet the final statement of purpose declared that it applied to "every red-blooded citizen." By implication, it excluded women from the general category of citizens, further confirmation that the state, and its constituent parts in a democratic society, was still being conceived of as a system of activities engaged in by men only. The Nation, as in Georgia, was seen as feminine, as something for which the masculine state apparatus existed.[74]

Neither public nor private individuals were shy about using the law to impose their own values on men who failed to meet certain standards of manhood. The county sheriffs of New Jersey met at Newark in March, 1918, and unanimously endorsed the "Compulsory Labor Act," as it was officially known, as the best way "to get every idle man in the harness."[75] Still, most local officials never found more than a few occasions to enforce the law. The sheriff of Cumberland County reported that he had placed "work or fight" posters in public places in every district, including county stores and post offices. City authorities had made "some arrests," he thought, but in personally looking after enforcement in rural areas of the county the sheriff found "that almost every one able to work is employed at present."[76] Even five months after the law took effect, the sheriff of Atlantic County reported that outside of Atlantic City, there was "not a single case" of an arrest or prosecution under the provisions of "Work or Fight." "Dread of publicity as being slackers," explained the low incidence of violations, wrote the sheriff. There were four cases in Atlantic City, but one of those charged, according to the sheriff, was "the victim of a miscarriage of justice." The man had been held in the county jail for twenty days before being discharged without a trial.[77] The Warren County Sheriff reported that "My office has picked up a few men who were in the 'hobo' business," one of whom he held as a German alien. Otherwise, he found "help scarce and very little loafing."[78]

However, sheriffs in several counties did aggressively enforce New Jersey's "Work or Fight" law. A month after passage of the Act, more than thirty men had been arrested for violating "work or fight" standards in Middlesex County. The town of New Brunswick accounted for twenty-five cases. Three of these had been confined to the workhouse, with the remainder apparently finding or being assigned to suitable labor. The remaining cases were in Perth Amboy. Of eight arrests there, three were sent to the workhouse and five found acceptable jobs. Other municipalities in Middlesex County "have given the slackers one week's notice to go to work or be confined to the Work-House," according to the sheriff's report. But the sheriff did not expect many more arrests because of the high wages and shortage of labor in his county.[79]

In two other counties, Hudson and Essex, authorities made widespread arrests under the Compulsory Labor Law. In Hudson County the sheriff reported by midsummer that law enforcement officials had arrested 406 men under the Act. Authorities had found employment for three-fourths of them, sent fifteen to the state hospital as "drug addicts," and convicted and sent to prison forty-three. Five more had been inducted into the armed forces and several cases were still pending.[80]

The most active enforcement of "Work or Fight," however, occurred in Essex County, in which Newark, the state's largest city, was the major municipality. Before passage of the law, Newark's own bureau of labor had been receiving between two and three hundred applications for work each day, according to the county sheriff. Since then, he reported, the bureau had been receiving one thousand to fifteen hundred applications a day. The sheriff attributed this large increase to the fact that "the Police

Departments, the officers of the Sheriff's office, and the citizens at large . . . are enforcing the law."[81]

The Essex County Sheriff was not exaggerating when he attributed the success of "Work or Fight" in part to enforcement by "citizens at large." Indeed, at times private individuals seemed to ferret out potential work "slackers" more effectively than did public officials. One letter to governor Edge from someone in Passaic urged the governor personally to use the "work or fight" law to straighten out one, Bob Montgomery.

[H]e lives on our street with his parents and his father is a old man and he works every day and Bob is 39 years and works only for rum money and then goes home and abuses the old folks and uses very bad talk that can be heard outside I have been told he use to belong to Co. A Northern Guards of New Jersey. . . . He should be in uniform and shouldering . . . [remainder of the letter missing].

The writer was certain that Montgomery had received a medal for being "a sharp shooter." The identity of the letter writer is unknown and only a portion of this letter survives.[82]

A report from the sheriff of Camden County suggests that "work or fight" could be enforced informally, with the threat of legal action used as a final resort. Camden's Sheriff W. Penn Carson created his own system that he called "persuasion and probation." Two months after passage of the Act, he and his men had only made one arrest. He preferred to "persuade" idle men to go to work. Any man thus "persuaded" then had to report to the sheriff from time to time as one would on probation. None of this was provided for in the statute, but Sheriff Carson thought it fulfilled the spirit of the law.[83] In Somerset County as well, authorities relied more on threats and public ridicule than on legal enforcement. Somerset's Sheriff reported that "police have warned the derelicts." "A number took warning and went to work," he added, noting that "the street corners and loafing places are deserted." Only seven men in his jurisdiction had been formally arrested under the statute. Four were "serving sentence," two were working, and one had been exempted. The sentences were not indicated.[84] The Bergen County Sheriff enlisted the aid not only of local government officials, but of businessmen, clergy, and hotel proprietors. On the day that all hotel owners in the county were required to appear in court to have their licenses renewed the county judge informed them that "it was their duty to see that no man . . . was allowed to loaf around Hotels." The Sheriff himself only knew of one man who refused to work. "I had him committed to the County Jail for ten days," he reported. After making him "work every day" around the jail "he was willing to work," according to the Sheriff. He added that "I then had inserted in all the papers what happened to this man and I think it had a good effect."[85] Finally, Sheriff A. Engle Haines, of Burlington County, thought that the mere existence of the law made enforcement unnecessary. "Many men went to work immediately after the passage of this act, who had been loafing for years," Haines reported.[86] Most sheriffs and other law enforcement officials in New Jersey thus did not engage in much overt enforcement of the "work or fight" law, but they did invariably express pleasure over its transforming effects on "loafers," "slackers," "derelicts," and "hobos."

An attorney sought advice from the governor on how to force the son of a friend to go to work. "He refuses to enlist or work," wrote the attorney.[87] Similar values, but a different relationship to the accused, inform the complaint of Thomas F. Carey. An undertaker from Jersey City, Carey criticized "undesirable citizens," in his neighborhood, and hoped that the new law would "make these characters who are stealing[-]hold-up men leave our corners." Carey contrasted such men with "our good honorable healthy Boys [who] have gone from us for what[?] to fight for us old men" and for the "undesirable citizens." They looked even more undesirable to him "when we look and see the moral characters go for what[?] to free the world of Barbarinism [*sic*] + slavery + for morality of our girls today." The work Carey thought acceptable for men who did not go to war was "in the mines or on the farms": in fact, any job that would get them out of his community. The draft, he believed, had created a shortage of policemen. "Make it not necessary for so many [policemen] please," he begged the governor. "Try and take these mien [*sic*] characters of[f] our streets."[88] But one wonders if Carey's concern might have been more about men loafing near his funeral home and making his patrons uncomfortable than about changing a few male characters into acceptable men. Yet even if this were his motive, it is significant that he would believe reference to a particular set of gendered social values would bring the law to his assistance in ridding the neighborhood of unacceptable men. One senses that the war did not bring about Carey's concern, but rather that wartime issues and new laws created a new social and legal milieu within which he was empowered to do something about a perhaps longstanding unpleasant situation.

Employers also thought that the compulsory labor law should alleviate the labor shortage created by the war, and they complained when it failed to do so. F. B. Stratford characterized the law as ineffective because Jersey City "is full of loafers who stand around smoking cigarettes and hang around the saloons while we are unable to get sufficient help to run the factory." His paper-manufacturing company was doing mostly work for the government yet local officials would not require the unemployed to seek employment with it. Blaming lax enforcement, Stratford demanded that the governor put "some responsible person . . . in a position to enforce this law."[89]

Some well-to-do citizens feared the law might deprive them of their servants. An apparently quite successful attorney, with offices both in Moorestown, New Jersey, and Philadelphia, wrote concerning "a colored man working for me" who cultivated his truck garden and did house cleaning. After reading a notice of the "work or fight" requirements this employee "has practically served notice on me that he will have to seek other employment." The governor was quick to respond that the estimable lawyer would not have to suffer through the war without a personal servant. "This act," he wrote, "was passed for the purpose of compelling persons who had no employment to get to work and was intended to reach hoboes, beggars, society lounge lizards, etc., and does not affect the man to whom you refer." The governor assured the attorney that such tasks as his "colored man" was doing constituted "a useful occupation."[90] More clearly than any other document, this response by the governor demonstrates that the purpose of the Compulsory Labor Law as he saw it, in addition to mitigating some labor shortages occasioned by the draft, was to enable the white middle class to rid society of certain males who were neither aspiring to nor meeting standards of normal manhood.

But at least one person also used the "work or fight" demands in conjunction with gendered ridicule to lodge class protest against white-middle-class men. An unsigned letter to the governor from "a citizen of Jersey City," questioned the manhood of bankers and similar professional men who did not work a full day, and who spent their leisure time engaging in morally questionable behavior. Although the author's sex is not indicated, the phrasing and nature of some of the specific concerns about women suggests that a woman wrote this letter:

> . . . [T]here are a number of Society Idlers—men who are employed in Banks, whose hours are very short from 9 or 9:30 to 3P.M. These men are Society Idlers—They go from their Bank to the Club Houses for the rest of the afternoon play cards—drink, smoke and hang around talking about women and trying to run women's characters down—these men are Society Idlers in the fullest sense of the word and they should be forced to occupy the whole day from 9 to 6P.M. like other office people. . . . They are a bunch of dressed up loafers. P.S. All these Democrats here in Jersey City . . . are a bunch of loafers, clerks and liars. They pretend . . . to be *your* [presumably the governor's] friend.[91]

The author of this letter claimed to have had some fairly intimate knowledge of what bankers in Jersey City did in their leisure time. It might have been either the wife of one of the men or a female clerk who resented having to work longer hours than the men. Whatever the case, the letter questioned the manhood of males who worked a short day, engaged in morally questionable pastimes, and who slandered women for entertainment.

As in Georgia and Illinois, women in New Jersey were among the most enthusiastic supporters of the "Work or Fight" law. Some women hoped that the law would provide a means of forcing husbands, sons, fathers, and brothers to secure "proper" employment that would better support their families, or that it would remove abusive men from the house. Their appeals to state officials relied on terms that defined Progressive manhood. Mrs. Joseph Williams, of Long Branch, New Jersey, thought that Edge might use the "Work or Fight" law to make her husband behave as a proper husband. He "dose [sic] not work and will not work to support my two little ones. As he dose [sic] nothing but gamble and hang out all hours of the nights in pool rooms and gamble houses . . . ," she complained. Mrs. Williams concluded her letter by requesting more information, apparently to help her in bringing her husband under the provisions of the "Work or Fight" Law.[92] Mrs. F. M. Steck, from Union, New Jersey, hoped the "Work or Fight" law would be used to help her son learn the value of hard work before it was too late. "My boy is . . . pretending to work every day," she wrote the governor. "Curtis is not a bad boy yet, but . . . if he associates with others who are older than he is, in this same lazzy [sic] life, then it will not be long before he will become a criminal for lazzyness leads to lying, and this leads to stealing." After this dire prediction for her son, Mrs. Steck concluded that there was hope for him, as he "is as strong and able to work as any of the other . . . boys." The other boys were apparently her sons who had learned proper work values.[93]

Complaints about the operation of "Work or Fight" were few. One, however, pointed out how compulsory labor worked to the disadvantage of some laboring men and to the advantage of employers. Stephen Colon, a self-labeled "ex-convict," wrote that the compulsory work law was "an injustice to all ex-convicts. Your anti-loafing rules," he told the governor, "forces [*sic*] a ex to work below living wages." Colon went on to say that everyone knew him as an "ex-con" and employers were able to use that in conjunction with "Work or Fight" to exploit his labor. As a result, he was unable to make more than twenty-one cents an hour, or $12.45 a week. Seven dollars a week of that went to room and board. "I would sooner go back to prison than work for 21 cent an hour," Colon concluded.[94]

The federal "work or fight" regulations took effect nearly four months after New Jersey began enforcing its "Compulsory Labor" Act. In operation these laws were enforced by different people and in different ways, but in both cases enforcement was by local officials who were able to use the laws to satisfy local rather than national concerns. Whereas police, sheriffs, and magistrates enforced the New Jersey statute, local draft boards enforced the federal one. The penalty for violating the New Jersey act could be prison. The penalty for violating federal "work or fight" was immediate induction. On paper the local draft boards were constrained by the oversight powers of District Boards and the Provost Marshal General's office. In practice, however, as in Georgia, Illinois, and California, local boards had considerable freedom to interpret and enforce the law as they saw fit.

The Selective Service District Board No. 2, which operated out of Newark, took a particularly activist approach to "Work or Fight." In July 1918 the board compiled a list of all registrants to whom it had granted industrial deferments and sorted them by employer. It then sent each, of which there were nearly a thousand, a list of its deferred employees. The board asked each employer to return the list, "indicating as to each man whether he is still in your employ, his occupation, the kind of work he is doing, the percentage of war work done by him, and his present monthly wages." For certain men, the board asked the employer "whether he is replaceable by a woman, or a man above draft age, and if not, why; and what efforts, if any have been made to replace him." In addition, the board requested the employer to notify it "immediately" when one of its deferred employees terminates his employment. This will "prevent any man who has left his employment from escaping our attention," the board chairman wrote.[95]

Immigrants and African Americans

In 1917, six in ten people in New Jersey were either immigrants or the children of immigrants. Thousands of African Americans were arriving every month from the South looking for jobs. Given a population that was so diverse and mobile, local and district draft boards struggled to keep up with all claims for exemption or deferment.[96] Foreign-born wage laborers and African American men living in New Jersey but registered with southern draft boards often found themselves helplessly snagged in the intricacies of Selective Service procedures. Often unable to read English, caught up in the separate world of an ethnic community, and sometimes dependent on persons in positions of power over them for information about the outside world, immigrant and migrant laborers might unintentionally forfeit some of their rights. Full access to the privileges of American white manhood was denied them as their choices were circumscribed.

This was graphically demonstrated during the first draft of 1917. Approximately five thousand men in New Jersey forfeited their rights to claim exemption or deferment under the draft when they failed to appear at their local boards for mandatory physical examinations. When a man missed a scheduled appointment to be examined at his local board, the board automatically placed him on a separate list to be inducted immediately. The exemption board would send this man an induction order, and in some cases the local police delivered the notice. As these people arrived at the local board they would be placed on a bus or train and sent to the office of the state adjutant general. From there they were transported to the nearest army training camp for induction. Frederick Gilkyson, the Adjutant General of New Jersey, reported to Washington that "a great majority" of these men were "foreigners [and] it was necessary to employ the services of an interpreter."[97]

But for Progressive federal officials such as U.S. Attorney Lynch, as well as for Gilkyson and Governor Edge, it was important that the law appear to function fairly. Not only was Gilkyson concerned about the appearance that the Selective Service Law worked to the disadvantage of immigrants whose English was limited, but he and Lynch also wanted to keep a close watch on the ways local draft boards treated foreigners. To such Progressive leaders, the legitimacy of conscription hinged on showing that it was both fair and efficient; these qualities were essential to the character of a "Progressive man."[98] Thus, when one of the Hoboken boards refused to grant an alien exemption to a man with a legitimate claim Lynch asked Gilkyson to order the board to reconsider. Antonio Genovese had filed suit for a writ of mandamus, and in Lynch's opinion the government would lose this case. John Lord O'Brian, a special assistant to the attorney general of the United States, concurred with Lynch that the nation could not afford "an adverse ruling from any court at just this time." Lynch thought there was too much "criminal business" coming into his office to permit him to represent local or district boards in court cases such as this. O'Brian thought that losing a case in federal court just when the first draft calls were being sent might hinder the government's ability to conscript men. At O'Brian's request, therefore, the Secretary of War, Newton Baker, sent instructions that the board should "reopen the case and grant Genovese's hearing." The board complied and granted Genovese's claim for exemption as an alien.[99]

The case was resolved with remarkable speed. Genovese submitted his petition for writ of mandamus on October 6, 1917, and by October 23 the board had reversed itself.[100] Yet the whole procedure was one that was not supposed to happen under the Selective Service System. Local board decisions were to be reviewed only by appeal boards. State and federal officials such as the adjutant general and the Provost Marshal General were not to have any influence over the votes of local board members. In other cases the Provost Marshal General had argued that the President himself should not be able to influence a local draft board. But in New Jersey when the appearance of legitimacy was threatened, the principle of local control was sacrificed.

Racial quotas posed unique challenges for New Jersey draft officials. White-middle-class New Jersey citizens showed little of the intense fear and resentment toward African Americans found in Georgia. Instead, they practiced a kind of *noblesse oblige*. At the time of the first registration in 1917, New Jersey still had a relatively small black population. Separate racial calls simply caused inconveniences for local boards. By mid-1918, the number of African American men registered for the draft in larger New Jersey cities had grown considerably. This was reflected in larger "colored" quotas. In July, New Jersey had sent more than 1,300 men to training camp in its "colored" call. The rapidly growing black community in Newark turned out *en mass* to see its young draftees off.[101]

The local board at Hackensack found an occasion to declare itself unprejudiced against "colored" men, and launched an attack on racism at a Virginia local board. The board had assigned one of its "colored" registrants to the Student Army Training Corps (SATC) at Hampton Institute, an all-black college in Virginia. In fall 1918 the board sent him with transfer papers to the draft board at Hampton expecting that board to prepare an induction order to Hampton Institute. The registrant returned to Hackensack a month later and told the board there that the Hampton board had refused to induct him because, with the signing of the Armistice, all inductions were canceled. The clerk of the Hackensack board wrote a strongly worded letter to the Hampton board demanding to know why the induction had not been completed prior to the termination of inductions on November 12. "What personal grudge do you have against this registrant?" he asked. "Is the reason because he is colored? He advises us that when he called at your office for information as to the delay in his induction he was ordered out of your office. What is the reason for this?" This letter also asserted that the Hampton board owed the registrant railroad fare from Hackensack to Hampton and twenty-two dollars to cover the fee for enrolling at the college. It then threatened to report the case to the Provost Marshal General "unless we receive an appropriate excuse." Returning to his charge of racism, the clerk's letter concluded that with the help of the Provost Marshal General he would try to

> . . . ascertain why Local Boards, as your, [*sic*] exist in this country. Although this registrant is colored he no doubt was more anxious to do his bit for his country than some white people. This case is the most unusual that has come to our attention . . . and from our view there must be some prejudice for the colored race.[102]

This letter drew an angry response from the Hampton board, which sent a copy of it to the Provost Marshal General. It was attached to a memo from one of the members that noted their "zealous endeavors to carry out properly the Selective Service regulations which were imposed on us at no solicitation of ours by the President." The board characterized the letter from Hackensack as "unwarranted and contemptible." It was a mild response for the benefit of the Provost Marshal General. A different letter from the entire Hampton Board to the Hackensack Board was of another genre. It presumed that the Board Clerk had written his letter without knowledge of the board members. It offered no explanation for why the registrant had not been inducted, but said that if he was thrown out of the office "I have no doubt there was some good reason for it and my only regret is that your chief clerk was not there at the time in order that we might kick him out along with the registrant." As to racial prejudice, Hampton's Board wrote, "this board has had more dealings with more negroes and probably has more respect for them as a whole than any individual of the mentality manifested by the communication from your chief clerk." Going on to belittle both the Hackensack Board and its clerk as insignificant and not worthy of respect, the letter continued, "your board is a very small part of the draft machinery . . . and we have found a number of incompetent clerks nearly as bad as yours." The Hampton Board hoped that the clerk would take the matter up with the Provost Marshal General, "whom the writer knows personally to be a gentleman . . . far above such petty ideas." The letter again repeated that the clerk was incapable of doing his job, characterized him as "obnoxious," and suggested that he should pay the registrant's expenses himself. Then, in case the insinuations had not been sufficient, the Hampton board made its gendered ridicule explicit: "If he [the clerk] has any semblance [*sic*] of manhood he should call on any member of this Board at any time and make himself known, in order that the matter may be handled personally face to face."[103]

This exchange shows both the sensitivity of the Virginia board to charges of racism, and the desire of the New Jersey clerk to assert his moral superiority over southerners on a question of racial justice. Both appealed to a shared ideology of manhood to shame the other. Whether the New Jersey clerk believed the black registrant counted as a man is impossible to know.

Conscientious Objectors, Resisters, and "Slacker Raids"

New Jersey men who opposed either the war or the draft found many ways to express their opposition. There were a number of conscientious objectors, men who opposed the war on political rather than the legally required religious grounds, and men who denied the right of the state to coerce them into the armed forces. Many of them simply left the country, with Cuba and Brazil, from which extradition was impossible, being the most likely destinations.[104] Others chose to confront the Selective Service System head-on, knowing that they had little chance of success. Much like national leaders, draft officials in New Jersey responded harshly to the actions of these men. Men who called themselves conscientious objectors elicited especially strong reactions from New Jersey draft officials, who went to great lengths tracking down and prosecuting the few acknowledged objectors in the state. The most vocal conscientious objectors threatened the dominant relations of power because while operating purposely outside the bounds of "legitimate" authority they claimed to adhere to the same standards and values upon which that authority was based. They violated the ideal of the Progressive white man not by rejecting ideals of strength, self-discipline, and reasoned exercise of choice, but by denying the social and political boundaries that marked the proper sphere of action for men. The investigation of such cases often lasted for the entire war. These people were different from the "religious" objectors provided for in the Selective Service Act. Objectors with no formal religious affiliation, or whose churches did not oppose all war had no legal recourse.

Frederick Stehr of Jersey City registered for the draft in 1917 and was ordered to appear before his exemption board for a physical examination on August 8, 1917. He complied with the order but brought a letter explaining his conscientious objection to war on personal moral and philosophical grounds. Although the law could not accommodate such persons, Stehr had written "conscientious objector" on his registration card. The board, of course, could have recommended noncombatant service had it wished to ignore the religious requirement in the law. Boards often bent other rules in the name of some local economic or political interest. But after the board informed him that his letter "did not constitute a valid claim for exemption under the law," Stehr did not expect sympathetic treatment. Predictably, he missed his scheduled induction six weeks later. It took a local police detective three months, with the help of the post office, to locate Stehr. But a year later the local board was still begging the Justice Department to take a greater interest in prosecuting him.[105]

From the beginning, Frederick Stehr directly confronted the Selective Service System. His letter to the local board revealed that he knew the law did not embrace objections such as his. He specified that he did not seek an exemption according to the provisions of the Selective Service Act. "These thoughts are not born of influence of the thoughts of others," he wrote. "My thoughts are wholly my thoughts" Stehr then described his view of war:

> War . . . is massive, monstrous murder. The slaying of human beings through the subterfuge of war, does not hallow the lowest of crimes to the loftiest of virtues. Because the State declares war, it does not sanctify killing, neither does it legalize the destruction of property. . . . To take up arms and slay, under the cover of war, is the same as to take up arms and slay for personal reasons. . . . To make war for ideals is no different than to make war for profit. . . . To make war for profit is common criminality, to make war for ideals is educated criminality.
>
> War for an ideal is the height of criminality. It may represent nothing more than the vision of a disordered mind, or the mind of a pervert whose pretended ideals make possible predatory conquest or unadulterated betrayal. But even if the ideal is just, if it is sound, if it is wholly devoid of selfishness, it does not make war or murder for such purposes less sinful.

A close reading of this letter suggests that Stehr and his local draft board probably shared more common ground than either of them recognized. He based his claim on what he assumed was a set of universal values. Societies universally reject murder. It is not something that civilized men do. In fact, crime in general has been a concept through which some men have used standards of social behavior to exclude other men from sharing the power and wealth produced by a society. If Stehr could successfully identify war as a crime he would have gone a long way toward emasculation of men who promoted or engaged in war. Thus the strategy was to persuade the board that war was murder. To do so he reverted to the same kind of gendered ridicule that government officials used to stigmatize the opponents of the war. The words "pervert," "predatory conquest," and even "unadulterated behavior," all deployed subconscious negative sexual innuendo to impugn the manhood of men who make war.

In turn, the local board characterized Stehr as "well educated and . . . a very dangerous man." To counter Stehr's attempted emasculation of warmakers the board portrayed him as someone incapable of thinking for himself and who was a mere mouthpiece for Germany. In other words, he was the direct opposite of true American manhood. By December, 1917, the board discovered letters that he had written to local newspapers that were "strongly pro-German and abusive of the Allies, and particularly of England." The board denied that his thoughts were, as he had put it "wholly my thoughts," characterizing them instead as "propaganda." "Whole expressions are familiar quotations from [the German papers]," insisted the local board chairman. In addition, the board asserted in a letter to the Justice Department that both Stehr and his brothers had offended their neighbors by making "many statements traducing the United States and praising Germany."[106] The social rejection of this family by the community in which they lived further legitimated the board's portrait. Given the surname involved and the nature of the terms by which the local board described Stehr and his brothers, any reader of the board's files in the case might conclude that the Stehrs were German immigrants. They were rejected by their community. They espoused "foreign" ideologies. They were incapable of independent thought and behavior. They had a German name. The board members went to such lengths to differentiate themselves, and by implication all true American men, from Stehr and his brothers that it made them appear to be foreign. The brothers, however, were all native-born U.S. citizens with middle-class backgrounds and white-collar jobs. Frederick Stehr, born in Jersey City in 1887, worked as a bookkeeper for an established Jersey City business. But by casting Stehr as foreign, the board could draw on the vast xenophobia being indiscriminately generated against foreigners and white ethnic minorities by the same groups that assisted with tracking down "slackers."[107]

Enoch Crowder had not exaggerated when he asserted at the end of the war that the success of the Selective Service System in providing manpower for both war and civilian industry had been due to "the universal watchfulness for slackers in every community, and the practice of neighbors informing on each other."[108] As expectations for America's entrance into the European War had intensified many white men sought ways to establish themselves as wartime leaders by founding or joining state or local chapters of the American Protective League, the National Security League, Liberty Bond Committees, local councils of defense, and similar organizations.

As in Illinois, Literally thousands of white men in New Jersey volunteered to serve either as investigators for the American Protective League's "secret service," or as deputies in slacker raids.[109] They reported their findings on standardized APL "operative" forms. APL officials disseminated either selected information or entire reports to whatever local, state, or federal government agencies they thought needed them.

Two "operatives" whose base was in Atlantic City were particularly enthusiastic about their work. Together Charles Ernest and John A. Barnshaw investigated the loyalty of African American men, searched fishing boats, examined the luggage on arriving passenger ships, and intercepted the mail of suspected German sympathizers. They went into factories and counted the number of Germans employed, and they made a list of the New Jersey firms owned by German Americans.[110]

The investigation of Barnshaw and Ernest into the loyalty of African Americans yielded a "disloyal" family living in Atlantic City. The family consisted of a draft-age male, his wife, an unspecified number of brothers, and a mother. As characterized in the APL report, the subject's attitude toward the United States "is that the American people have never done anything for the colored people and why should he stand up for the President or anyone else who has declared war." In phrasing that sounded suspiciously close to what APL operatives expected to find, Ernest and Barnshaw wrote that "he claims that the German people will do more for them than the white people of America." They reported that he said he would not willingly go to war, and that interviews with his mother and brothers elicited responses of a similar nature.[111] While there is enough reliable evidence elsewhere to conclude that many African

American men viewed the war as a white man's fight, these APL reports primarily indicate the social attitudes and expectations of APL secret police rather than the attitudes of African American men on the war or the United States in general. In this case, the subjects were easy targets for two white males who clearly used the process of investigation as a form of mastery over those whose race or ethnicity placed their eligibility for full citizenship in question. It is implicit in these reports that the investigators represent the unspoken, but real, standards by which white manhood should be judged. They found a family from whom they differentiated themselves racially, socially, ideologically, and especially in terms of inclusion and exclusion. By claiming that the objects of their investigation willingly excluded themselves from the national community of men, Ernest and Barnshaw reinscribed dominant values of gender and race in their report.

The predisposition of Ernest and Barnshaw to perceive the actions of males around them in terms that differentiated the objects of investigation from accepted patterns of behavior, easily descended to the absurd, further calling into question the reliability of their report on the African American family in Atlantic City. While en route to an investigation, they spied "two strangers making road sketches" near Robbinsville, New Jersey. Interrupting their journey, Ernest and Barnshaw found a vantage point from which they could observe the strangers. They made detailed descriptions of the strangers and recorded their every move for a period of hours. Convinced they had caught two German spies mapping the roads of New Jersey, Ernest and Barnshaw hurried to present their report to the state's military authorities. After a brief investigation, the commanding officer of the Second New Jersey Infantry reported to the state adjutant general that Ernest and Barnshaw had caught red-handed two surveyors from the State Road Department. Undeterred, and probably unamused, by this finding, the two operatives continued their investigations until the end of the war, receiving encouragement along the way from the state adjutant general.[112]

On a much larger scale, on Tuesday morning, September 3, 1918, an alliance of public and semipublic vigilantes carried out a massive "slacker raid" throughout all of urban New Jersey and metropolitan New York City. Private detective agencies, APL agents, and police from dozens of jurisdictions participated. Newspapers described a "dragnet" in which an estimated 20,000 to 25,000 operatives swarmed saloons, pool halls, factory entrances and other places where young men might assemble. One newspaper account reported agents stopping automobiles and trolleys. "Two men would board a trolley, directing the motorman to hold the car while they made all men who seemed to be of draft age exhibit cards or accompany them from the car." Tens of thousands, by newspaper estimates, were arrested and held over night in city armories. In Newark, an estimated 3,000 were held over night in the Armory. In the morning, most were released as mothers, wives and friends showed up with the men's draft cards. Several hundred who could not prove their draft status were put on trains to local army camps.[113] These were perhaps the largest slacker raids anywhere in the country during World War I. They netted an insignificant number of actual draft resisters relative to the effort put forth, and they demonstrated the fragility of Constitutional guarantees against unreasonable searches and arrests without probable cause or warrants. Newspapers and public officials seemed unconcerned by the Constitutional violations.

But when reports surfaced that some agents had shaken arrestees down for money officials sat up and paid attention.

The Bureau of Investigation was the first federal agency to receive information that the New Jersey "slacker raids" might have involved fraud in July 1918 when one of the arrestees complained to its Division Superintendent in New York City.[114] Pasquale John Boracci, a native of Long Island, New York, reported that while employed at a New Jersey munitions plant, he and dozens of other draft-age men were rounded up by a private detective agency and imprisoned in the Middlesex County workhouse. According to Boracci's letter to the Department of Justice he was working the night shift as a time keeper at the Camp Raritan plant when a fellow worker informed him that his brother had been "pinched." He knew that his brother had both a registration and classification card and so he went to see what the charge might be. He was stopped by detective T. H. Brindle of the Interstate Detective Agency. Like his brother, despite having his draft cards with him, the detective arrested him and had him taken to the Middlesex County workhouse. After three days he was approached by a man who told him "he had been working hard on my case as a result of which I was now a freeman." Boracci said he thanked him and got ready to leave when the man "called me aside and said, 'I want five dollars for this job.' I absolutely refused after being unjustly locked to pay to get out when I shouldn't have been put in. 'Then you ain't out,' he says. Having run down considerable from lack of proper nourishment and yearning to see my mother I thought it worth while to see me [sic] to give the five and get out." The agency released him but did not return his draft cards. Boracci, who was in Class I at the time, had by now been ordered for induction. "Now I am called and as a result of exposure and deprivation I am in bed with fever," and would have to seek a delay. The letter from Boracci ended with a list of other men, including his brother, who had also been committed to the workhouse by the Interstate Detective Agency.

The investigation, initiated by the Bureau of Investigation, and then continued by the APL, military authorities at Fort Dix, New Jersey, and a representative of the Provost Marshal General's Office, revealed that a small group of men had engaged in a systematic attempt to use mass arrests of draft-age men for their own pecuniary interests. This case demonstrates that the line between formal state authority and private power was as permeable in New Jersey as in Georgia. The Interstate Detective Agency, consisting of T. H. Trimble and Leo Gannon, conspired with the county detective of Middlesex County, Richard A. Peltier, and a Middlesex County draft board to conduct indiscriminate sweeps of draft-age men for the purpose of either detaining them until a bribe was paid for their release or delivering them to an army base where a fifty-dollar reward for delivering a deserter would be claimed. Eventually this enterprise expanded to include the county custodian of the court house, a driver for the county workhouse, and a justice of the peace. One report suggested that Peltier had sought out the Interstate Detective Agency because detective Leo Gannon was a nephew of "the Democratic political boss of [Middlesex] County." Two APL agents who also investigated the case "suspected that [Trimble and Gannon] went there and opened an agency to recover rewards for the apprehension of slackers, and otherwise to profit from the raids conducted by them." There were also intimations that the county sheriff and the State Adjutant General Gilkyson might be implicated, but this was never pursued.[115]

When making arrests, detectives Trimble and Gannon, sometimes accompanied by the county detective, carried with them a letter from the New Jersey adjutant general to Peltier authorizing him to "apprehend delinquents and to assist local boards in locating men who had failed to return their questionnaires." The letter requested the "cooperation and support of all those who he may come in contact with in carrying out [the arrests]." During the subsequent investigations most of the persons involved invoked this letter to justify their cooperation with Trimble and Gannon. Indeed, given the vague wording of the letter, it was easy to assume that the private detectives were legally assisting county detective Peltier.

The detectives would typically arrive at the main gate of a plant where many draft-age men worked at the end of a shift and inspect the men as they left. A Bureau of Investigation agent observed the process at the California Loading Company on a Saturday afternoon. "Peltier demanded that the workmen show their registration cards and those who did not have any he made stand in a group." According to this BI agent similar raids at plants in New Brunswick, Parlin, Morgan, and Perth Amboy had resulted in the payment of deserter rewards to the detectives when they delivered men to Fort Dix. This agent previously had witnessed what he called another "haul" at a plant in Morgan.

Once the detectives had detained the men, they had them transported to the county workhouse by the county employee assigned to drive the workhouse auto. According to the warden, "men were brought to the workhouse without any commitment at all. [He] simply obeyed the orders of the detectives making the arrests, and released the men on receiving memoranda from the detectives." The warden estimated that between two and three hundred men had been brought to him by Trimble and Gannon. In several cases a local justice of the peace had signed commitment papers, but when questioned as to which section of the Selective Service Law the men had been committed, he informed investigators that "he didn't know the Selective Service Law as he had not read it, that the men were committed as alleged draft evaders upon advice of the Interstate Detective Agency." The justice of the peace admitted that the Agency had paid him a fee for the commitments, and that he had probably authorized about one hundred. Some of the men sent to the workhouse stayed only a few days while others languished for six to seven weeks, but their release was determined by a private business rather than by any government official.

Through either a Middlesex County local board or New Jersey Adjutant General Gilkyson, Trimble and Gannon were able to secure copies of telegrams naming men who had been reported to be either draft delinquents or deserters. When they arrested men against whom no charges could be made the detectives apparently turned the names over to the court house custodian who would locate the men in the Workhouse and offer to get them out for a fee. He split this fee with the workhouse driver who had first told him that "money could be made by visiting the detective agency on behalf of those under arrest." But Peltier, fearing such a scam was too obvious, quickly put a stop to this aspect of the operation.

Among the men wanted for some violation of the Selective Service Law were those who had failed to return questionnaires and those who had not appeared when ordered by their local board for physical examinations. Later investigations would conclude that a large percentage of these men had not broken the law willfully, but owing to inability with the English language were unable to understand communications from their draft boards. Their status as foreigners and their language difficulties made them further susceptible to manipulation. Trimble and Gannon had worked out a deal with a local draft board in Middlesex County whereby such men would be brought to the board, examined, and immediately inducted as delinquents. Then Trimble and Gannon would take them to Fort Dix where they would collect fifty-dollars reward for each man accepted as a deserter.

The end of the war, and thus of draft inductions, did not immediately bring the activities of Trimble and Gannon to an end. Although outstanding induction orders of nondelinquent men were canceled when the Armistice was announced, local boards continued to induct delinquents and army camps continued to accept deserters. Five months after the war ended, Trimble and Gannon were still delivering alleged deserters to Fort Dix and collecting rewards. Finally, the commander of that base instituted his own investigation. A large number of men brought in by Trimble and Gannon had physical maladies so extreme that any layman, according to the Fort Dix commander, could see that they would not be suitable for military duty. In a report to the Provost Marshal General, the commander gave several "typical" examples. On February 28, 1919, Trimble and Gannon brought a man by the name of Gobar Bodnar to Fort Dix as a deserter. In exchange, the military authorities paid them fifty dollars. Bodnar was Hungarian-born and had been in the United States only three years before the United States entered the war. When the draft was instituted he was living in West Virginia and registered with a local board there. He moved to New Jersey in search of work in August 1917. With the assistance of an interpreter he notified the West Virginia board of his new address and inquired about the classification questionnaire. The board did not answer his letter, but apparently sent him a classification card indicating that it had placed him in Class 5-E: enemy alien ineligible for induction. The Fort Dix investigative report describes the rest:

> He was arrested by H. L. [sic] Trimble at Milltown at his place of employment, given no opportunity to go to his home. Taken before Local board for Div. #1, Middlesex Co. New Jersey where, without an interpreter or any other investigation, aside from a telegram produced by the said Trimble from the Adjutant General of the State of West Virginia, he was determined a willful deserter, so classified by a certificate. He was then examined by Surgeon Chas. J. Sullivan who marked him "Group A" "Qualified for General Military Service" when it was apparent that he was unfit. . . . This man had a fractured leg which had been improperly set and it was apparent that he was unfit for General Military duty, being unable to stand erect or to walk any distance. . . . [116]

The Camp Dix investigator concluded that board number one in Middlesex County was guilty of complicity in "many hundreds" of such cases. He called "particular attention to the activities of . . . Local Board for Div. #1, Middlesex Co., New Jersey; the member signing E. I. Cronk, the examining surgeon, Dr. Chas. J. Sullivan," who, along with Trimble "composing the trio affecting the cases cited." He requested "that action be taken to stop the illegal apprehension and apparent disregard for the Selective Service Regulations by this particular section of New Jersey." The report concluded "that Middlesex County contains a large number of industries employing thousands of this type of employees and there is a large field for [such] operatives and operations."

The simultaneous investigation being conducted by Frank R. Stone, a "secret Service" agent of the APL concluded that the Interstate Detective Agency had "entered into a conspiracy with certain members of the Local Board at New Brunswick, N.J., the object being to defraud the Government in the matter of rewards." Stone estimated that the detectives had received about $20,000 from the U.S. government for delivering "about 400 alleged deserters." In addition to Camp Dix, according to Stone, Trimble and Cannon had collected rewards at four other army camps in New Jersey. He speculated that "these men have split the rewards with the board members who have certified the men as 'wilful delinquents,' " and with the board doctor who "has certified as physically fit certain palpable defectives."[117]

Despite overwhelming evidence of widespread fraud and abuse of draft registrants, U.S. Attorney Lynch concluded that no federal law had been broken. A disappointed Stone obviously desired that some individuals be prosecuted. He laid the primary blame at the feet of Peltier for turning the "slacker raids" over to Trimble and Gannon. "The whole thing reeks with cheap graft," he charged, "and there is evidence of a prostitution of power entailing gross abuse, illegal restraint and unwarranted hardship." Lynch referred the case to the Prosecutor of Middlesex County who showed no inclination to proceed with it. Stone hoped that the Provost Marshal General would ask Governor Edge to pressure state authorities to prosecute, but that too came to naught.[118]

Conclusion

Stone's characterization of the operation was accurate and his outrage justified. But Trimble and Gannon demonstrate how the war offered possibilities for self-aggrandizement. Structures of state power in transition permitted white men who were otherwise excluded from the operation of state power to assume roles not meant for them. Legitimization of state authority is always determined by contexts of time and place. In this instance, white men who were neither elected nor legitimately appointed to any government position were able to seize the appearance of state power and make it real power. Ironically, that is precisely what Stone and his fellow "agents" of the American Protective League had done. The phenomenon recalls Frederick Stehr's argument against war. The distinction was in the motivation more than in the acts of men themselves. Stehr thought that killing for ideals was as unacceptable as killing for personal aggrandizement. So also might some argue that private assumption of power over life and death in the name of the state, whether for financial gain as by Trimble and Gannon, or for patriotic ideals as by the APL, is never legitimate.

Finally, it is inconceivable that the activities of either Trimble and Gannon or of the APL could have been undertaken by any men of color or by women. The race and sex of the persons who carried out these operations enabled them to pass themselves off as representatives of state authority. To the extent that such persons were able to impress fully the strength of their white manhood on others they were able to assert power in the name of the state. It was not that men of color or women were unable to assert power or even to seek aggressively the ends of the state. But as would-be rep-resentatives of state authority, men of color or women in the early-twentieth-century United States could not have legitimately exercised state authority in the eyes of white men, nor perhaps in the eyes of other men of color or women.

CHAPTER FOUR

CALIFORNIA: "PLEASE FORWARD CHINESE, JAPANESE AND AMERICAN INDIANS, BUT NO NEGROES"

Less than a month after draft boards had begun inducting men in the fall of 1917, the Adjutant General of California, J. J. Borree, instructed all draft boards in the State: "You are authorized to forward Chinese, Japanese and American Indians, but no Negroes, with the third contingent."[1] Governor William Stephens and his adjutant general thereby acquiesced to the insistence of federal authorities that there were only two races in the United States—"white" and "colored." In this binary racial system only persons of African descent were "colored," and anyone else would be classified as "white" for purposes of the Selective Service System and the racially segregated armed forces. This surely came as a surprise to Californians who, since 1854, had lived with a state Supreme Court decision that ruled just the opposite. In *People v. Hall*, the court agreed that there were two races in California—white and nonwhite—but that for purposes of the law, Chinese, other Asians, and American Indians, who it found were obviously not white, should be placed in the same racial category as "Negroes." A string of federal court decisions, including several notable U.S. Supreme Court rulings, in the late nineteenth and early twentieth century had generally confirmed this view. Immigrants from China, Japan, the Philippines, and India all faced an impenetrable barrier to U.S. citizenship because federal courts declared them not "white."[2] California, and eight other states, had barred such immigrants from owning land on the grounds that their nonwhite legal status disqualified them from becoming citizens.[3] In so doing, these states explicitly defined whiteness as a narrowly restricted social and political status. In particular, they confirmed that whiteness involved special privileges with respect to land.

The white men who governed the State of California expected that federal racial categories would conflict with those in California, but it did not play out as they had anticipated. Since passage of the Chinese Exclusion Act in 1882, thousands of Japanese immigrants replaced the declining Chinese population as the numerically dominant Asian group in California. Leaders of the Japanese immigrant community understood the intensity with which many white people held the Chinese in contempt. In response, they sought to distinguish themselves as racially distinct from Chinese, rejecting categorization as "Mongolian," which was the official designation for Chinese. Some Japanese, in fact, strenuously insisted they were white. Takao Ozawa, a Japanese immigrant seeking U.S. citizenship, argued in a federal district court in 1917 that: "the Japanese are free. They are white persons having European and Aryan root stock. They are a superior people, fit for citizenship."[4] Japanese leaders and white officials in California agreed, for the most part, that the Japanese were racially distinct from the Chinese. It mattered most that Japanese in California organized gender relations for reproduction and production in ways that defined whiteness. In particular, unlike the Chinese before them, Japanese immigrants by 1917 often lived on family farms, and within nuclear families headed by males, often converted to Christianity, and were likely to learn English. The division of labor between men and women in the Japanese American communities was similar to that expected of middle-class-white people. In short, Japanese men appeared to have all the characteristics expected of successful white men—characteristics that the federal government had made a condition for citizenship in the case of American Indians. Furthermore, the Selective Service System provided exemptions for men who exhibited such qualities by being married and/or directing productive agricultural or industrial enterprises. Japanese leaders were proud of these qualities. They argued that Japanese had "Americanized," that Americanization equaled becoming white, and this was their primary argument against anti-Japanese measures such as immigration restrictions, the Alien Land Law, which intended to bar Japanese from owning land in California, and prohibitions against Japanese children attending public schools with white children.

But the very characteristics of which the Japanese were so proud struck fear into the hearts of California's white leaders. In the face of strong evidence that Japanese men behaved in nearly every important social and cultural way just like white men, the governor fell back on appeals to immutable racial differences. He wrote:

The Japanese, be it said to their credit, are not of servile or docile stock. "Proud of their traditions and history, exultant as they justly are at the extraordinary career of their country, they brook no suggestion of any dominant or superior race. Virile, progressive and aggressive, they have all the race consciousness which is inseparable from race quality."[5]

Where white people in California considered Chinese inferior partly because they viewed them as an effeminate race, Governor Stephens, as well as Japanese leaders explicitly characterized the Japanese as a masculine race. Since the Gold Rush, as Gary Okihiro has written, "because of white men's choices and the dearth of women, work such as cooking and cleaning and washing were open to Chinese men, who, according to a prevalent idea, were lesser men belonging to a feminized race."[6] Okihiro quotes Scottish writer, Robert Louis Stevenson, who observed during his brief stay in Monterey, that, "the young Chinese man is . . . like a large class of European women."[7] Japanese leaders sought to distance themselves from these stereotypes that had dogged the Chinese, and to a significant extent, they succeeded. They were content to let white Californians portray Chinese as effeminate, and Japanese as masculine. Both Japanese and white Californians would have agreed with Okihiro's conclusion that in Progressive Era racial ideology, "masculine races were superior to feminine races."[8] Japanese were "manly" in the very ways that Theodore Roosevelt and other Progressives saw white America as "manly." But ultimately this only made the Japanese seem more threatening than the Chinese. To support their characterizations of the Japanese, both Stephens and Japanese leaders relied almost exclusively on evidence of Japanese ability to outperform white men in agriculture. According to Stephens:

- "The Japanese in our midst have indicated a strong trend to land ownership and land control, and . . . have gradually developed to a control of many of our important agricultural industries."
- "The Japanese, with his strong social race instinct, acquires his piece of land and, within an incredibly short period of time, large adjoining holdings are occupied by people of his own race."
- "California views with alarm the rapid growth of these people within the last decade in population as well as in land control, and foresees in the not distant future the gravest menace of serious conflict if this development is not immediately and effectively checked."[9]

The similarities between Governor Stephens' characterizations and those, which the Japanese Association of America made to President Wilson in 1919, are remarkable. Citing the immense contributions Japanese farmers in California had made to the war effort, the authors of this statement filled their document with statistics on the number of acres cultivated by Japanese farmers and the amounts of fruits, grain, cotton, and other crops they had produced in 1918. Governor Stephens and the Japanese used the very same evidence to make two very different arguments. The Japanese cited the following to show how "Americanized," and therefore "white," they had become, while Stephens used it to illustrate the "threat" the Japanese posed:

- "In 1918 Japanese farmers in the Sacramento Valley contributed more than 1,000,000 sacks of rice to the food supply of the United States and its allies."
- "Japanese were not the first to try rice in California, but they were the first to make it a commercial proposition."
- "The Japanese farmer in California has always been a great developer and improver. Where he has taken over lands that were in use before his time he has almost always, if not always, put them to a far higher use, and made them far more valuable than they were before."
- "The Japanese in California are assimilated to a degree unrecognized by anti-Japanese Americans. The native born Japanese are one hundred per cent American, while foreign born Japanese are at least fifty per cent American in spite of the many obstacles put in their way. Their Spiritual attitude toward, and material contributions to, the various enterprises of the late war eloquently testify to this effect."[10]

Precisely because of their behavioral similarities to white men, Japanese men presented a more serious racial dilemma to the white men who would administer the draft in California. During the spring of 1917, as state officials made preparations for California's role in Selective Service, they had asked Provost Marshal General Enoch Crowder how to racially classify Japanese. In so doing, they showed remarkable concern that Selective Service racial policies not offend the Japanese by associating them racially with Chinese. Ralph Merritt, whom Governor Stephens had named to run a "State Bureau of Registration," wrote to Crowder: "Relative classification of races desire instructions regarding Japanese. You understand peculiar local conditions existing California and Japanese sensitiveness against classification as Mongolians. Please advise." Crowder replied unhelpfully: "Use race classification ordinarily used."[11]

The two racial categories, "white" and "colored," seemed relatively unproblematic in the eastern United States, but in California, officials simply were not prepared to think about whether Japanese, or other Asians, were "white" or "colored." Rather, they *assumed* that Selective Service officials in Washington would implement a racial classification system that included at least two distinct Asian races—Mongolian, for Chinese, and some other classification for Japanese, and perhaps even additional categories for "Hindus" (South Asians), "Kanaka" (Hawaiians), and Pacific Islanders. Most likely, they thought it would be absurd to ask whether the Selective Service System would lump all Asians into either "white" or "colored" draft quotas. California officials believed that Asians were not white. Lacking a satisfactory instruction from Washington, Merritt notified the county councils of defense, who were directing registration, to "use the term denoting nationality rather than race" in order to avoid offending Japanese registrants.[12] Confusion over racial categories initially created local variations in the treatment of Asian registrants. As registration commenced in June, some California draft boards still assumed their Chinese and Japanese registrants belonged on their "colored" lists. In San Diego, several precincts listed small numbers of "colored" registrants, most of whom had either Chinese or Japanese names.[13]

When boards began calling men for induction, Japanese, Chinese, and at least a few Filipinos, Koreans, Hawaiians, and South Asians, were lumped together as one race, not as "Mongolian," but as "white." The boards had little choice. The only way to designate "colored" on the 1917 registration cards was by tearing off the lower left hand corner of the card where there was an instruction that read: "If person is of African descent, tear off this corner."[14] Members of San Diego's Local Board Number 2 must have felt strange when they called four men of Chinese ancestry as part of their September 28, 1917, white draft call.[15]

San Diego County: The Community and Selective Service

"Chinaman." The word leaps off the page, repeated a dozen or more consecutive times on an official population spreadsheet of the 1910 manuscript of the United States Census for San Diego, California. On pages designed to name individuals and reveal details unique to each, each entry contains identical information. In columns for name, relationship to head of household, age, race, place of birth, occupation, and so on, the census taker has reduced everything to a racially gendered slur, a number and a state of economic dependency. The images are startling as they go on for a page and a half: Chinaman no. 1; Chinaman no. 2; Chinaman no. 3; Chinaman no. 4; Chinaman no. 5; . . . In the margin, the census taker wrote, "Mission Valley Ranches, Hong Far Co. owners."[16]

Here, in one visually simplified schematic, was a stark expression of the intersection of race, gender, and land as commercial property in early-twentieth-century San Diego. The single word, chinaman, simultaneously racialized and gendered.[17] The status of these men as labor/property and as racially marked males superseded even their rights to individual names. It also made them a mere element of the landscape of Mission Valley, as though the census taker were counting livestock or trees. The United States' Naturalization Act of 1790 barred them (as well as all other non-white immigrants) from citizenship unless they were born in the United States. Even those of Chinese ancestry born in the United States lacked the basic rights of citizenship under California's racially restrictive laws.[18] They lived their lives in a state of civic liminality. The laws of white men in which they had no say and an economic system that defined them as suitable for only certain kinds of labor circumscribed their everyday lives.

What a dramatic reversal of status, then, was a Selective Service policy that proposed to transform some of these men into white U.S. soldiers. If the men labeled "Chinamen" on these census pages were of draft age in 1917 or 1918, the law required them to register with Selective Service. As with other men of Asian ancestry, San Diego County's three local draft boards had to determine whether they were U.S. citizens or aliens, and process the U.S. citizens as white, draft-eligible men. As agricultural laborers, however, their relationship to the land and production for the market determined whether or not they were drafted. This was surely a confusing and contradictory exercise for the draft boards and registrants alike, but as it turned out, not nearly as confusing as it would be to determine the racial categories and citizenship statuses of the California Indians living in San Diego County. We will return later to the responses men of Asian ancestry had to the draft.

The experiences that the California Indians of San Diego had with the Selective Service System show quite baldly the links between whiteness, manhood, citizenship, and private ownership of land or other natural resources. Understanding these will help us make better sense of the ways in which race and gender played out with respect to other groups in San Diego. The Indians' varied and often ambiguous responses to the draft reflect nearly a century and a half of indigenous peoples' relations with Europeans in San Diego. The story begins with the Spanish, continues through a period of Mexican rule, and ends up with San Diego under the control of the United States. To understand Indian responses to these various regimes, we have to know something of the land itself and the competing traditions of human engagement with the land since 1769 when Spanish missionaries arrived in San Diego to convert the natives to Christianity. Conversion meant not only adopting a belief in the Christian God, but adopting European attitudes toward the earth and the European system of patriarchal gender relations. The Spanish Christians taught that men should be separate from and in control of nature, and of women, whom they associated with nature. They labeled those who could not or would not separate themselves from the natural world in order to take control of it as "*sin razón*," or without reason. To live in and be one with nature was to be heathen, savage, uncivilized. Later, in the nineteenth century, in both Latin America and the United States, to be civilized and in control of nature was also part of what it meant to be white.[19]

The indigenous people of present-day San Diego County prized the land for its beauty and as the source of their sustenance. Historian Edward D. Castillo, a contemporary Cahuilla Indian has written, "Indians of California teach that the blessings of a rich land and a mild climate are gifts from the Creator. The Indians show their love and respect for the Creator—and for all of creation—by carefully managing the land for future generations and by living in harmony with the natural environment."[20] But the first Europeans to settle here hardly saw it this way.

The Spanish missionaries and soldiers alike found the Indian cultures abhorrent. One described the Cahuilla as "the most unhappy people in all the world. Their habitation is among the arid and bleak rocks of these sierras. . . . The clothing of the men is nothing at all, and the women wear some tattered capes made of mescal fibers. . . . [J]ust as the Sierra de California, because of its unfruitfulness and rockiness, looks like the wastebasket of the world so the Indians who inhabit it are the dross of human kind."[21] More than a century later, white men seeking profits and political power at the Indians' expense would echo these sentiments. The land in present-day San Diego County that the Indians found rich and sustaining, white men found harsh and threatening. They therefore sought to take control and reshape it according to European ideals.

San Diego County covers a very large amount of land. Occupying the southwest corner of California on the Mexican border, it is approximately eighty miles from north to south and averages about the same distance from east to west. There is more diversity of geography and climate here than in all the states east of the Mississippi combined. It has more than seventy miles of Pacific Ocean coastline to the west. On the east approximately one-third of the county is high desert. In the middle of the county its mountains rise to nearly seven thousand feet. The coastal littoral consists of a maze of canyons and mesas that extend inland for anywhere from ten to thirty miles. Where mesas reach the coast, they end at cliffs of up to a hundred feet above the beaches below. Many canyons become coastal wetlands within a few miles of the ocean.

The southern coastline is broken by San Diego Bay, which curves inward protected by a two-hundred foot high mesa/peninsula that juts into the ocean about twenty miles north of Tijuana, Mexico. The city of San Diego began on the low land along this bay. Half a dozen rivers and many creeks flow into the Pacific along the San Diego coast. None are large enough to support large boats, and many become dry or nearly dry during the summer.

San Diego's climate is ideal for a small human subsistence population that does not intend to cultivate any significant agricultural crops. For centuries the scarcity of year-round fresh water limited the size of human populations and made any kind of large-scale agriculture problematic. Rain is seasonal, falling mostly between October and March. Summers are usually dry. Annual average rainfall of eleven inches is less than the southeast might receive in a few days.

The white American men who came to San Diego in the late nineteenth century had two strategies for dealing with what they considered the land's shortcomings: first, separate indigenous communities from their ties to the land by converting individual Indians into private property owners; and second, find a way to manage the water flowing through rivers and streams to make up for the lack of rainfall. Both strategies would end up significantly shaping the local operations of the Selective Service System in San Diego in 1917 and 1918. The Federal Government had already created a plan to accomplish the first.

In 1887, in a move that many white men saw as a last-ditch attempt to civilize "savage" Indians, Congress passed the Dawes Allotment Act (also known as the Dawes Severalty Act). It sought to break up tribal identities by forcing reservation Indians to claim plots of land as their individual private property. Once Indians had taken possession of their allotted land, the Dawes Act declared that they had become U.S. citizens and were no longer citizens of their Indian nations.[22] The Bureau of Indian Affairs allotted reservation land to those who agreed to this plan. Each allotment removed land from tribal sovereignty and made it part of the United States. Most Indians rejected this attempt to force them to become white men. But incrementally, acre-by-acre, allotment undermined the social and cultural integrity of tribes. Indians who had accepted allotment were considered to be "civilized" and private citizens of the United States rather than members of an Indian tribe. The association of individual private property ownership with citizenship is remarkably literal and direct in this federal law. Conversely, this law regarded as "uncivilized" any culture in which people's primary identity is defined by a group or tribe, and where individual men did not own private property.

California Indians posed a unique problem for officials seeking to "civilize" Indians by making them owners of private property. Because the Senate had not ratified treaties with the California Indians that had been negotiated in the 1850s, there were few reservations and little reservation land available in California to allot to Indians in 1887. Thus, in 1891 and 1892 Congress created reservations specifically for the former mission Indians of California primarily within San Diego County. These laws not only created reservations, but contained a formula for immediately breaking them up through an allotment system similar to the Dawes formula. The U.S. government gave the Indians of San Diego two choices. Individual heads of household could become private landowners and "take up civilized ways," or they could continue to live as reservation Indians. Those who took the first option became U.S. citizens. If they took the second choice they claimed no land. After twenty-five years the United States would turn over all the land that had not been claimed for private ownership to the tribe. Those Indians who chose the second option would not become U.S. citizens, but would remain citizens of their Indian nation. During the 1890s a federal commission assigned more than a dozen tribes to reservations in San Diego. Like Indians elsewhere in the United States, California Indians mostly declined the offer to claim individual private ownership of land.[23]

The California Reservation Indians, living under dire conditions mostly on nonarable reservation land in San Diego County, had largely become by World War I a curiosity for the amusement of white society. Their threat to "civilization" had been neutralized while white writers romanticized them in bestselling novels and travel books.[24] But by 1916 the romanticized, tragic, Indians of San Diego County had become an obstacle to white progress. This obstacle would become, improbably, the centerpiece of a scandal involving Selective Service officials, water rights, and a draft exemption for one of the wealthiest men in the county.

In San Diego, one of the goals of white men's laws was to create an eastern landscape and that would invite a larger white population to settle in southern California's semiarid climate. For this, white men needed to move water around. The battle over water in San Diego reintroduced the debate about civilizing the Indians at just the time Selective Service officials had to determine which Indians were "civilized" and thus liable to be drafted. This is also a story of political intrigue and undercover wheeling and dealing pitting two giant newspaper magnates against each other in the relatively sparsely populated and apparently insignificant county of San Diego.

"Water Is King"

In 1912, Ed Fletcher, of San Diego, wrote to his friend and business partner, ". . . There is no doubt that Water is king, throughout this whole southern territory, and the value of same, will greatly increase, with intensified farming."[25] He was right, of course, and his belief in the importance of water to the future of San Diego would make him wealthy and secure him an appointment as a Selective Service official. Thus began the long and successful political career of Ed Fletcher.

Besides needing a dependable supply of fresh water, white people in San Diego who wished to build towns or establish agriculture in the style of Europe and the eastern United States, also had to control wild rivers and streams that tended to flood during the rainy season and go dry in the summers. San Diego needed development, said one, but development required that Congress give them "the privilege of stopping that water that rushes by and destroys the valley and rushes through the city and destroys our improvements," even if it meant breaking legal contracts with San Diego Indians.[26]

Ed Fletcher was a white man who had moved to California from Massachusetts as a young man of sixteen in 1888. He briefly returned to Massachusetts in 1896 to marry Mary Batchelder. Like many other propertied white men at the time, he kept his political and business affairs separate from his private family life. Fletcher's voluminous correspondence with friends, foes, associates, and business partners rarely, if ever, mentions either Mary or the ten children she bore. Similarly, his memoirs focus mostly on his public and business life. Yet surely, without Mary's management of his household, Fletcher would have had far less time to pursue his myriad interests in business and politics. Just as certainly, Fletcher would not have succeeded had he not been white, or had he been a woman. Nevertheless, marriage, whiteness, and maleness did not by themselves guarantee success. Fletcher worked extremely hard to achieve the fullest potential of white manhood through his continuous struggle to gain mastery over the people and landscapes of San Diego County.

For thirteen years, Fletcher traveled the rough backcountry of San Diego County by bicycle and horse-drawn cart selling fresh produce and other goods to a scattered population of whites, and Indians living on reservations. Few white men would have known the semiarid canyon and mesa terrain and rugged mountains of San Diego County better than Fletcher did by 1901. In that year he would use his knowledge of land and water in San Diego County as an agent for railroad and land tycoon, Henry Huntington. He successfully managed the creation of a major water project for Huntington inland from the City of Oceanside on the San Luis Rey River, and negotiated the purchase of thousands of acres of coastal lands for development.[27]

By 1908, Fletcher no longer had to make a living working for others. He owned his own real estate company and two water companies. He owned thousands of acres throughout San Diego County. As white men had done in Coweta County, Georgia, Paterson, New Jersey, and Adams County, Illinois, Fletcher helped establish a regime in San Diego County founded upon the domination, reordering, and control of nature. This required dispossessing the Indians of their lands and of their ability to subsist independently of white society. It required the surveying, mapping, and privatization of land.[28] It required the carving of roads through hills and mountains and bridging rivers and streams. And finally, it meant controlling those rivers and streams, capturing their flow, and moving the water to places where farmers could use it to irrigate and residents for drinking and bathing. What cotton was to Coweta County, Georgia, what silk was to Paterson, New Jersey, and what corn was to Adams County, Illinois, water was to San Diego County. Without the ability to control and own it as a marketable commodity, white men in San Diego could not be what it meant to be white men elsewhere. The ownership of land, power to direct the labor of others, and control of governmental authority meant little in San Diego unless one had some say in the distribution of water. Water would become the source of Ed Fletcher's power.

Political leaders in the City of San Diego, and some of the smaller municipalities served by Fletcher's water businesses, increasingly resented his stranglehold over their water supplies. Fletcher had frequently raised his rates, and when the City protested he sent a veiled threat to cut off the water.[29] It should not be surprising then, that the city should secretly hire an engineer to draw up plans for a city-owned waterworks that would end their dependence upon Fletcher. But the only way the city could challenge Fletcher was by damming the San Diego River and flooding nearly all the lands belonging to the El Capitan Grande Indians. Unaware of these plans, the Indians continuing to occupy the reservation communally had every right to expect that the entire reservation, minus ten alloted acres, would become the permanent territory of the El Capitan Grande tribe in 1919.

The Department of the Interior and the Bureau of Indian Affairs initially opposed the plan. The Bureau's agent on the reservation reported that the plan angered the Indians, and that they could only be removed by force. The Act of 1891 provided that at the end of twenty-five years (counting from March 1894 when the initial patent to El Capitan Grande was made), "the United States will convey the same or the remaining portion not patented to individuals . . . to said Capitan Grande Band or Village of Mission Indians . . . free of all charge or encumbrance whatsoever." By 1916, twenty-two years after the initial patent, individual Indians had only claimed private ownership of about ten acres of land within the El Capitan Grande Reservation.[30]

Ed Fletcher stood at the center of an unlikely confluence of events in San Diego. As the battle between Fletcher and the City over the El Capitan Grande Indian Reservation continued, Governor William Stephens appointed him to the Selective Service District Appeals Board for the First District of Southern California, a position that helped him to secure a powerful ally in his fight against the City. It pitted wealthy white men in San Diego against each other, set competing newspapers to calling each other's owners unpleasant names, unified most of the local politicians against Ed Fletcher, and got two sons and a nephew of one of the wealthiest men in San Diego excused from the draft.

Water, Newspapers, and Draft Exemptions

James Scripps, a twenty-eight-year-old white man of San Diego, appeared before the San Diego County Local Draft Board on November 26, 1917, to request an exemption from the draft on the grounds he was the "manager of an enterprise essential to the war effort." Scripps was the son of E. W. Scripps, the founder and owner of the Scripps newspaper empire, and owner of United Press wire service. Young Scripps managed the Scripps newspaper in San Diego, *The Sun*, one of three major dailies there. By his own estimate, he was a millionaire. Two of the most influential white men in San Diego accompanied him to meet with the draft board on that day. One of these men, a Mr. Harper, was a lawyer for the Scripps newspapers. The other, Ed Fletcher, represented San Diego on the Selective Service District Appeals Board for Southern California District 1. This board reviewed all decisions of the local draft boards in the counties of San Diego, Orange, and Los Angeles. The draft board, although highly skeptical of Scripps's application for exemption, temporarily excused him, giving him a month to transfer management of his newspaper to someone else.[31] Although Scripps's claim was officially about an industrial deferment, in reality it was about white men's entitlement to ownership of land and water.

The day after the hearing, Fletcher wrote in a letter to his business partner, William Henshaw: "I came home yesterday with Mr. Harper, San Diego representative of Mr. E. W. Scripps, and a brainy man. He represented E. W. Scripps at the Exemption Board meeting yesterday, and was very appreciative of my assistance in getting temporary exemption for Scripps' son, James Scripps. . . ." Harper had explained a strategy by the City of San Diego to secure riparian [water] rights along the San Diego River. The City's proposed dam on the river, which would force the El Capitan Grande Indians off their reservation land, would also block Fletcher's plans to build his own dam further down the river and guarantee that the City would not become dependent upon Fletcher's Cuyamaca Water Company for fresh water. But as insurance against lawsuits by landowners downstream from the dam, the City also needed to secure the downstream riparian rights. If Fletcher could persuade a few large landowners along the river not to cooperate with the City, he might be able to stave off the City's dam indefinitely through a series of lawsuits. As an owner of several hundred acres of riverfront land, E. W. Scripps occupied a strategic position in this struggle. According to Harper, a city representative had secretly approached him to get Scripps to support the project. "Harper said that . . . he refused to be a party to it," wrote Fletcher. "We certainly are indented [*sic*] to Mr. Scripps and Mr. Harper."[32]

Fletcher would repay E. W. Scripps for his support on the water dispute by tirelessly seeking a permanent exemption for son James. Fletcher stood literally alone in support of Scripps's exemption against the otherwise unanimous opposition of both the local draft board and the district appeals board. He made public statements and sent letters to the newspapers defending his stance. The *San Diego Union*, a newspaper owned by John Spreckels, and the major competitor to Scripps's *San Diego Sun*, ran almost weekly stories on the case, ridiculing both Fletcher and the Scripps family. Fletcher's stance only makes sense in the context of his ongoing water war with the City of San Diego at the same time. The *Union* covered the water war at the same time it was reporting on the Scripps case, yet it never connected the two issues. In fact, the *Union* published a Fletcher letter opposing the City's proposed dam only three days before it published another in which he attempted to justify his support for the Scripps exemption. It is only Fletcher's private letter to William Henshaw that proves the link.

Publicly, Fletcher was hard pressed to explain his support for Scripps. James Scripps made no claim on his own behalf. Rather, the three senior partners in the Scripps Corporation, including E. W. Scripps and Mr. Harper, had produced all the documentation and Harper had appeared before both the local draft board and the district board to argue the case. They requested a draft classification of IV-D, exemption on grounds he was "the sole managing, controlling and directing head of a necessary industrial enterprise." There were three issues of fact to be determined: (1) Whether Scripps was the only person who could perform his duties; (2) whether the enterprise could survive without him; and (3) whether a newspaper chain qualified as "a necessary industrial enterprise" in time of war. Clearly, Scripps was not the "sole" director or manager of the Scripps firm. Just as clearly, no reasonable person could believe that the Scripps newspaper empire would collapse without young James at the helm. This was a major corporation that operated nationwide. No single person is indispensable in a large corporation. But Fletcher insisted that those who would have to take over the young Scripps's duties were too old to manage them—not because age incapacitated them, but because age entitled them to rest. They "are all men between 60 and 70 years of age," he wrote, "and believing they are entitled to be relieved of the heavy burdens of business, have asked that the responsibility of the successful management of their business be put upon the shoulders of younger men." What made a newspaper chain a "necessary industrial enterprise" in time of war, according to Fletcher, was its propaganda function. The Scripps chain owned more than twenty newspapers in the United States, as well as the United Press wire service. Through the wire service it reached "a million readers daily." Further, Fletcher wrote, "no one denies the loyalty of these papers nor their power for good in supporting the president of the United States in this hour of emergency."[33]

So far, Fletcher's arguments, though implausible, came within the scope of his duties as a member of the District Appeals Board. But Fletcher played fast and loose with the Selective Service regulations in order to get Scripps excused. It was the job of this board to rule on all agricultural and industrial claims. It did not have jurisdiction over dependency claims except in cases that it received on appeal from an adverse local board decision. Nevertheless, Fletcher wrote that he had voted to excuse Scripps partly because he had a dependent wife and four dependent children. Scripps had not asked the local board for exemption on these grounds. Acting on his own initiative, Fletcher introduced evidence of Scripps's dependents. "Being a neighbor of his," he wrote, "I am aware that James Scripps is the father of four children. . . . When it has been conclusively shown that we have more single men and volunteers than we can clothe, arm and prepare for service, certainly the time has not yet come to call into service the father of four small children." In addition to the procedural irregularity of basing a claim for industrial exemption partly on evidence completely irrelevant to that claim, Fletcher added that he voted for Scripps in order to make it possible for him to appeal to the Presidential Appeal Board. Claimants could not appeal unanimous decisions of the District Board. "My vote in this case would make it unanimous," Fletcher wrote, "and there could in that case be no appeal to the president."[34]

Fletcher's actions so outraged the San Diego County draft board that it refused to certify the presidential appeal of James Scripps. The *Union*, a Spreckels-owned news paper in competition with Scripps's *Sun*, relished this event. It placed the story smack in the middle of page one. The headline paraphrased a board member's statement that "One of Publisher's Sons Ought to Serve for Country." It was the *Union*'s longest news story that day, and it contained a nearly complete transcript of the debate between the local board and Scripps's lawyer. Every Scripps man of draft age in San Diego County had sought exemption. E. W.'s other son, Robert had also sought exemption and been placed in Class II, still liable for induction, but only after all from class I had been drafted, which was not likely. The nephew of E. W. Scripps, Thomas O. Scripps, had sought exemption on the grounds that he was the sole support of his "infirm and dependent parents." Indeed, the Thomas Scripps case was a virtual comedy. His father, Fred T. Scripps who was a wealthy man in his own right, claimed that Thomas contributed nine hundred dollars a year to his and his wife's support. But it turned out that the nine hundred dollars came out of a much larger salary that his father paid him. The *Union* speculated that this was "the first time a parent has claimed dependency while actually paying his son a salary."[35]

The Chairman of the County draft board justified its refusal to certify the case of James Scripps to the Presidential Appeal Board because none of the Scripps men had shown a willingness to go to war. "If Robert Scripps had shown a willingness to go, we would have consented to the exemption of James G. Scripps," Chairman R. C. Allen told Scripps's lawyer. The local board thus admitted that it did not make its decision on the basis of the facts of each Scripps case, but on a belief that someone in that family should go. Further, Scripps's lawyer pointed out that Claus Spreckels, the son of *San Diego Union* owner John Spreckels, had also requested an exemption on precisely the same grounds that James Scripps had. The board had denied his claim for an industrial deferment, but it did place him in Class II on grounds that he had dependents.[36]

Scripps's case did go to the president on orders from Provost Marshal General, Enoch Crowder. Amid rumors that the case was fixed, the *Tribune*, another Spreckels paper, asked: "What secret diplomacy is conniving in this fierce democracy. Is there a back stairs entrance to the White House?"[37] As predicted, Scripps won his appeal to the President. Crowder ordered the local board to classify James Scripps IV-D, deferred on industrial grounds.[38]

One might reasonably ask what this case has to do with race and gender. Neither was an explicit issue here. It is a question of what people believe they are entitled to and the grounds for that belief. To explore this, we might return to the epigraph that precedes the introduction to this book. W. E. B. Du Bois asked: "What is whiteness that one should so desire it?" The answer, he concludes, after long and careful observation of white people is that "whiteness is the ownership of the earth forever and ever, Amen!" But the essay that follows this statement makes clear that this is an ideal, a goal, rather than a constant state of being. Whiteness is the right "to swagger and swear and waste," behaviors that white men viewed as impudent or aggressive when people who are not white engaged in them. In this essay, "The Souls of White

Folk," Du Bois explains what he has observed as the "white" nations of the world fought a world war amongst themselves to decide which white people would own which parts of the earth where brown and yellow people lived. It was this sense of entitlement that allowed Fletcher to justify intervention on behalf of Scripps, and to use his position to protect his personal economic interests. And it appears the contested ground of white manhood was the only arena in which Fletcher could imagine negotiating his demands for rights to sell water from the San Diego River. He cajoled the San Diego City Council. He published an open letter in the local newspapers. He met with members of Congress, the Secretary of the Interior, the Commissioner of Indian Affairs, and the white Superintendent of the San Diego Indian reservations. But he made no attempt to negotiate these rights with the El Capitan Grande Indians, who on moral grounds, as well as technical legal grounds, were the only ones with the right to offer him the water. He would presume to speak in their interests when those coincided with his own, but he would not invite them to the bargaining table as equals.[39]

Ed Fletcher used his position on the District Appeals Board to dominate the administration of the draft in San Diego. In none of the other three communities we have looked at have District Board members played such a prominent and decisive role. Fletcher's colleagues on the District Board turned over to him the authority to review all cases from San Diego County. In addition, they gave him oversight over all agricultural claims from Los Angeles and Orange counties as well. During the dispute over the Scripps case in March of 1918, Fletcher noted that he had personally reviewed 7,200 appeals and made recommendations to the District Board. The Scripps case was one of only two in which the board did not unanimously agree with Fletcher.[40]

San Diego "Mission Indians" and the Draft

It is curious that Fletcher showed no concern for how the draft affected the so-called Mission Indians of San Diego County. Before his appointment as a Selective Service official, he had shown great interest in Indians as a source of amusement for white people and profits for himself. With his business partners he had built a tourist ranch at Warners Hot Springs where he expected to host annual fiestas to celebrate Indian cultures of San Diego County. "I expect to have four or five hundred Indians there," he wrote his partner, the State Supreme Court Justice F. W. Henshaw. "The fiesta will last a week and I expect ten thousand people. . . ." Henshaw, revealing a common prejudice against California Indians, wrote back that bringing the Indians to the hot springs was a good idea, adding, "it certainly won't do a Digger Indian any harm to give him a bath. . . ."[41] In his correspondence with the superintendent of the San Diego reservations as well as the Bureau of Indian Affairs, Fletcher presented himself as a friend of the Indians. The Indians, however, may not have seen him as such. While Fletcher's water company and other enterprises sold water to the reservations and built roads through them, which he said was for their benefit, the Indians let the superintendent know that they did not trust him.[42] Nevertheless, there was a confluence of interest between Fletcher and the Mission Indians when it came to preserving the Indians' rights to remain on the reservations. It was in Fletcher's interest that

Indians not leave the El Capitan Grande Reservation in particular. Their continued presence was an obstacle to the dam project proposed by the City of San Diego.

The Indians on the San Diego County reservations were in a bind. In order to preserve their individual cultures and rights to the land as indigenous people, they had to live on the reservation. They could not take private ownership of land, or take up life as individuals or families separate from their tribe. But the United States had confined them to areas too small to sustain much of a traditional way of life, and on land that was of marginal economic value. The Indians who remained on the reservations had to accept a life of economic dependency upon the U.S. government in exchange for the right to maintain their distinct identities as Indians. Furthermore, as long as they lived as tribal members on the reservations, they did not have any of the rights of U.S. citizens. The Dawes Act of 1887 prescribed what an Indian had to do to be a citizen:

> Every Indian born within the territorial limits of the United States who has voluntarily taken up, within said limits, his residence separate and apart from any tribe of Indians therein, and has adopted the habits of civilized life, is hereby declared to be a citizen of the United States, and is entitled to all the rights, privileges, and immunities of such citizens.[43]

In the decades following passage of this statute, courts and subsequent legislation further defined what might make an Indian a citizen. The children of Indians who had become citizens under the Dawes Act were declared to be citizens. Indians who had declared their intention to claim an allotment of reservation land were declared citizens. Indians who moved off the reservation in order to take jobs frequently became citizens whether or not this was their intention. The Selective Service Act of 1917 exempted noncitizens, whether they were foreigners or American Indians. Selective Service administrators and the Bureau of Indian Affairs agreed that reservation superintendents would appoint registration boards and oversee the registration of all Indian men within the draft ages. The same superintendents would then determine which Indian men were citizens and which noncitizens. They would forward the draft cards of citizens to the local draft board that had jurisdiction in the region, and send the draft cards of the noncitizens to the Commissioner of Indian Affairs in Washington, D.C.

The Selective Service records relating to the Indians of San Diego County suggest that many reservation Indians struggled to maintain their social cohesion and common identity in the face of the economic necessity for men and women to seek jobs off the reservation. Young men, in particular, moved about so much that P. T. Hoffman, the superintendent of the Pala Indian School District, which included El Capitan Grande, was unable to keep track of them. His Selective Service files contain numerous scraps of paper with notes about laws and court decisions that defined citizen and noncitizen Indians. Hoffman was hard pressed to provide the government with the names and current residences of draft age Indian males under his jurisdiction. These records offer a picture of a young male population in constant movement apparently in search of jobs. This was the conundrum he faced. If a reservation Indian left the reservation to take a job, could he be said to have taken up "residence separate and apart from any tribe of Indians . . . , and . . . adopted the habits of civilized life?" If so, this would make him a citizen and subject to the draft. This was further complicated by current racial ideology. What should Hoffman do about a man who would be a noncitizen Indian except for the fact that he had one parent who was a white citizen.

The case of William Nelson particularly worried Hoffman. When he forwarded the names of Indians registered for the draft who he judged were noncitizens, Hoffman added a note asking the Commissioner of Indian Affairs to determine Nelson's status. His mother, Maria Nelson, was officially an Indian. Hoffman thought she had received an allotment of land, but could not find her name on the San Diego County allotment lists. Even if she had received an allotment, it would not yet make either her or her children citizens if the government still held her land patent in trust for her. Under the Acts of 1887 and 1891, the government held patents in trust for twenty-five years after the initial allotment. During this time, the Indian holding the allotment was prohibited from selling any portion of it. This provision was to prevent unscrupulous land speculators from taking advantage of cash-starved Indians by convincing them to sell below a reasonable market rate. At the end of twenty-five years, the government issued "a patent in fee" to the allotted Indian, which meant he or she now owned the land outright and was free to sell it. In 1906, in order to open up more Indian land for sale to whites, Congress removed the patent in trust provision, making all allotments issued after that year direct patents in fee. If Maria Nelson had been allotted before 1906, she did not yet hold "a patent in fee."[44]

Hoffman concluded that Maria Nelson was not legally a citizen according to the Dawes formula. But what of her son William? Receiving no reply from the Commissioner, Hoffman decided that William Nelson was a citizen. An unsigned and undated document among Hoffman's records in the National Archives lists the draft age male Indians under his jurisdiction who have been determined to be citizens, and therefore liable for induction. The last entry reads:

WILLIAM NELSON: Son of white man; therefore considered citizen. Subject to approval by Indian Office.

In at least one other case, Hoffman again declared a man a citizen solely on the grounds he had a white father. In forwarding the registration card of Joseph Lancaster to the San Diego County draft board, Hoffman wrote: "While this boy has Indian blood, yet his father is a white man and under precedents established heretofore in similar cases, should be adjudged a citizen."[45] This particular official associated whiteness with U.S. citizenship, and a person could be white with only one white parent.

In San Diego County, California, on Indian reservations under federal jurisdiction, the racial criteria that distinguished black from white was reversed. Historically in the United States, before the end of slavery, the free or slave status of the mother determined the status of the child. Under such a regime, tens of thousands of the children of white men were born slaves to their fathers because their mothers were slaves. After slavery, any child, or descendent, of either a black man or a black woman would be considered black. Having a white father was not sufficient to secure the privileges of citizenship to anyone believed to have "a drop of black blood." Now, Hoffman ruled that the racial status of the white father determined that the racial status of the child was citizen/white. This says something profound about the meanings of race at this particular time in U.S. history. It has very much to do with the rights of white men to make the rules for everyone else. At a time when black people in the United States demanded their rights as citizens, as supposedly guaranteed by the Fourteenth Amendment to the United States Constitution, every level of government, from the federal and state to the local conspired to deny them those rights. As only the most immediate case, the federal government ordained the segregated draft calls of 1917 and 1918, but local and state officials supported and enforced them in every state. Simultaneously, the federal government had decided that Indians would no longer be permitted to be primarily citizens of their individual Indian nations. The government would force them to become U.S. citizens. It would strip them of their language, their spirituality, their kinship relations, and their sense of belonging as a group to a particular area of land. It would make Indian men into individualistic, acquisitive, and competitive imitations of white men and at the end of this process call them "citizens." Simply, white man's racial ideology of this time decreed that an Indian man could become a white man. Senator Henry Dawes and Colonel Richard Pratt, inventor of the Indian School, had laid out an explicit plan of deracination. Indian schools, such as the Pala School in San Diego County, would erase the culture. Allotment would force them to become selfish, a trait that Senator Dawes said was the foundation of civilization. "Till this people . . . give up their lands," declared Dawes, "and divide them among their citizens so that each can own the land he cultivates, they will not make much progress."[46]

Many Indians in San Diego County apparently remained unconvinced. On many reservations no one signed up for allotments. In his Selective Service report to the Commissioner of Indian Affairs, Hoffman listed six reservations on which no Indians had claimed allotments. "No citizens, since unallotted. These reservations patented to bands, not to individuals," he noted.[47] Under the Act for Relief of the Mission Indians of California of 1891, any reservation land not allotted remained the collective property of the tribe in perpetuity. This was a protection Indians elsewhere in the United States did not have under the Dawes Act. The Indians of El Capitan Grande seemed to be particularly insistent on keeping this protection and maintaining their cultural and geographic integrity. During the debate over whether or not the City of San Diego would get the legal authority to dam the river and flood their reservation, the Indians told Hoffman that they would never leave voluntarily. It would take force to remove them. In this respect, the El Capitan Indians and Ed Fletcher should have been natural allies. But consistent with the pattern of white supremacy elsewhere in the United States, the Indians were not accorded the opportunity to participate in the public and private negotiations that would eventually cost them their land and homes. Neither their potential ally, Ed Fletcher, nor their expressed enemy, the City of San Diego, saw them as agents of their own destiny. Fletcher negotiated behind the scenes with other wealthy white men, and publicly with Congress and the Bureau of Indian Affairs, using the plight of the Indians as part of his argument. He would lose his fight with the City, but as a member of the State Legislature in the 1940s, he would be instrumental in bringing Colorado River water to San Diego, and become a hero of later City governments.[48] The Indians of El Capitan Grande lost their only productive land to the City's reservoir in the 1920s, forcing them into greater dependence upon the federal government.

Cato Sells, the United States Commissioner of Indian Affairs, saw himself as a champion of the Indians in the tradition of Senator Henry Dawes and Richard Pratt. He was anxious to use Indians in the military service as examples of their fitness for U.S. citizenship. He asked the reservation superintendents to "keep in touch with the Indians of your jurisdiction and obtain full and complete information concerning each one drafted." The purpose of this information would be so "that our records may stand as a fitting tribute to the Indian race."[49] With more than a hint of paternalism, Sells insisted that superintendents should make sure that all draft eligible Indian men under their jurisdiction should have their rights under the Selective Service Act protected. The Indians literally were theirs. "You should advise your Indians . . . in regard to their rights to deferred classification on the grounds of noncitizenship and on such other grounds as they may be entitled to. . . ." Further, "as superintendent in charge of and responsible for the welfare of your Indians," he wrote, "you should exercise [the right to claim exemption or discharge on their behalf as warranted]." They should keep in mind that "the rights of Indians may not otherwise be protected." In recognition of the poor health of many reservation Indians, Sells emphasized that Indians with physical impairments or other health problems should not be "drafted and sent to camp only to be discharged, . . . thus involving annoyance to the Indians and expense to the Government."[50] But another Sells letter assumes the individual and nuclear families count more than the community: "Those who have no dependents and are the best specimens of physical manhood are of course most desired to make up the army."[51] Here was a major goal of the Selective Service System stated in a nutshell. Preserve nuclear families. Take only single men on whom no one depends for survival, and who are physically fit. This policy does not account for collective communities in which each individual is important to the whole. But this did not matter. Those Indian men who lived as part of such communities in San Diego County were probably not citizens, and therefore not subject to the draft. In virtually all cases in which Hoffman declared Indian men in San Diego County to be citizens he did so on the basis of his judgment that they had "taken up residence apart from the tribe and adopted habits of civilized life." Quite simply, this meant that they had gone off the reservation to live and had taken a job for wages.

Whether they wanted to be drafted or not Indians of San Diego County were forced to wait upon a white man's determination of their citizenship. Two Indian men from the Rincon reservation, which Hoffman reported had no citizen Indians, went to the San Diego County local draft board and registered as citizens. The board chairman and Hoffman conferred with each other about whether or not to accept them, and concluded that since they wanted to be drafted they should be permitted to claim citizenship.[52] Others, however, apparently did not wish to be drafted, but Hoffman declared them citizens and forwarded their cards to either the San Diego or Riverside County draft boards. Three others claimed to be underage, and Hoffman reported that he gave them the benefit of the doubt because they "are all engaged in work as agricultural laborers."[53] Another Indian insisted that he was not a U.S. citizen, but Hoffman declared him one on the grounds that he "has lived on land leased by his mother" outside the La Jolla reservation where he was born.[54]

The U.S.-Mexican Border

While the natural geography and climate of San Diego County helped to shape how Indians and Selective Service officials dealt with each other, the man-made seventy-mile boundary between the United States and Mexico generated a host of other complications for San Diego's draft boards. Mexican citizens, including many Indians whose traditional territories spanned the international border, had moved back and forth between Mexico and Southern California with relative freedom since 1848 when the United States wrested California from Mexico. If they resided primarily on the U.S. side of the border, Mexican men of draft age were obligated to register for the draft as aliens. If they had declared an intention to become U.S. citizens, they could be drafted. White men in San Diego who employed Mexican laborers feared this would stimulate an exodus of Mexicans back to Mexico. Other white men, those who felt the pressure of the draft upon them, resented the possibility that they could be sent to fight and possibly die in France, while Mexican men took their jobs. Enoch Crowder anticipated the first of these concerns in a letter to the governors of Texas, New Mexico, Arizona, and California a few days before the first registration. "Misapprehensions among Mexicans in border states . . . may cause serious exodus of labor," he predicted. Governors should make a proclamation in Spanish and have it published in Spanish language newspapers throughout their states.[55]

The San Diego draft boards shared these concerns and took steps to mitigate them. The *San Diego Union* reported that when six Mexican requested expedited physical exams so that they could go back to their railroad construction jobs two hundred miles east of San Diego, the board obliged. But at the same time, the three local boards shared with the newspapers their frustrations over the large numbers of aliens who were unwilling to be drafted. The *Union* reported:

> Many aliens have applied for exemption in both the city and county divisions and cannot be drafted. Only one alien has so far expressed a desire to serve. Most of these aliens are strong, husky young men who passed the physical examination, but who will remain in San Diego, where they are not citizens, while Americans go out to fight.[56]

Someone at E. W. Scripps's newspaper, the *San Diego Sun* feared the large number of registrants in San Diego who claimed to be aliens would force draft boards to move through their lists of eligible men too quickly. A telegram from the *Sun* to Crowder complained that the County board had "accepted registrants statement in registration that he was an alien without investigation." This seemed to be one reason that the board reached all the way to draft lottery number 556 in its first call.[57]

The press focused its ire especially on Mexicans, a sentiment local draft board members seem to have shared. The *Union* complained that most of the aliens claiming exemption were Mexicans who had "declared they did not desire to become American soldiers. . . . They are young men who have derived their living from American industry and were told that they could not be compelled to serve the United States, but were asked if they would follow Old Glory of their own free will. To a man, they shook their heads and claimed exemption." But the paper did note that among the recalcitrant aliens were "several Englishmen," as well as "several Italians," and "two Greeks."[58]

But some of this may have been the fault of the City and County's own boosterism during the decade before the United States entered World War I. Indeed, although the population had grown with amazing speed during the first decade of the twentieth century, San Diego, if the U.S. census is to be believed, was uniquely homogenous among growing urban centers in the United States at the time. While the population doubled between 1900 and 1910, according to the U.S. census, the number of people it categorized as alien or nonwhite showed no increase. Thus, in a population of 40,000 in 1910, only about 3,000, or 7.5 percent, were labeled either alien or nonwhite. By comparison, El Paso, Texas, another border city of approximately the same size, was approaching 35 percent nonwhite during this period.[59] There is good reason to suspect the census both undercounted nonwhites in San Diego in 1910 and over-counted whites as part of a larger campaign to attract even more whites to move to the city. Hugh S. Johnson, second in command in the Selective Service System, in fact suggested this was the case for the three Pacific Coast states. "I have a very definite idea about this matter," he wrote the adjutant general of California, "and it is apparent that the chickens of the boosters out there are coming home to roost and that the apparent discrepancy will be found in a padding of Census returns in 1910." Overcounting in general would have swelled local quotas disproportionately to the rest of the country, exacerbating the built-in need to draft more white male citizens in jurisdictions having many exempt aliens.

For San Diego, the evidence that aliens and nonwhites were purposely under-counted in the Census is reasonably strong. A comparison of the names of draft registrants from the 1917 registration with city directories between 1910 and 1917, shows that large numbers of residents were not counted, and that nonwhites and aliens were less likely to be listed in the directories than whites. Perhaps equally significant, eighty percent of those missed in the directories resided in the jurisdiction of Local Draft Board Number Two. Throughout the war, this board in particular would complain repeatedly to local newspapers that it could not meet its quotas because of the large numbers of aliens among its registrants. According to draft registration records, twenty-six percent of all 1917 draft registrants in the jurisdiction of Local Draft Board Number Two were considered either alien or colored.[60]

In addition to increasing the numbers of noncitizen residents, the border also provided a convenient way for U.S. citizens to escape the draft. Numerous reports from U.S. consuls in Ensenada, Baja California, Mexico, and other border cities indicated that hundreds, if not thousands, of draft-eligible American men had taken up residence there to wait out the war. The American consul in Matamoros, Mexico, across from Brownsville, Texas, recommended in November 1917 that draft boards near the Mexican border take photographs of all draft-eligible men in their jurisdictions and provide them to immigration officials at border crossings.[61] But attempts to stop the flow of American men into Mexico ran afoul of the business interests of Claus Spreckels, and his father, John D. Spreckels, owner of two newspapers, the *San Diego Union*, and the *Evening Tribune*. Claus was invested in racetracks in Tijuana and Mexicali. John held controlling interest in the San Diego and Arizona Railroad, whose primary business was transporting Americans from San Diego to racetracks and other amusements in Mexico.

John D. Spreckels called on his close friend and political ally, Congressman William Kettner, to oppose any order to close the border to draft age men. Kettner referred him to another California Congressman, Republican Julius Kahn, ranking minority member of the House Committee on Military Affairs. In a letter to, "My Dear Julius," Spreckels assured the Congressman that northern Mexico was not an inviting place for "slackers." It is "a wild and rough country." There are "few places where a man could live at all." The whole territory was "thoroughly policed by Governor Cantu, [who] can be depended upon to round them up." Then he waxed paranoid, asserting that proposals to close the border were part of a Los Angeles conspiracy against San Diego. The campaign "to close up the line as tight as possible," was started by the Customs Collector in Los Angeles, who has been trying to choke off San Diego's growth. In addition, there was a minister from Los Angeles trying to start "a bone-dry movement in San Diego," which would prohibit the sale of alcohol. This minister, said Spreckels, was part of a Los Angeles conspiracy to force the closure of the Tijuana racetrack. Another minister, apparently part of this conspiracy, was actually a member of the San Diego City Council. He "is naturally a highly prejudiced person," according to Spreckels. "He stands for bone-dry and every other ism that is usually associated with the long-hair." Kahn forwarded the letter to the Secretary of War with a note referring to Spreckels as "one of the leading citizens of California."[62]

But Secretary of War, Newton Baker, showed little sympathy for Spreckels. He wrote back to Kahn that local boards in southern California "would be justified in taking such reasonable action as would be necessary" to staunch a flow of draft-eligible men into Mexico. The War Department had in hand evidence that during the fall 1917 draft calls American men were fleeing into Mexico to escape the draft. One reported "three stages full of alleged slackers arrived at Ensenada, two of them from Tijuana, the other from Tecate, trying to go further south." Another, from Army Intelligence, estimated "over 100 slackers in Ensenada." At approximately the same time Spreckels was praising Mexican Governor Cantu of Baja California for his diligence in rounding up American draft evaders, U.S. Customs agents in Baja were complaining that he had done nothing. In December 1917, the agent in Calexico said that Governor Cantu "had yet to turn over any slackers." Spreckels' own newspaper had reported in September that "Ensenada is said to be full of Americans who have attempted to evade answering the draft summons." It added: "A number of these slackers, it is alleged, are scions of wealthy California families."[63] However, by April 1918, the paper reported that "the slacker colony at Ensenada has dwindled" to "fewer than ten." American men had tired of "laborious work in the mines" of Mexico and had been making their way back north "with the hope of crossing the line unmolested."[64]

Winners and Losers

Although the World War I draft disrupted, and ended, the lives of some San Diego men, as a system it provided protection for the economic and political interests of the County's wealthiest and most influential white men. The investments of John and Claus Spreckels in railroads and racetracks did just fine. The local draft boards adopted a policy of granting temporary passes to draft registrants that permitted them to take short trips into Mexico. Claus Spreckels was placed in Class II and was not drafted. The *San Diego Union* was the only daily newspaper in San Diego to survive the twentieth century. James Scripps remained at home for the rest of the war to manage the family empire, and he had the company of his brother Robert, and cousin Thomas. The Scripps name lives on as a newspaper chain, a school of oceanography, and an upscale residential neighborhood. Ed Fletcher lost his battle to stop the city from damming the San Diego River and flooding the El Capitan Grande Indian Reservation, but he survived both economically and politically. In the 1930s he became one of San Diego's most powerful politicians, serving six terms in the State Senate. The Colonel Ed Fletcher Middle School in San Diego stands today as a monument to him.

From 21,422 registrants, San Diego draft boards conscripted 1,974 men for regular army service. They excused 2,535 for dependency, 107 as essential for agriculture, and 67 as essential to industry. They found 757 men physically unfit. They drafted a few hundred more for limited service due to mild physical conditions. The remainder, more than fifteen thousand, simply had high lottery numbers. A small percentage of those enlisted. San Diego's drafted men included American Indians, Japanese Americans, Chinese Americans, and Mexican Americans, all called as part of the "white" quota. Den Chow left his laundry business when he was drafted on April 19, 1918. On March 28, 1918, San Diego City Board Number Two drafted four truck drivers, all white men with no dependents. In the same call, it drafted a waiter, a peddler, a tailor, an office clerk, a farmer, three mechanics, a stenographer, and a storekeeper. All were white men whom the board judged had no one dependent solely upon them. I was unable to locate any record of a general "colored" call. But City Board Number One called Paul Tardy (colored) on February 20, and sent him off to Camp Lewis, Washington. From there, the army would have sent him to one of several camps in the South reserved for black draftees. Newspapers across the nation called men such as these, "The Flower of American Manhood." It was a ruse. In truth, these were the men draft boards found disposable—nonessential to the economy and nonessential to the American [white] family. They were men upon whom no one depended, or at least no one whose welfare mattered to the draft boards. The nation sent them off to fight. If they proved themselves in war and survived, they might return as better approximations of what it meant to be white men, unless they were actually black, or brown, or red or yellow.

Statewide Selective Service in California

Statewide officials of the Selective Service System in California, ranging from the governor and adjutant general down through district boards, local boards, and law enforcement struggled to define whiteness. They consistently linked it to manhood and citizenship. In no other state was the debate over whiteness in relation to the draft so explicit, and nowhere else did the racial lines dictated by the Selective Service System so contradict the racial histories and traditions of the state. But draft officials were not alone in their quandary. Some Japanese Americans tried to claim they were white by holding white Californians to their own definitions.

If it tells us anything about race in America, the World War I Selective Service System in California demonstrates that official "whiteness" can mean many things, and is frequently internally illogical and incoherent. This often depended simply on what was most convenient for officials needing to fill quotas. In the case of California Indians, they tried to justify it by linking official whiteness to citizenship and land ownership, except that they did not consistently apply these standards. Philosopher Charles Mills has rightly observed that "the membership requirements for Whiteness are rewritten over time. . . ."[65] In California during World War I, white men wrote simultaneously competing requirements for whiteness, applying them either to different groups in the same place, or to similar people in different places.

Japanese and Chinese Experiences

By all indications, most draft age men of both Japanese and Chinese ancestry in California responded favorably to the draft. Leaders told the public that both groups enthusiastically supported the war and were anxious to aid in mobilization. When Toyokichi Iyenaga of the East West News Bureau spoke to a crowd in Long Beach in June 1917 he asserted that "there are hundreds of Japanese in the United States who would like to enlist in the American Army, but they cannot, because they are denied citizenship."[66] Scattered evidence indicates that few men of Asian ancestry intentionally resisted conscription. Some California boards took special pride in noting the enthusiastic responses of some Chinese and Japanese to the draft. The Weaverville board announced at the end of registration day, June 5, that, "among the registrants are two American-born Chinese who declare they are anxious to join the Army." Likewise, the Stockton board reported that, "Chinese-Americans of Stockton showed their patriotism today when up to noon, without a single exception, all Chinese who registered waived exemption from draft." San Francisco boards attributed an initial reluctance of Chinese men to appear for registration to the dangers of the ongoing Tong Wars. Once assured of protection, "Chinese in flocks appeared for enrollment," reported the *San Francisco Chronicle*.[67]

A 1932 study called *Oriental Crime in California*, by Walter Beach, offered statistics comparing Chinese and Japanese wartime violations. It reported that there were no Japanese violations of the Selective Service Act and no Japanese charged with desertion, while four were identified as "slackers," presumably under the "Work or Fight" regulations. By contrast, Beach reported forty-one Chinese violators of the Selective Service Act, eighteen Chinese deserters, and five Chinese "slackers."[68] If these figures are correct (Beach does not explain how he got them), they would lend credence to the idea espoused by both Japanese and white male leaders that Japanese were more "Americanized," even more "white," or at least more able and willing to assimilate into white California than were Chinese.

The Military Intelligence Branch (MIB) records, which reported that in order to avoid the draft, many aliens were leaving California and returning to their native lands, offer some support for this hypothesis. A few of these were Chinese with obligations to California draft boards. The U.S. Postal Censorship program, in coordination with the MIB, intercepted a number of telegrams between draft-age Chinese men in California and family members in China, which described arrangements to have the men return to China in order to avoid the draft. Other intercepted cables reported that draft-age men in China had cancelled plans to immigrate to the

United States for fear of being drafted. One of these intercepted cables, which seems to be from one of two brothers in the San Francisco area to their uncle in Canton, China, shows not only the fear that some Chinese men had of being drafted, but suggests other factors may have been as important. The cable, as the MIB translated it from Chinese, reads in part: "Chew Kim Wing as you know is very irregular person—no one can give him any advice. . . . [H]e is working at the Stafford [*sic*] University but was arrested for fooling with the girls there. His friends are all afraid to bail him out as he is of draft age, so they left him in prison instead of being drafted by the government."[69]

These cables reflect a misunderstanding of the draft law. While all men of draft age residing within the United States had a legal obligation to register for the draft, aliens who had not declared an intention to become naturalized citizens were exempt from actually being drafted. Because of the 1882 law that barred most Chinese immigration to the United States, there were few recent immigrants from China in California. Thus, most men of Chinese ancestry in California who were of draft age would have either been born in the United States, and therefore were U.S. citizens, or they had somehow eluded the restrictions of the Chinese Exclusion Act. If they had entered the United States illegally, registering for the draft possibly made them more vulnerable to prosecution as illegal immigrants.

Chinese communities in California also tended to consist predominantly of single males. Chinese men, therefore, were unlikely to have dependent wives, children, or elderly parents, who would help them qualify for exemption from the draft. Unlike Japanese communities, which usually consisted of relatively stable nuclear or extended families, Chinese communities appeared to whites to lack the social stability that families often bring. In combination, these factors perhaps made it more difficult even for long-time Chinese residents of California to see themselves as Americans. And perhaps not seeing themselves as Americans, they felt particularly vulnerable to unfair treatment from local draft boards. It would surely be the case that, unlike many white men, men of Chinese ancestry would not have much in common with the members local or district draft boards. Given the history of their experience in the United States, it seems surprising that Chinese men cooperated with the draft as much as they did.

One Chinese American leader did believe that numbers of Chinese men of draft age had violated the draft law because they misunderstood what the Selective Service System required of them. Frank Yeo Lee, who identified himself as "Chief Inspector, California State Chinese Auxiliary, Oakland Society," wrote to the Provost Marshal General Crowder in May 1918 that, "the Chinese boys in many different cities that have to registered [*sic*] do not understand this as they should and therefore many of them have run away." He volunteered to assist in locating "these boys . . . in any way which you might suggest."[70]

Although Lee suspected there might be a large number of Chinese draft evaders, Crowder did not seem to share these suspicions. In particular, he did not altogether trust the reports of Chinese violations that he received from California. Instead, his suspicions with regard to reports of Chinese violators may have been directed at white officials. His response to one case suggests he believed that some military officials welcomed the delivery of accused Chinese delinquents or deserters to their camps, particularly if they needed draftees to perform duties stereotypically associated with Chinese men. Thus, the Commander of Camp Fremont cabled the Provost Marshal General: "Soo Hoo Fong, Chinese, called for Selective Service, Pinal County, Arizona, apprehended in this camp. Request authority to assign him to duty here as cook." In his reply, Crowder questioned whether the man actually was a deserter. In a return cable he wrote: "If man is not a deserter there is not authority to assign him to duty with you. In any event, communicate with his local board."[71] Perhaps, like their belief that African American draftees in the South should go to work on cotton plantations, military authorities in the West believed that they should put Chinese draftees to work cooking and doing laundry.

Final statistics nationwide reported that rates of "colored" and "alien" violations were three times higher than those of white-citizen registrants. In the aggregate, statistics for "alien" and "Colored" violations in California are nearly identical to the national average. If Walter Beach's 1932 figures are correct, however, both Chinese and Japanese draft registrants in California were atypical of either "colored" or "alien" registrants nationwide. But the Japanese were especially so. Why were there apparently almost no violations by Japanese men? Evidence from each draft board we have examined in this book suggests that the more an individual resembled local draft officials, the more likely he was to try to do as the draft board instructed him. That is, white-middle-class men, married heads of households, who were active in local churches and other community organizations, and those engaged in industrial or agricultural enterprises that were well established in their communities, were very rarely reported as draft violators.[72] Like many white farmers around them, some Japanese farmers of draft age requested agricultural exemptions, and a few whose claims were denied felt strongly enough about it to appeal their cases to the President of the United States. But when the Presidential Appeals Board rejected their claims, as it did in every case, these men apparently accepted the rulings and appeared for induction when their boards called them.[73]

It appears that many draft age men of Japanese ancestry, especially those engaged in successful farming enterprises, did see themselves as fully American. They explicitly based their claim that they were not racially distinct from white men on the fact that they could out-perform most white men when it came to exploiting the land for profit. Thus, in spite of a brutal history of legal and extralegal oppression against them by the white male state, they believed not only in their right to all the privileges and benefits of white men, but in their inevitable achievement of those privileges and benefits.

With all men of Asian ancestry classified as "white" for purposes of the draft, what, then was the status of men of Mexican ancestry? The absence of any discussion in Selective Service records over whether or not Mexicans were white may seem, from the perspective of twenty-first-century California, to be a huge gap. But this is not particularly surprising given the history of earlier legal debates over the definition of whiteness in California. The delegates to the first California Constitutional Convention in 1850 struggled for several days to find language that would restrict the full rights of citizenship, and especially the right to vote, to white males without violating the Treaty of Guadalupe Hidalgo, which had transferred California territory from Mexico to the United States. It guaranteed the "rights and privileges of U.S.

citizenship" to all residents of California who had been citizens of Mexico, provided that they had resided in California for at least two years prior to U.S. takeover. They resolved this difficulty by declaring that some Mexicans were white and some weren't, thus, avoiding a blanket exclusion of Mexicans from legal whiteness. Rather, the constitutional convention delegates declared that those Mexicans who were found to be Indian, or of African descent, could not be considered white. But since many, and perhaps most, of the former Mexican citizens of California had at least some Indian ancestry, the delegates needed a standard for determining who was actually Indian. At first, they drew a line between "wild" and "domesticated" Indians. But some delegates feared this opened the door to wholesale enfranchisement of "full-blooded" Indians. So instead, they borrowed literally from the laws of the State of Louisiana, which used "blood-quantum" to determine the race of individuals who had some African ancestry. They agreed that in order to be white in California, a person with Indian ancestry could not be more than one-fourth Indian. A new constitution in 1879 removed the provision limiting the vote to "white males."

By 1917, most persons who descended from the early Mexican inhabitants of California as U.S. citizens would have been considered white by law. But there was a much larger number of relatively recent immigrants and temporary residents from Mexico working primarily in agriculture and railroad construction in California. Historians such as Tomas Almaguer, Martha Menchaca, and Neil Foley have shown that throughout the Southwest during this period, whites generally treated Mexican laborers as racially inferior. In her study of Santa Paula, California, Menchaca reports that such racialization of Mexicans extended beyond ideology and custom to local ordinances that segregated Mexicans from whites much the same way that Jim Crow laws in Georgia segregated African Americans from whites. All three authors document ways in which white men used the legal system in support of an extralegal pattern of racial violence designed to keep Mexicans in bound labor arrangements similar to the peonage systems of the deep South.[74] It is thus not surprising that some draft-age Mexican men in California went home rather than take their chances on the draft. Much like the Chinese men described by Frank Yeo Lee above, many draft-age Mexican men, not understanding that as "aliens" they were exempt from the draft, or, perhaps not believing that the draft boards would respect their exempt status, headed back to Mexico in the early months of the draft.[75] Such men could, however, volunteer for induction. Absent evidence of African ancestry, they should have been placed in the "white" quota. Local draft boards in California did draft a large number of men who had Spanish surnames, and they always counted these men as part of their white quotas. It appears that draft officials in California had no reservations about drafting men of Mexican ancestry as white men.

It is clear, then, that the racial binary of black and white that dictated race relations in most other places in the United States, made no sense at all in California. For one thing, there were very few blacks in California—so few, in fact, that most black men who were drafted from California were called individually. California issued its first and only statewide call for men in the "colored" quota over a five-day period at the end of October 1917. Thereafter, men classified as "colored" were called individually or in small groups of two or three.[76] Thus, San Diego's first "colored" call consisted of one African American man, Paul Tardy, who was sent off on the train alone, in contrast to the first white calls for which the city arranged day-long holidays and great patriotic parades. San Francisco, with the highest proportion of blacks to whites among major population centers in California, had only 260 black draft registrants in 1917, compared to 38,484 registrants on the white lists.[77] Even after draft liability was extended to include all men between nineteen and forty-five for the September 1918 registration, California only had a total of 9,712 black men eligible to register, or about one percent of all draft-age men in California.

But once the decision had been made to classify as "white" every California draft registrant who was not clearly of African descent, neither draft officials nor the press paid much more attention to those men placed on the "colored" list. Although the white men who controlled the economy and government in California cared intensely about race, the black population was too small to attract their attention. California drafted a smaller proportion of its "colored" registrants than did Georgia, New Jersey, or Illinois. However, like the rest of the nation, all four states studied here inducted a higher percentage of their "colored" registrants than of their "white" registrants.[78] In the final analysis, only about 900 of the approximately 67,000 men drafted from California were classified as "colored."

Americanization and Radical Labor

Everywhere in the United States, successful operation of the Selective Service System required state and local governments to employ a combination of police coercion, community pressure, and ideological persuasion. In Georgia, police coercion predominated. In rural Illinois, community pressure and the ideology of Americanization foundations sufficed to keep antiwar German Americans in line. California, like urban Illinois and New Jersey, with a very large immigrant population, relied heavily on ideological persuasion, backed up by a few well-publicized examples of police coercion for their deterrent effect. The ideology of "Americanization" was at its center a racial ideology that racialized various ethnicities and nationalities differently in relation to an idealized whiteness. How the agents of Americanization approached any given ethnic or national group depended on whether or not they believed the group could legitimately aspire to whiteness. In California, as in Illinois and New Jersey, the American Protective League and local Councils of Defense ran most Americanization projects. As the Japanese case discussed above illustrates, Americanization was a useful concept that could function in many different ways when it came to mobilization. While Japanese leaders who used the term explicitly linked it with both whiteness and citizenship, it is not likely most white leaders meant it that way. For example, when local councils of defense reported on their work "Americanizing" Mexicans, it is not clear whether they sought to make them citizens and equal to white people, or simply to "domesticate" them in order to elicit more support for the war. Under the heading of "Americanization," the San Bernardino council reported: "Splendid work done among the Mexican boys and girls, particularly in teaching them how to make and care for a war garden." The San Diego council "organized a unit of Mexican women in San Diego City with a membership of sixty, which meets once a week in a downtown office room for Red Cross and sewing for Belgian relief and Home Economics instruction. At each session, Spanish-speaking women give talks on the meaning of America." It reported that the Mexican embassy provided a thousand work census cards in Spanish for "a complete registration of Mexican women."[79] These activities were the same kind that women's committees of the Council of National Defense were organizing for women and children of all races and ethnic groups around the nation. So, it appears on the surface that these were genuine attempts to assimilate Japanese, Chinese, and Mexicans into mainstream white California.

Nevertheless, these coexisted alongside continuing popular agitation among significant groups of whites to exclude these very groups from California, and perhaps to send them back to their countries of origin. Federal immigration reform legislation passed in 1917 (Congress overrode a veto by President Wilson) had broad support among the white people of California. This legislation sought to strengthen the exclusion of "inferior stocks" of immigrants through literacy tests and more stringent physical examinations.[80] In order to understand the contradictory responses of white Californians to racialized immigrant groups, we must look at another group that supporters of the war found far more threatening than any immigrant group, at least during the war. This group was radical labor, and in particular, the Industrial Workers of the World.

As in New Jersey and Illinois, radical labor and anarchist movements, such as the Industrial Workers of the World (I.W.W.), had long been active in California. From the beginning of the war, state officials, the American Protective League (APL), and the Council of Defense, expected trouble from these movements, and they got it. Only a year before the draft began, radicals had bombed a preparedness day parade on Market Street in San Francisco. The trial of radical labor activist Tom Mooney for this bombing was under way in San Francisco as the first Selective Service registrations began in 1917. On registration day, Wobblies (I.W.W. activists) and other anarchists protested the war and the draft at registration sites from San Diego to San Francisco. In Oakland, someone set fire to tents that had been put up for draft registration. In San Francisco, anarchists positioned themselves at the North Beach registration site on Columbus and Green Streets, where they passed out antidraft literature and made speeches against the war. APL "Secret Service" agents arrested one man, and a deputy registrar threw two other men "bodily from the booth," according to the *San Francisco Chronicle*.[81] Officials in Folsom arrested a member of the I.W.W. for distributing antidraft literature.[82]

Despite these early events, San Francisco newspapers, like newspapers in towns and cities across the nation, proclaimed that the actual number of draft opponents in San Francisco was small compared to the rest of the nation. However, by mid-June, I.W.W. and anarchist activism had undermined the official view that San Francisco was home to few war objectors. Officials changed their tune and began issuing dire (and, it turned out, overstated) warnings. They organized large-scale "slacker raids," which were among the first of their kind in the country. The raids, which the newspaper said were carried out by "secret service" officers, were probably the work of the APL. On Saturday, June 16, they rounded up twenty-five men. By the end of the day, eleven had been released because they were able to produce their registration cards. Officials held the remaining men in the City Prison. As the newspaper described the raid, officers arrested fifteen men in a sweep of North Beach. Bars and saloons were special targets. Men who could not produce registration cards within a few hours were held in the prison and the newspaper printed their names.[83]

The manager of a San Francisco hotel was arrested for distributing anti-registration and antiwar pamphlets on a train in the area of Santa Rosa. The district attorney called the pamphlets "treasonable," and reported they "advised men to use the guns they would receive in the Army 'for their rights.'" The police labeled the suspect, D. A. White, a "radical socialist."[84]

It was in their responses to radical labor and other opponents of the war and conscription that Governor Stephens and the other white men in charge of the California Council of Defense revealed the more sinister and white supremacist aspects of Americanization. In mid-May, 1918, Governor Stephens made "Americanization" the key to controlling labor, both radical and non-radical, when he presided at a series of "California war conferences" in Los Angeles and Sacramento that was organized by the Council of National Defense. First on the agenda was the issue of farm labor. The conference emphasized the important role community organizations played in mobilization, especially in labor management.[85] In his opening speech, the governor urged increased support for "a real Americanization programme" to "promote universal desire among persons of foreign birth to preserve and maintain the privileges they are enjoying under the American flag." Americanization meant, among other things, said Stephens, that immigrants adopt the English language. "It was Abraham Lincoln who said that America could not endure half-slave and half-free. It is equally true that America cannot endure half-American and half something else. What we need, if we are to endure as a Nation, is the acquirements of a common language for all of our peoples. That to my mind is the fundamental principle of a real Americanization programme. . . . We need an intelligent public opinion that will remove racial prejudices and discriminations, and that will at the same time discourage foreign associations that tend to keep people in America apart."[86] The governor's bid to convince immigrants to move quickly toward assimilation, however, clearly did not encompass Asian immigrants. In other statements, the reader will recall, Stephens had insisted that Japanese and Chinese could not be assimilated, and that attempts to do so would be both futile and tragic.

Rather, the governor's remarks targeted specifically those immigrants who made up a significant portion of anarchists and the Industrial Workers of the World, and who challenged not only the right of the nation to conscript men for war, but also the traditional arrangements between labor and capital in California. These immigrants tended to be mostly European, except for a few radical Mexicans, such as Ricardo Flores Magon in southern California, who linked radical labor in the United States to the ongoing revolution in Mexico.[87] It frustrated authorities in California that many radical activists carried on their communications in Russian, German, or Spanish. As Stephens put it: "One of our big problems right now is to stamp out in California every trace of disloyal propaganda and sentiment. We shall tolerate no seditious utterances in California. There is not any room in this great commonwealth for that cowardly, sneaking and disloyal element known as the Industrial Workers of the World."

Stephens then linked the radical labor movement and non-English-speaking immigrants to the crisis in labor supply by immediately adding, "there isn't room in

California for any loafers." He may have been referring to an instruction issued by the San Francisco I.W.W. office calling on all workers to "go to work on Government contracts and take the money, but don't do any more work than you have to."[88] The federal "Work or Fight" policy that was at that moment under consideration by the Wilson Administration might, then be useful not only to guarantee adequate labor in the State's most essential industries and agricultural sectors, it could also assist the state in its battle against the I.W.W. Anticipating the "Work or Fight" policy, Stephens commended "those cities and counties where the authorities already have initiated drastic measures to suppress idleness and seditious disturbance." He suggested the state legislature might consider its own California version of "Work or Fight," as Georgia, New Jersey, and several other states had already done.[89] But for a variety of reasons discussed below, this did not happen. Even though police in some jurisdictions used the draft to justify increased arrests of men for vagrancy, "Work or Fight," as an official policy, would not come to California until federal officials made it part of the Selective Service law in the spring of 1918. The most likely explanation for this is the unique nature of the agricultural labor force in California.

Agricultural Labor

Although agricultural employers periodically screamed that the war took their laborers away, California did not actually need a "Work or Fight" policy in order to protect its essential labor from being drafted. California's most important industry, then as now, was agriculture. As in Georgia, many of California's agricultural enterprises were extremely labor-intensive. But unlike Georgia, California had a large agricultural labor pool that was not liable to be drafted. By the beginning of the twentieth century, most of California's marketable agricultural products were produced on large corporate farms employing dozens or hundreds of wage laborers.[90] Many growers relied almost exclusively on temporary or migrant labor, a significant portion of whom were noncitizen immigrants and therefore not liable to be drafted.

Nevertheless, the white men in charge of mobilizing California for war offered dire predictions of draft-induced labor shortages in agriculture. A. H. Naftziger, vicechairman of the State Council of Defense toured agricultural counties in the Central Valley in early June 1917 to discuss with county councils the effects the draft might have on 1917 harvests. The news report of this tour stated: "It is believed that not less than 20,000 extra laborers will be needed to help save the immensely increased peach, raisin grape, grain and other crops."[91]

Another news report warned that wealthy fathers might be purchasing farms for their draft-age sons to permit them to seek agricultural exemptions. Ralph Merritt, Director of the State Selective Service Bureau of Registration, announced on June 12 that local draft boards would not be deciding these cases. Rather, as national regulations prescribed, district boards, that were less susceptible to local public pressures, would handle all claims for agricultural and industrial exemption. "Farmers coming before this board," announced Merritt, "will be required to show how many acres they farm and how long they have been engaged in agricultural pursuits. Those who have become farmers since war was declared and men who sit in offices and direct their farms over the telephones are likely not to be classed as legitimate farmers."[92]

Some people proposed programs to have children and adolescents help make up for the expected labor shortage in agriculture. Perhaps confirming that commercial agriculture is a kind of war against nature, the University of California College of Agriculture suggested that school children could aid the larger war effort by waging a small war against wild squirrels. Reporting that each ground squirrel "costs the farmer $1.50 annually," the college suggested that children could be recruited to assist in mixing poison in grain before it was sown as a way of killing the pests. "A single family of squirrels can destroy a quarter to half an acre of beans, sugar beets, barley, or similar field crops," reported the college. "Similar damage to range and pasture-grasses is fully as extensive."[93] Such work done by children, while not actually replacing adult laborers, would presumably increase the productivity of those adults who remained working on the farms.

As in Illinois, Council of Defense officials in California developed plans to use teenage boys to fill in as farm laborers for those men who had been drafted off of farms. An undated report made by an inspector from the Council of National Defense in Washington, D.C., probably in early 1918 reads as follows: "Boys Working Reserve: California: The State Council thinks that our Bulletin on the Boys Working Reserve applies to the States where boys will be sent individually to farms. In California boys will be sent out in groups and will be housed in camps under careful supervision."[94] Conveniently, state officials had mandated camps for migrant agricultural workers near the turn of the century. As geographer Don Mitchell has shown, these camps reflected white Progressives' instincts for heavy-handed social control, but at the same time the best camps offered significantly improved living conditions for migrant laborers. Existing camps thus seemed ready-made to receive teenage city boys to do agricultural labor. But in the final analysis, the war hardly affected the pool of agricultural wage labor, and only a relatively small number of boys were sent to the Boys Working Reserve in California. The significance of the Boys Working Reserve in California, then, lies not with its impact on agricultural labor, *per se*, but rather in what it tells us about the political strategies of the white men who ran the state of California. Rather than dispute growers' dire predictions of war-generated labor shortages, state officials quickly adopted a program that was already in effect elsewhere in the United States. It both mollified growers and enhanced the potential authority of the state over teenage boys too young for the draft.

A comparison of agricultural labor in Georgia and California during World War I offers instructive similarities and contrasts. Selective Service records have helped us tease these out. In both states, agricultural workers labored on large commercial monocrop enterprises in harsh conditions, and for pay that was barely enough to subsist on. In both states, agricultural laborers were racialized as either nonwhite, or as inferior forms of whiteness, which justified excluding them from participation in decisions that affected their lives individually and collectively. But the draft had a tremendous impact on agricultural labor in Georgia where black sharecroppers became pawns in a largely white struggle for state-sanctioned power. Whatever they lacked in the way of citizenship rights, under the Fourteenth Amendment to the United States Constitution black men in Georgia were U.S. citizens. This made them subject to the draft and consequently the focus of a struggle among white plantation owners to keep them out of the draft. In California, as immigrants, many of whom were ineligible to become citizens under federal law, tens of thousands of agricultural laborers were not subject to induction under the Selective Service Act. They were external to the white supremacist state in ways that African Americans in Georgia were not. Their function, as far as white California was concerned, was simply to labor in the fields and no more. Unlike plantation owners in Georgia, California growers had no need to ask local draft boards to delay draft calls until the harvest was in, or to request large numbers of farm furloughs, or to intercede with district boards to secure deferments for their workers. Least of all did they need a "Work or Fight" law to protect their labor force.

"Work or Fight"

The white men who ran the State of California probably knew from the start that the war would not significantly reduce the number of men working in "essential" jobs. For them the Boys Working Reserve, Americanization programs, and campaigns against radical labor, offered multiple ways to increase their control over those they viewed as not-quite-white or not-quite-men within the California population. We can only understand the application of "Work or Fight" principles in California as part of this complex of systemic, yet individualized, strategies for exercising power. City authorities in Los Angeles, for example, could hardly wait for the draft to get under way so that they could begin sweeping up men of whom they disapproved. In the late summer of 1917, during the period between registration and the first draft calls, Los Angeles Police Chief John L. Butler, announced a campaign to make every idle man in Los Angeles "go to work or go to jail." On the first day of this campaign, Los Angeles police arrested forty-two men, charging them with vagrancy. The city court gave sixty-day suspended sentences to twenty-seven who pleaded guilty on the condition that they find suitable work, and sentenced one man to either ten days in jail or a ten-dollar fine. The others demanded jury trials or were held for further investigation.[95] From the start, then, local officials used wartime mobilization as a rationale for increasing their surveillance and social control over a whole class of men. The control of other men enhanced their own agency (which was key to their exercise of white manhood). Reducing the agency of the arrested men became a process that both feminized them and marked them as individuals incapable of exercising the full privileges of whiteness. (Recall Governor Stephens's discussion of racial "quality" as having virile characteristics for which self-agency and control of others is evidence. The fact that Japanese men had demonstrated racial quality in these precise terms was what Stephens thought made them both a "superior" race and a racial threat to white men in California.)

Elsewhere in California, authorities agitated for new state laws or local ordinances that would increase their power over "idlers" in their jurisdictions. The police chief in San Diego found the state and city vagrancy laws "inadequate . . . to secure convictions" of many idle men they swept up in various raids. He called on the city attorney to draft an ordinance "whereby all able-bodied men are compelled to work so many days per week." He hoped it would "cover that class of loafers who work just enough to evade the state vagrancy law." The chief thought the situation merited an emergency response, as they were "gathering in dozens of these loafers, and then it is almost impossible to convict them." The ordinance was required "at once," he insisted, "if we are to rid the city of this class of undesirables." The chief's desires coincided nicely with those of the San Diego County Farm Bureau, which had announced its intention "to enlist farm labor from the ranks of the city population," and especially "from among the ranks of those who are not in the habit of working regularly," reported the *San Diego Union.* "The police department turned over a number of alleged vagrants to ranchers," on May 14, 1918, and apparently growers were waiting at the county jail in hopes authorities would release additional men to work for them as they secured vagrancy convictions.[96] The police chief, the growers, and the newspaper editors, all white men, joined forces in categorizing and labeling a group of men as "vagrants," "undesirables," and "loafers." By implication, what made a man desirable was that he did not hang out on the streets doing nothing productive, and that he filled his time with activities that other white men recognized as productive. Loafing and hanging out on the streets were behaviors that justified denying men the most fundamental privileges of white manhood—in particular, the right to choose how to spend their time

But California officials would never enact a California version of "Work or Fight." In his May 1918 speech to the California War Conference in Los Angeles, Governor Stephens suggested a "Work or Fight" policy for California. "It is outrageous to tolerate either the idle rich or the idle poor. There is work for everybody, and it is up to us to see to it that in California everybody does work."[97] Less than ten days later, Provost Marshal General, Enoch Crowder, announced the new federal "Work or Fight" regulations that would take effect nationally on July 1.

The *San Francisco Chronicle* predicted that the new policy would "work a sweeping change in the life of San Francisco," changes that would alter all those qualities, which made San Francisco unique and wonderful among American cities. In the *Chronicle's* report, a picture of San Francisco emerges as the home of a substantial wealthy elite, dependent upon butlers, chauffeurs, and other servants; a town with a thriving night life of theater, opera, saloons; and the center of a vibrant business community dependent upon messengers, elevator boys, and thousands of clerks. It would eliminate an estimated twelve thousand clerks—"shoe clerks, drug clerks, in fact, clerks in every sort of merchandising store." The paper predicted that the new policy might spell the disappearance of "the dapper young men that are much in demand at afternoon teas and dinner dances." Baseball parks, amusement parks, swimming pools, and other "amusement centers" would be hit hard. It "may wreck" the "Pacific Coast Baseball League," predicted the paper. "Every saloon and roadhouse will have missing faces. Bartenders belong to a non-useful occupation, according to the Provost Marshal-General's order." The *Chronicle* estimated that "300 or more bartenders and porters in San Francisco . . . will be missing from their stations behind the polished mahogany when the order goes into effect. The lobbies of the principal hotels will be shorn of the 'tango lizards'; new faces will appear in many of the cabaret shows, and the young idler who stays up all night and sleeps all day will don an Army uniform or get busy in some useful occupation."[98]

According to the *Chronicle*, Warren Olney Jr., chairman of District Exemption Board No. 1, said that the effects would generally be beneficial. He predicted that women would fill those nonuseful jobs vacated by men, which the policy characterized as "harmless," while nonuseful jobs considered harmful would simply "go out of business." These, he said, included "gambling, fortune telling, palmists, race track touts and roustabouts and bucket shop gamblers."[99]

It is impossible to calculate how many men, and perhaps women, were pressured into doing "approved" work in California as a result of "Work or Fight" policies. What is more important for our purposes than labor market or production statistics, is that "Work or Fight" policies in California help us identify and explain how the choices of specific white men who claimed to embody the power of the state constituted multiple interlocking regimes of power through which they controlled or limited the choices available to other men and women. "Work or Fight" enforcement in California simply strengthened the work of enforcement that officials had begun with the first registration. It was part of a larger regime of surveillance and control carried out by that particular group of white men who acted under government authority. As in Georgia, Illinois, and New Jersey, federal law in the form of the Selective Service Act enhanced the power of local and state officials to compel specific kinds of performance from lesser men and women, nearly always to the benefit of the wealthiest white men—the growers, industrial employers, the land speculators, the business tycoons. Major urban newspapers, all owned by very wealthy white men, supported these interlocking regimes, in part by repeating the language used to shame resisters: "slacker," "undesirable," "vagrant," "loafer." They offered other white individuals the choice of either falling under the category of one of those names, or enhancing their own individual power by joining the regime of surveillance, watching their neighbors, turning in names.

Beginning in the spring of 1917, Registrar Zemansky in San Francisco had made draft cards available to the public, in alphabetical order by precinct, as a way of encouraging people to determine whether there were "slackers" in their neighborhoods. According to the *San Francisco Chronicle*, the state's largest newspaper, this "list affords a convenient method for tracking the suspected slacker. Anyone having reason to believe there are slackers in his or her neighborhood has but to consult the alphabetical list of the precinct in which they live and see at once whether the names are there." Eligible men who had not registered on June 5 often showed up a day or two later in response to community pressure. The newspapers reported an array of reasons for failures to register. One man, Harry Pawluk, who was a chef, told the registrar "he did not feel just like killing anyone." According to the news report, "it was explained to him that he would not have to slay, except, perhaps, sheep and oxen, as the Army would need good cooks." A couple of German men reportedly said they preferred not to fight the German people. Another man claimed he was too drunk to register on registration day.[100]

Conclusion

The uniqueness of each individual response to the draft comes across in these documents, but so does the monotonous similarity with which officials across the nation lumped hundreds of thousands of individual acts of resistance under broad undifferentiated categories. The three very different cases described in the previous paragraph became simply part of the mass of humanity called "slackers." It is part of the privilege of white manhood to be recognized for what distinguishes you as an individual from the rest of society. In this respect, the denial of unique individual forms of resistance to the draft became a way of denying white manhood. The concluding chapter explores this theme in more detail through an examination of the Provost Marshal General's *Final Report*. In that document, the power of social scientific universalization, categorization, and homogenization obscures the messy contests that individual men and women across the nation engaged in under the rubric of the Selective Service System.

CHAPTER FIVE
"THE FINAL REPORT"

Never in the history of this or any other nation had a more valuable and comprehensive accumulation of data been assembled upon the physical, economic, industrial, and racial condition of a people.

—Enoch Crowder[1]

Nine months after the end of the war Enoch Crowder submitted his *Final Report* on the operations of the Selective Service System from 1917 to 1919. If the reader has not yet been convinced that the fundamental goals of draft officials at the local, state, and national levels were to protect privileges associated with property, patriarchy, and white supremacy, while providing men to fight the war, perhaps the words of the Provost Marshal General will finally make the case. This report graphically illustrates the ways in which draft officials made decisions with the intent to promote patriarchal, nuclear families and to preserve white male mastery of the material world. And in both its substance and its format, Crowder's "Report" reveals the ways in which categorical scientific ways of ordering the world sustained the power of married white men who engaged in sanctioned economic pursuits. As Crowder reported, draft officials called only those unmarried white men whose occupations they deemed inessential to the material needs of a nation during wartime. These men they deemed expendable enough to send to kill and perhaps die in Europe. Black men, with a few exceptions, were drafted only to be sent to work on the plantations of the South. Most other men of color became officially white for purposes of the draft.

As head of the Selective Service System in World War I, Crowder had carefully sought to balance the interests of propertied white male leaders of local communities and states with the desire of the nation's leaders for men to fight the war. He largely achieved this goal by giving the leading white men of every community an interest in the success of the draft. The local and district board system increased the power and prestige that propertied white men already held in most American communities by making them agents of federal authority. Then the Selective Service offered these men the power to single out those young men in their communities whom they judged marginal, nonessential to their interests, or simply social nonconformists, and to send them away where they would not only enable the United States to win a war, but would be socialized to join the mainstream of white American manhood—unless, of course, they were members of groups permanently barred from acquiring "whiteness." The first consideration, said Crowder, was to protect the family. "We shall have, in every community, immediately available for military service single men and a few married men whose removal will not disturb the reasonably adequate support of their dependents," he had written to board members. Yet those white men who controlled the draft frequently believed that men stamped with the badges of racial inferiority were themselves "dependents" of propertied white males, and thus logically could not have their own dependents. The second consideration was to protect the interests of the propertied elite—the mostly white men who owned industrial and agricultural enterprises. As Crowder put it, boards called those "men who have not especially fitted themselves for industrial or agricultural pursuits."[2] The system thus assumed that for the protection of the social order it should spare those white heterosexual males who headed patriarchal households and who through either ownership of property or gainful employment in industry or agriculture supported dependents—wife, children, and possibly elderly parents.

The classification and selection process identified and defined each American man of prime working age according to his proper place in a great system that served the needs and desires of the propertied white men who controlled local and national economies. This system "scientifically" organized the economy and manpower of the nation so that each separate economic interest would, by cooperating in it, benefit itself. "The Nation is rapidly becoming a great system," wrote Crowder. "The principle of selection" was good for business, and "the wonder is that a people so devoted to business efficiency should have hesitated to adopt it."[3]

But white patriarchy, although ubiquitous, was not monolithic. The Selective Service System shows us how a national policy sustained local elites in their own unique ways of functioning. The foregoing chapters show that the response of each local board and the people within its jurisdiction was shaped both by local factors and the extent to which they believed they were participants in a larger national community of common wartime purpose. But board members often found that the policies set by Selective Service officials in Washington did not serve their local interests. More often than not, the local interest took precedence over national policy.

Actual day-to-day records of local and district draft boards present a picture very different from Crowder's. They show that by manipulating the classification system, "work or fight" regulations and the furlough system, men and women, white men and men of color, rich and poor, officials and private individuals, constructed new relationships of power, or reinforced old ones. Historical traditions in local communities combined with the daily experiences of individuals to shape how these relations were worked out. From the standpoint of the all-white male administrators and enforcers, men who possessed the authority to compel other men to behave in particular ways stood above the compelled in power and in prestige. Men with certain kinds of occupations stood above others; employers usually above employees. Men in good health who were physically fit and had "normal" bodies stood above the sickly, the unfit, or the physically deformed. Adult men stood above boys. In Georgia, white men stood above African American men; in New Jersey native-born white men above immigrant men; in Illinois ethnic hierarchies were contested, especially between white men of German and non-German extraction, but in the crucible of forced mobilization, ethnic Germans largely embraced the culture of whiteness by abandoning their German identity. In California, propertyowning white men stood above Chinese, Japanese, Mexican, and American Indian men. Intersecting all of these male hierarchies was the hierarchical relationship that placed men above women.

Ironically, the war to save the world for democracy brought to the United States sharper social segmentation. While Roosevelt and Wilson were condemning "hyphenism" and promoting assimilation through "100 percent Americanism" the Selective Service System, as well as many other wartime agencies, demanded sharper distinctions among men and between men and women. Through classification, physical typing, and intelligence tests, government officials at all levels encouraged people to look for difference not in ways that fostered equality or even democracy, but that constructed inequality.[4] As the records show, without being coerced neither men nor women could be counted on to construct these differences in accordance with the needs and desires of the white men who constituted the state.

Willingness to go to war was, in fact, far less common among draft-age men than traditional accounts of the U.S. home front during World War I have suggested. In both Georgia and New Jersey, approximately five out of every hundred men called actually risked court martial and did not respond to the draft. In Illinois and California the official rates of failure to report for induction were approximately four percent.[5] But these figures surely understate the truth. They are the Provost Marshal General's official figures for desertion, or only violations of the draft law committed after a man's number was reached. The figures do not include the much larger numbers of men who were classified as "delinquent" for violating the Selective Service Law before their number was called. By administrative sleight-of-hand in 1919 officials dismissed nearly all of these cases, permitting Crowder in his *Final Report* to conclude that draft resistance was negligible.[6] Local boards, composed of men who were presumed to have the best knowledge of their registrants, submitted tens of thousands of delinquent reports in each of the four states studied here. Even if one accounts for the possibility that a local board mistakenly reported men delinquent on occasion, it would be absurd to accept the Provost Marshal General's finding that the majority of reported delinquencies were unfounded. Well before the end of the war the U.S. attorney for Northern Georgia had received 28,000 delinquent cases. His counterpart in southern Illinois was holding 15,000 cases and in New Jersey, Charles Lynch complained of a comparable load.[7]

Of course there is also good evidence that many men went willingly, even enthusiastically, perhaps because they believed the rhetoric of "Progressive Manhood," or that it was truly a war to save the world for democracy. The pages of local histories— mostly written by supporters of white male elites—are filled with reports of these men. Nevertheless, the evidence is clear from the communities studied here that most draft-age men tried to avoid conscription and had little desire to go to war. Most, of course, found the system worked well for them, and so they worked within the bounds of the system, a compromise that enhanced the authority of local draft officials. But, as Crowder tells us, the sudden end of the war brought an equally sudden end to the authority of local board members. At five a.m, on November 11, 1918, in the Forest of Compiegne, France, representatives of Germany and the United States signed the Armistice that ended World War I. Only two months earlier, fifteen million additional men between the ages of eighteen and forty-five had been required to register for the draft. Before that day ended, every local draft board in the United States received a telegram from Washington ordering it to cancel inductions into the active army. There were a few exceptions to this order, the most important being the continued induction of eighteen-year-olds into the Student Army Training Corps (SATC). As a result, thousands of young men enrolled for the first time at American colleges and universities.[8]

The speed with which the War Department demobilized abruptly changed the lives of both Selective Service officials and draft registrants alike. Boards stopped conducting physical examinations on November 16 and initiated no new classification actions after November 19. No one explained why any of these actions continued after the Armistice, but the Provost Marshal General was disappointed that demobilization took place before the fifteen million men who registered in September 1918 could be classified. Addressing the Secretary of War in his final report, Crowder wrote: "Undoubtedly, a complete classification of the entire registration between the ages of 18 and 45 would have produced very interesting results. But the Nation had been through such strenuous days and the stress and strain of the emergency had been so severe that you wisely concluded that the value of such a complete classification would be far outweighed by relief from the onerous duties [of] the preceding 18 months."[9] Local board members now turned their attention away from classifying, examining, and inducting men and began putting their records in order and closing up. State and national officials drew up plans for collecting and storing draft records and closing down draft operations. Clerks at local and state Selective Service offices were given thirty days' notice on November 28. During that period of rapid demobilization boards tallied the results of their work in the previous eighteen months and prepared final lists of delinquents and deserters that were forwarded to U.S. attorneys for prosecution. Demobilization, therefore, at first increased the work for Selective Service officials, and at the local level work that probably felt isolated as board members now ceased seeing a daily stream of draft registrants. They were now also performing dull clerical work that did not carry any of the rewards of power. "These same men," wrote the Provost Marshal General, "weary from the strain of many months of service, . . . were again called upon in time of peace to perform a task that was no less onerous."[10]

The first part of Crowder's *Final Report* contains a nine-page essay in praise of local and state Selective Service officials. Part one of the *Final Report* concludes with an impassioned plea for formal congressional recognition of the essential military functions that local officials had performed. "Never in the history of the Nation had there been a more urgent call for the unselfish exercise of patriotism and never has there been a more universal and whole-souled response than was found in the administration of the selective draft." With these words Enoch Crowder pled with Secretary of War Newton Baker to seek congressional recognition of "the service rendered by the civilian members of the selective-service organization."[11]

Like a good bureaucrat, Crowder was preoccupied with structure and the importance of rewarding those who made structures work. The heroism of draft officials, and by extension his, was that in the face of the chaos and disorder that characterized prewar

American society they recognized their place in a hierarchy of policy-making and enforcement and did their duty within the confines of that hierarchy. They served the interests of the institution, often at great personal sacrifice, he wrote. At each point, Crowder was careful to note that every action local officials took was in response to an order or directive from a duly constituted higher authority. "The local boards had been instructed" to take each action taken. Crowder, or his assistants, had issued instructions only at the direction of the Secretary of War, who administered the policies of the President and Congress, who had taken their instructions from the people. It was a vision of democratic institutions that were running along like perpetual motion machines, and one that was quite different from what we saw when we looked at local draft boards and state draft bureaucracies up close.

In the second and largest part of Crowder's *Final Report* the preoccupation with structure and orderliness becomes literally graphic. It consists of more than 250 pages of statistical tables, quantifying almost every imaginable aspect of the Selective Service operations. The tables, black with numbers, with everything in straight lines or at right angles, impose the image of orderliness on a process that had been, in fact, quite messy. Crowder was prouder of nothing more than the ability of his system to construct a single portrait of American manhood through the discipline of numbers, graphs, and tables:

> Never in the history of this or any other nation had a more valuable and comprehensive accumulation of data been assembled upon the physical, economic, industrial, and racial condition of a people. [This was] the first and only record of the man power of this nation. It would be of untold value to the physician, the economist, the sociologist and the historian for many decades. This generation owed it to posterity that it be preserved.[12]

Quite aside from the fact that the Selective Service System was explicitly concerned with men and not with women, this passage demonstrates underlying and unconsciously gendered meanings that characterize the entire report. Everyone who might be expected to read this report would know that all the data collected was about men. Yet Crowder argued that this data revealed virtually everything of consequence about "a people." Crowder and his report universalized males and by implication exceptionalized females. The male population, in accordance with its universal human character, had been organized and represented in well-ordered columns. The female other remained the unquantified, the unorganized, the chaotic and unstructured.

Yet equally insidious, in the *Final Report* Crowder went out of his way to exclude from universal American manhood those men who did not follow the dictates of the system. He did recognize that not all Americans had supported the Selective Service System. Some had not cooperated. Some had actively resisted. In some places, resistance even came from those asked to administer the draft. The duty to draft their neighbors, Crowder admitted, had been "onerous" to many local board members. It was the unique quality of statistics that enabled Crowder both to recognize these facts and to deny their significance. As any good statistician does, he discarded statistical "outliers," or those that are so far out of what he considered normal that including them would skew his averages. But he had his own justifications. First he simply erased thousands of delinquencies from the records by attributing them to "mistake, ignorance, or mishap." Then he limited his reported statistics on draft law violations to those in the legal category of deserter, so that the sole measure of either resistance or apathy to the draft was failure to appear when called. The resulting statistic, that only 1.41 percent resisted the draft, "proved" what Crowder wanted to prove: that the proportion of draft age men who resisted conscription was so small as to be insignificant. This showing by American men was, he said, "truly remarkable."[13]

Now that the war was over, the chief value of the Selective Service System according to Crowder was what its records told about Americans. According to the *Final Report*, many draft registrants left a "record of patriotism to which [they] and their descendents would look with greatest pride." For the 1.41 percent, "a record of ignominy and unpunished delinquency" would be a source of shame. "The pride, the sorrow, the sacrifice and the patriotism of the Nation were contained within the records of the local boards."[14] But in the *Final Report*, pride, sorrow, sacrifice, and patriotism took the form of numbers neatly lined up in rows and columns. The numbers were stand-ins for individual men whose real lives were partly reflected in local board records—records, which in truth, were tossed unsystematically into thousands of boxes and sent into deep storage.

This report was, in its instrumentality, its imposition of regularity and orderliness, its obedience to structure, its reification of hierarchy and duty, a literary reflection of the same manly virtues extolled by the nation's political leaders in a time of chaos. It perfectly represents the values and paradoxes of Progressivism—the tensions between individual freedom as an American ideology and the orderly state that depended upon categorization, surveillance, and conformity—between the America that espoused democracy and the America that imposed its imperial will on people it defined as racially inferior. In particular, it is surely no mere coincidence that the statistical charts of the *Final Report* resembled in both appearance and purpose the census records created in the nation's newly acquired colonies in the Philippines, Cuba, Hawaii, and Puerto Rico. No better characterization of the *Final Report* could be found than the words of Filipino American scholar, Vicente L. Rafael, in describing the 1905 census taken by U.S. colonial authorities in the Philippines: "Enumerated on the sheet, one can imagine one's existence flattened and neatly spread out as a set of numbers across a table. It is as if becoming a subject of the colonial state entailed taking on a different kind of particularity. Plotted on a grid, one's identity becomes sheer surface and extension, abstracted from any historical specificity." Rafael adds that this process divorces "identity from biography. Where biography entails the articulation of the subject as an agent of its own history, the schedule positions its subjects as a series of aggregates locatable on a table of isolated and equivalent values."[15] My project has been to excavate these records, to provide the historical specificity and to construct the biographies in part to undermine such positivistic props in the system of white supremacist patriarchy.

It was precisely the white supremacist and manly elements in the report that would enable scholars to construct a profile of the American people that had never before been possible. Never mind that by leaving out women the profile would be a lie. It would also provide a guide for men in the future to plan for other wars. The *Final Report* said that the Selective Service System had supplied 2.7 million men to the armed forces and an additional 800,000 had volunteered. But, according to the Provost Marshal General the 3.5 million men who entered the armed forces during the war could have been expanded to 8.7 million "without invading any of the deferred classes." On the other hand, it was only possible to know this in retrospect. The data collected during World War I and organized in the *Final Report* would make it possible to predict accurately how many men the nation could call upon to fight in future wars.[16]

Once placed in rows and columns, numbers are rigid, didactic, uncompromising, and impersonal. They tell a kind of legitimate story, but at the same time they suggest that their truth is a higher kind of truth than stories told by other means. Charts, graphs, and statistical tables, in other words, tend to create a hierarchy of truths in which numbers occupy the most revered position. But this study has been an attempt to tell a different story from the one contained in the *Final Report*. One of the most striking impressions left by the records of the Selective Service System between 1917 and 1919 is how intensely personal this particular exercise of the state was. Conscription offered some men an arena of power in which to pursue personal agendas. That power was felt by draft registrants as personal coercion. It affected their relations with family, with neighbors and with employers, and it could alter their economic conditions, or even cost them their lives. For both administrators and registrants, the process of conscription could affect their sense of themselves as men. The women who knew these men often were able to take advantage of these personal effects, although they might be compromised in the process.

It is perhaps ironic that the most basic assumption underlying this study is one of the tenets of the middle-class ideology of Progressive manhood. That is the assumption that men and women made choices that determined how they would experience or exercise authority. I have assumed that draft officials exercised power in certain ways because as propertied white men they chose to do so. Similarly, draft registrants, their families, and their employers chose the ways in which they would respond to conscription. The result of such acts of volition, multiplied by millions, was a plethora of unequal contests over the exercise of state authority. Few were passive in this process. Institutions in this story never had total power to direct human action. Institutional needs often exerted tremendous pressure on people to make particular choices, but people always had the choice to serve the institution or not. The Selective Service System from 1917 to 1919 had no existence outside of the things people did in response to their belief in its existence. It was made up of people whose daily decisions constantly constructed what the institution would be and what it would mean to society. In terms of the theoretical framework with which I began this book, the Selective Service System became a "field of engagement" in which individuals who were positioned differently relative to each other by race, gender, or class, and by their roles within that system, negotiated the power to determine how the system would impinge on the lives of each one.[17]

The Selective Service System in World War I surely demonstrates that government institutions are first and foremost instruments of human will and not the other way around. The men who constituted that system used it in thousands of ways to impose their will on other men. Despite the presumed popular legitimacy of such a system in a democratic government, hundreds of thousands of men and women resisted the imposition of other men's wills on them. Many forms of resistance reinforced the underlying bedrock beliefs about gender, race, economic relations, and state authority. The system thus depended upon both forms of human action—cooperation and resistance. The daily performances of men and women in relation to the Selective Service System, whether cooperative or resistant, continuously reconstituted and reshaped it without seriously challenging the fundamental ideology that made it work.

NOTES

Introduction

1. W. E. B. Du Bois, *Darkwater: Voices from within the Veil* (Mineola, N.Y.: Dover Publications, 1999, 1920).
2. Information in this paragraph, and the next two, is based on my interview with Milton and Ruth Brackbill, October 14, 1987, Sarasota, Florida.
3. Gyan Prakash, "Subaltern Studies as Postcolonial Criticism," *American Historical Review* 99 (1994): 1475–1490.
4. Christopher Capozzola, "The Only Badge Needed Is Your Patriotic Fervor: Vigilance, Coercion, and the Law in World War I America," *Journal of American History*, 88 (March 2002): 1356.
5. The only general history of the World War I draft in the past fifty years is the excellent John Whiteclay Chambers II, *To Raise an Army: The Draft Comes to Modern America* (New York: The Free Press, 1987). See also, John Whiteclay Chambers II, "Decision to Draft," *Magazine of History* 17 (October 2002): 26–33.
6. The most complete description of this system is, Enoch Crowder, *Second Report of the Provost Marshal General on the Operations of the Selective Service System through December 1918* (Washington: GPO, 1919).
7. Enoch Crowder, *Final Report of the Provost Marshal General to the Secretary of War on the Operations of the Selective Service System to July 15, 1919* (Washington: GPO, 1920), 9.
8. Enoch Crowder, *Report of the Provost Marshal General to the Secretary of War on the First Draft under the Selective Service Act of 1917* (Washington: GPO, 1918), 28.
9. Selective Service General Rules and Regulations, December 1917, Records of the Selective Service System, 1917–1919, Historical Files, Box 317, RG 163, National Records Center (NRC), College Park, MD.
10. Crowder, *Second Report*, 22–24; and Selective Service General Rules and Regulations, December 1917, Part XI.
11. U.S. attorneys complained frequently to the Justice Department about this problem. Their correspondence may be found in the Department of Justice (DOJ) correspondence files of the U.S. attorneys, 1910–1920, RG 60, NRC, College Park, MD. See also references in chapters 1 and 3, and Conclusion.
12. Peter Kolchin, "Whiteness Studies: The New History of Race in America," *Journal of American History* 89 (June 2002): 172.
13. George B. Tindall, *The Emergence of the New South, 1913–1945* (Baton Rouge, Louisiana: Louisiana State University Press, 1967), 186–187, has the Wilson quote; Joel Williamson, *The Crucible of Race: Black–White Relations in the American South since Emancipation* (New York: Oxford University Press, 1984), 175–176, explores the film's origins and content and notes the use of live orchestras; *Newnan Herald* (Newnan, Georgia, April 27 and May 4, 1917, describes the arrival of sets in a boxcar, the twenty-piece orchestra, and the general excitement in the white community at the film's opening.

14. Responding to black protests, officials in several jurisdictions, including in the State of Illinois, either banned it or ordered portions censored. Mary Frances Berry and John W. Blassingame, *Long Memory: The Black Experience in America* (New York: Oxford University Press, 1982), 382–383.

Chapter One "The Darkness in Georgia"

1. On the historical gendering of racial identity that constructs the citizen in the United States as white and male, see Robyn Wiegman, *American Anatomies: Theorizing Race and Gender* (Durham, N.C.: University of North Carolina Press, 1995), chapter 4. See also two books by David R. Roediger, *The Wages of Whiteness: Race and the Making of the American Working Class* (London and New York: Routledge, 1991), and *Toward the Abolition of Whiteness* (London and New York: Routledge, 1994), and Ruth Frankenberg, *The Social Construction of Whiteness: White Women, Race Matters* (Minneapolis: University of Minnesota Press, 1993), 13, 16–18.
2. Mrs. F. H. Anderson, Danburg, Wilkes Co., Ga., to Governor Hugh Dorsey, July 30, 1918, Farm Furloughs File, Box 3, World War I, Georgia State Council of Defense (GSCD), 1917–1918, R. G. 22-1-14, Georgia Department of Archives and History (GDAH), Atlanta, Georgia.
3. According to Dolores Janiewski, "A common inheritance 'naturally' endowed southern white men of every class with the right to dominate the 'naturally' subordinated members of southern society, who included all women and black men." Janiewski, "Southern Honor, Southern Dishonor: Managerial Ideology and the Construction of Gender, Race, and Class Relations in Southern Industry," in Ava Baron, ed., *Work Engendered: Toward a New History of American Labor* (Ithaca and London: Cornell University Press, 1991), 72. See also LeAnn Whites, "Rebecca Latimer Felton and the Wife's Farm: The Class and Racial Politics of Gender Reform," *The Georgia Historical Quarterly* 76 (Summer 1992): 354–372, and Ted Ownby, *Subduing Satan: Religion, Recreation and Manhood in the Rural South, 1865–1920* (Chapel Hill: University of North Carolina Press, 1990), 38–39, 49.
4. A history of Coweta County, Georgia, published in 1919 summarized in a brief biography of one local citizen qualities that could define southern white manhood: (1) Service in the Confederate Army; (2) Successful management of a significant enterprise; (3) Success in politics; (4) Membership in a fraternal order such as the Masons; (5) Marriage and fatherhood. These qualities were said to have made H. M. Couch "a fine type of manhood." Mary G. Jones and Lily Reynolds, *Coweta Chronicles for a Hundred Years* (Newnan, Georgia: Daughters of the American Revolution, 1919), 65.
5. The word "negro" as commonly used in early-twentieth-century Georgia denoted a specific kind of gendering. When not accompanied by a modifier, it signified generic African American male in much the same way as the words "man" or "men" may signify the universal human. Just as the word "man" has been used to universalize the experiences of males as *the* human experience, the word "negro" universalized the African American male as the universal African American. In addition, unmodified, it nearly always meant male African American laborer, assumed to be both relatively unfree and dependent. If he was anything other than this, the sources added a modifier. Thus we find "negro preachers," "negro teachers," "negro doctors," "negro lawyers," and, most disturbing to white people, "negro soldiers." Where authors wished to indicate African American women they wrote "negro women," or, in some cases, "colored women."
6. Hall, *Revolt Against Chivalry: Jessie Daniel Ames and the Women's Campaign Against Lynching* (New York: Columbia University Press, 1979), 147–148. David T. Wellman argues that "being an American is . . . culturally and ideologically constructed to mean being not black." *Portraits of White Racism* (Cambridge: Harvard University Press, 1993), 245. I would add that historically it also means not being a woman. See also Toni

Morrison, *Playing in the Dark: Whiteness and the Literary Imagination* (New York: Vintage Books, 1993), 6–7, 38.

7. My analysis here is inspired, in part, by the work of Edward Said, most recently in *Culture and Imperialism* (New York: Vintage Books, 1994), who is masterful in detecting ways in which meaningful silences in public discourse signify relations of power. See also the helpful "AHR Forum" on "Subaltern Studies" by Gayan Prakash, "Subaltern Studies as Postcolonial Criticism," Florencia Mallon, "The Promise and Dilemma of Subaltern Studies: Perspectives from Latin American History," and Frederick Cooper, "Conflict and Connection: Rethinking Colonial African History," *American Historical Review* 99 (December 1994): 1475–1545.

8. Dozens of Georgia sheriffs initially defied the law by refusing to serve on local draft boards to which the president had appointed them. See Hooper Alexander, United States Attorney for Northern Georgia to The United States Attorney General, July 4, and 6, 1917; J. Van Holt Nash, Adjutant General, Georgia, to Alexander, July 7, 1917. DOJ Correspondence File No. 186233–68, R.G. 62, National Archives, Washington.

9. The term "King Cotton" appeared frequently in the local weekly newspaper, *The Newnan Herald*. See also, Harold D. Woodman, *King Cotton and His Retainers* (Lexington: University of Kentucky Press, 1967).

10. Cheryl Harris, "Whiteness as Property," in Kimberle Crenshaw, Neil Gotanda, Gary Peller, Kendall Thomas, eds., *Critical Race Theory: The Key Writings that Formed the Movement* (New York: The New Press, 1995), 279–280.

11. Interview with Lynch, January 24, 1989, Newnan, Georgia.

12. *Fifth Census; or Enumeration of the Inhabitants of the United States* (Washington: Printed by Duff Green, 1832), 14–15, 96–97; *Population of the United States in 1860; Compiled from the Original Returns of the Eighth Census* (Washington: Government Printing Office, 1864), 72; *Twelfth Census of the United States, Taken in the Year 1900*, Population, Part I (Washington: United States Census Office, 1901), 533; *Thirteenth Census of the United States, Taken in the Year 1910*, Vol. II, Population (Washington: Government Printing Office, 1913), 378–379; *Thirteenth Census*, Vol. VI, Agriculture, 346–337; and *Fourteenth Census of the United States, Taken in the Year 1920*, Vol. III, Population (Washington: Government Printing Office, 1922), 210; and *Fourteenth Census*, Vol. VI, Part 2, Agriculture, 306–307. On the changing nature of the planter class and the source of its power after the Civil War see Steven Hahn, "Class and State in Postemancipation Societies: Southern Planters in Comparative Perspective," *American Historical Review* 95:1 (1991): 75–98; Gavin Wright, *Old South, New South: Revolutions in the Southern Economy Since the Civil War* (New York: Basic Books, 1987), 47–50. Jonathan Wiener, "Class Structure and Economic Development in the American South, 1865–1969," *American Historical Review* 84 (1979): 970; and Pete Daniel, *The Shadow of Slavery: Peonage in the South, 1901–1969* (Urbana: University of Illinois Press, 1972).

13. Pete Daniel, *Breaking the Land; The Transformation of Cotton, Tobacco, and Rice Cultures since 1880* (Urbana: University of Chicago Press, 1985); Theodore Rosengarten, *All God's Dangers: The Life of Nate Shaw* (New York: Vintage Books, 1984). United States Bureau of the Census, Agricultural Reports, 1910.

14. Lynch, interview.

15. *Newnan Herald*, May 18, 1917.

16. Arthur Link, *Woodrow Wilson: Revolution, War, and Peace* (Arlington Heights, IL: Harlan Davidson, 1979). John Whiteclay Chambers II, *The Tyranny of Change: America in the Progressive Era, 1890–1920*, 2nd ed. (New Brunswick, N.J.: Rutgers University Press, 2000); John Milton Cooper, Jr., *The Warrior and the Priest: Woodrow Wilson and Theodore Roosevelt* (Cambridge, MA: Harvard University Press, 1983). On the preparedness movement, see Arthur Ekirch, Jr., *The Civilian and the Military: A History of the American Antimilitarist Tradition* (New York: Oxford University Press, 1956), 140–176; John Garry Clifford, *The Citizen Soldiers: The Plattsburg Training Camp Movement, 1913–1920* (Lexington: University

of Kentucky Press, 1972). Christopher C. Gibbs, *The Great Silent Majority: Missouri's Resistance to World War I* (Columbia: University of Missouri Press, 1988).

17. *Newnan Herald*, April 13, and May 11, 1917.

18. "Jesus and 'Peace at Any Price,' " *Newnan Herald*, May 11, 1917, p. 1.

19. See Gail Bederman, " 'The Women Have Had Charge of the Church Work Long Enough': The Men and Religion Forward Movement of 1911–1912 and the Masculinization of Middle-Class Protestantism," *American Quarterly* (September 1989), 432–465.

20. This point has been made in various ways by historians of the Civil War. See LeeAnn Whites, "Gender, War, and Southern Culture," in *War and Southern Society* (Oxford, Mississippi: University of Mississippi Press, 1989); Gerald Linderman, *Embattled Courage: The Experience of Combat in the American Civil War* (New York: The Free Press, 1987), 87–89, 91–92, 277; Bertram Wyatt-Brown, *Southern Honor: Ethics and Behavior in the Old South* (Oxford: Oxford University Press, 1982), 35–36. A poster commemorating the mustering into federal forces of a Georgia National Guard Squadron in 1917 shows a woman representing the nation, a woman seeing a soldier off to war, and women providing the hero's welcome home. Original poster is in Box 9, State Council of Defense Records, RG 22-1-14, GDAH.

21. *The Newnan Herald*, April 13, 1917.

22. Ibid.

23. *Newnan Herald*, April 27 and May 4, 1917; D. W. Griffith, *The Birth of a Nation* (1915); For an example of the extremes to which Creel and the cooperative U.S. press would go to dehumanize Germans see the green monster that fills the cover of *Leslie's Magazine*, July, 13, 1918.

24. More than two thousand white people, including many families with picnic baskets, joined the carnival-like gathering to witness the 1899 lynching of Sam Hose in Newnan. Hose was accused of murdering his employer and raping a white woman. Ida B. Wells published an independent investigative report indicating Hose had killed his employer in self-defense, and showing that there was no evidence he had committed rape. See Ida B. Wells-Barnett, *Lynch Law in Georgia* (Chicago Colored Citizens: Chicago, 1899); Mary Louise Ellis, "Rain Down Fire: The Lynching of Sam Hose" (Ph.D. diss., Florida State University: Tallahassee, 1992).

25. The equation of "American" with whiteness has been explored my many scholars, including Grace Hale, *Making Whiteness: The Culture of Segregation in the South, 1890–1940* (New York: Pantheon, 1998); Lee Haney-Lopez, *White by Law: The Legal Construction of Race* (New York: New York University Press, 1998); Alexander Saxton, *The Rise and Fall of the White Republic: Class Politics and Mass Culture in Nineteenth-Century America* (London; New York: Verso, 1990); Noel Ignatiev, *How the Irish Became White* (New York: Routledge, 1995).

26. Frederick C. Luebke, *Bonds of Loyalty: German Americans and World War I* (De Kalb, IL: Northern Illinois University Press, 1974), 85.

27. Luebke, *Bonds of Loyalty*, 146,

28. *Newnan Herald*, April 6, 1917.

29. *Newnan Herald*, May 25, 1917.

30. *Newnan Herald*, June 1, and June 8, 1917.

31. *Twelfth Census of the United States Taken in the Year 1900*, Population, Part I (Washington, D.C., 1901), xl; *Thirteenth Census of the United States*, Population, Volume II, 378; *Fourteenth Census of the United States*, Population Reports, Volume I, 378.

32. According to the published census, the population of Coweta County in both 1910 and 1920 was approximately 56 percent African American with a roughly equal sex ratio in both the European and African American populations. My random selection of 550 males from the 1910 manuscript census who would have been draft age in 1917 or 1918 resulted in a list that was 55.5 percent African American. *Thirteenth Census of the United*

States, Taken in the Year 1910, Vol. I, Population (Washington: Government Printing Office, 1913), 378–379; *Fourteenth Census of the United States, Taken in the Year 1920*, Vol. III, Population (Washington: Government Printing Office, 1922), 210.

33. The men who administered the draft in Coweta County and who owned farm property apparently held between 200 and 300 acres each. On the other hand, a large planter in the county would own between 1,000 and 3,000 acres of farm land. It should be noted, however, that if a Coweta resident owned land outside the county it would not show up in the Coweta tax records that I have used here. Nevertheless, I am confident that the *relative* social and economic positions of the persons identified here are reasonably accurate.

34. *Newnan Herald*, June 15, 22, 29, and July 6, 13, August 3, 1917.

35. *Newnan Herald*, June 15, 1917.

36. *Newnan Herald*, June 29, 1917.

37. *Newnan Herald*, August 3, 1917; Newnan-Coweta Historical Society, *History of Coweta County* (Roswell, Georgia: W. H. Wolfe Associates Historical Publications Division, 1988), 332; "Returns of White Tax Payers for the Year 1917," Fifth Militia District, No. 646, Coweta County, Georgia.

38. *Newnan Herald*, August 3, 1917. On Miss Olivia Young, see Newnan-Coweta Historical Society, *History of Coweta County*, 103.

39. *Newnan Herald*, July 6, 1917.

40. Lynch interview, 1989.

41. *Newnan Herald*, July 6, 1917.

42. *Newnan Herald*, Friday, June 29, 1917, and Friday, August 3, 1917.

43. *Newnan Herald*, Friday, August 10, 1917.

44. *Newnan Herald*, August 10, 1917.

45. Jones and Reynolds, *Coweta Chronicles for a Hundred Years*, 439.

46. "List of Men Ordered to Report to this Local Board for Military Duty . . . ," PMGO Form 164-A, Local Board for the County of Coweta, Georgia, September 6, 1917, September 19, 1917, October 4, 1917, and October 5, 1917, Records of the Selective Service System, 1917–1919, RG 163, National Archives, Atlanta Regional Branch; Crowder, PMGO, to Governor of Georgia, September 9, 1917, M. J. Daniel, Actg. Adjutant General of Georgia, to Provost Marshal General, September 10, 1917, Crowder to Governor of Georgia, September 11, 1917, Crowder to Governor of Georgia, September 22, 1917, File 61-1, States File—Georgia, SSS Records, 1917–1919, RG 163, WNRC, Suitland, MD.

47. E. J. Reagan, Chairman, District Board for Northern Georgia, to the Adjutant General, Atlanta, September 25, 1917, File 41-7, Box 112, States Files-Georgia, SSS Records, 1917–1918, WNRC, Suitland, MD.

48. *Second Report of the Provost Marshal General to the Secretary of War on the Operations of the Selective Service System to December 20, 1918* (Washington, D.C.: Government Printing Office, 1919), 45; Enoch Crowder, *The Selective Service System: Its Aims and Accomplishments—Its Future* (Washington, D.C.: Government Printing Office, 1917), 1–13.

49. Draft Registration Card of Marvin Kirk, Coweta County, SSS Records, 1917–1919, RG 163, Atlanta National Archives Branch, Eastpoint, GA; Form 164-A-P.M.G.O., "Lists of Men Ordered to Report to This Local Board for Military Duty"; Docket Book for District Board for Northern District of Georgia, Local Board for Coweta County, SSS Records, 1917–1919, RG 163, WNRC, Suitland, MD.

50. Draft Registration Card of Johnnie Poach, Coweta County Draft Registration Cards; "Classification Lists," Local Board for Coweta County, GA, (Microfilm) SSS Records, 1917–1919, RG 163, Atlanta National Archives Branch, Eastpoint, GA; United States Bureau of the Census, Manuscript Population Schedules, Thirteen Census, 1910, Coweta County, GA, Enumeration District 32, Sheet No. 27B; *Newnan Herald*, April 13, 1917.

51. Memo from A.W. MacMahon, "Some more light on the darkness in Georgia," April 11, 1918, Georgia File, States Division, Council of National Defense Records, Box 785,

R.G. 62, Washington National Records Center (WNRC). According to this memo, "the attitude of the boards in Georgia has been 'go to hell' and they have actually used these words."

52. For an excellent account of southern resistance to the draft, see Jeanette Keith, "The Politics of Southern Draft Resistance, 1917–1918: Class, Race, and Conscription in the Rural South," *Journal of American History* 87:4 (March 2001): 1335–1361.

53. Memo from Joel B. Mallet, Officer in Charge of Selective Service Law, State of Georgia, to The Provost Marshall General, Washington, D.C., March 11, 1918, File 17-38, Box 109, States Files: Georgia, R. G. 163, SSS Records, 1917–1919, WNRC.

54. Memo from Major Harry T. Matthews, Inspector General, Camp Wheeler, Ga., to the Commanding General, Thirty First Division, Camp Wheeler, Ga., "Report of Investigation Concerning Negro Deserters," October 10, File 17-14, Box 109, States Files: Georgia, SSS Records, 1917–1919, R. G. 163, WNRC.

55. Ibid, exhibit A.

56. Ibid., exhibits B, D, E, F.

57. John L. Hayden, Brigadier General, Commanding, to the U.S. attorney, Southern District of Georgia, Macon, Ga., October 16, 1917, File 17-14, Box 109, States Files: Georgia, SSS Records, R. G. 163, WNRC.

58. E. J. Reagan, Chairman, District Board, Northern Georgia, to Adjutant General of Georgia, September 25, 1917, File 41-7, Box 112, States Files: Georgia, SSS Records, 1917–1919, R. G. 163, WNRC; Hubert Work, Major, M. R. C. (for Crowder, P.M.G.), to Joel B. Mallet, June 5, 1917, "Subject: Rejected Negroes," File 32-11, Box 112, States Files: Georgia, SSS Records, 1917–1919, R. G. 163, WNRC. The latter document reads, in part: "Many complaints come to this office from army camps that local boards are inducting into service registrants who are utterly worthless for any purpose in the army and presumably were equally useless at home. . . ." File 32 in this box contains many individual cases of "negroes" sent to camp missing various limbs and appendages or suffering from debilitating illnesses.

59. Emmet J. Scott, *Scott's Official History of the American Negro in the World War* (New York: Arno Press, 1969, 1919), 9, 69.

60. "Lists of Men Ordered to Report for Induction," local board for Coweta County, SSS Records, 1917–1919, R.G. 163, National Archives Branch, East Point, GA.

61. Erwin, CB Camp Gordon, to P.M.G., December 3, 1917, "Re: Telegram Dec. for explanation of the discrepancies between number of men called and those accepted at this cantonment," File 62-4, Box 114, States Files: Georgia, SSS Records, 1917–1919, R. G. 163, WNRC.

62. Jane Lang Scheiber and Harry N. Scheiber detail the concerns of southern Congressmen over the drafting of large numbers of black men. "The Wilson Administration and the Wartime Mobilization of Black Americans, 1917–1918," *Labor History*, 10 (Summer 1969), 439–444. On the southern belief that military service should be a specifically white male privilege and responsibility, see also Janiewski, "Southern Honor, Southern Dishonor," and Bertram Wyatt-Brown, *Southern Honor: Ethics and Behavior in the Old South* (New York: Oxford University Press, 1982), 35.

63. Thomas Lee to "Mr. Bartlett," Georgia Council of Defense, July 15, 1918, Farm Furlough File No. 4, Box 3, GSCD, R. G. 22-1-14, GDAH.

64. On blacks in southern industries between 1890 and 1930, see Gavin Wright, *Old South, New South: Revolutions in the Southern Economy since the Civil War* (New York: Basic Books, 1986), 179–180. On the exclusion of blacks from southern cotton mills see Woodward, *Origins of the New South, 1877–1913* (Baton Rouge: Louisiana State University Press, 1951), 222; David L. Carlton, *Mill and Town in South Carolina, 1880–1920* (Baton Rouge: Louisiana State University Press, 1982); Douglas Flaming, *Creating the Modern South: Mill Hands and Managers in Dalton, Georgia, 1884–1994* (Chapel Hill: University of North Carolina Press, 1993).

65. See "Memorandum of Proceedings of Meeting of the Committee on Labor—Georgia State Council of Defense, Held in the Office of H. M. Stanley, Chairman of the Committee, 319 State Capitol, Atlanta, Georgia, April 23, 1918," Labor File, Box 2, GSCD, RG 22-1-14, GDAH.
66. Price Gilbert to Fleming, Council of National Defense, August 10th, 1918, "Negro Organization File," Box 3, GSCD, R. G. 22-1-14, GDAH.
67. R. G. 22-1-14, GDAH.
68. Wright, *Old South, New South*, 178–181.
69. "Memorandum of Proceedings of Meeting of the Committee on Labor—Georgia State Council of Defense, Held in the Office of H. M. Stanley, Chairman of the Committee, 319 State Capitol, Atlanta, Ga., April 23, 1918," Labor File, Box 2; and letter of May 28, 1918, from the Chairman of the Georgia State Council of Defense to the Council of National Defense, p. 9, File 4, Box 2, GSCD, R.G. 22-1-14, GDAH, pp. 1–12.
70. On the concept of racializing poor whites as something less than white, see Matt Wray and Annalee Newitz, eds., *White Trash: Race and Class in America* (New York: Routledge, 1997), 6–8. But it is also important to heed Toni Morrison's advice that characterizations of black people in America by privileged whites tell us little about black people and a great deal about those who have constructed these images of blackness and the nature of the power they have held. Morrison, *Playing in the Dark: Whiteness in the Literary Imagination*, 6–11, 38–39.
71. "Memorandum of Proceedings." This document constructs images of African American men in terms remarkably similar to those used by British imperialists with reference to Javanese workers in 1904: "It has been impossible to secure the services of the native population by any appeal to an ambition to better themselves and raise their standard. Nothing less than immediate material enjoyment will stir them from their indolent routine." Quoted in Said, *Culture and Imperialism*, 167–168. See similar comments regarding Indians in Said, 203.
72. Telegrams from Swift, CB Camp Gordon, to Provost Marshall General, September 21, 1917, and Crowder, Provost Marshal General-Army, to Commanding General, Camp Gordon, Georgia, File 54-1, States Files: Georgia, SSS Records, 1917–1919, WNRC. Crowder's telegram also instructed the local draft board to call another man to replace the one temporarily discharged.
73. R. W. Grow to Governor Dorsey, June 29, 1918, "Farm Furloughs," Box 3, GSCD Records.
74. New York *Age*, August 1917, report contained in Herbert Aptheker, ed., *A Documentary History of the Negro People in the United States: Volume 3, From the N.A.A.C.P. to the New Deal* (New York: Citadel Press, 1973), 183–184.
75. Letter from Chief Clerk, J. F. Mcleod, Local Board for Floyd County, Rome, Ga., to Bureau of Farm Furloughs, Atlanta, undated, "Farm Furloughs" File, Box 3, GSCD Records.
76. Robert N. Hardeman, Local Board for County of Jones, Gray, Ga., to Marion Stump, August 18, 1918, Farm Furlough File No. 2, Box 3, GSCD Records.
77. H. S. White, Attorney at Law, Chairman, County Council of Defense, Sylvania, Georgia, to Marion Stump, August 15, 1918, Farm Furlough File No. 2, Box 3, GSCD Records.
78. Copies of the furlough application forms are in File 2967–10, Box 3, GSCD records, R. G. 22-1-14, GDAH. See also the federal regulations issued for the administration of this program in General Orders No. 31, War Department, Washington, April 2, 1918.
79. Archibald Campbell, Col., Coast Artillery Corps, Commanding, Ft. Screven, Ga., to Director, Bureau of Farm Furloughs, Georgia Council of Defense, Farm Furlough File No. 2, Box 3, GSCD Records.
80. The tone of one of Stump's letters to an applicant suggests relations were not good between the State's Selective Service Administration and Camp Wheeler: "If your sons are sent to Camp Wheeler . . . we will not be able to render any help as Camp Wheeler does

not cooperate with this Department." Director, Bureau of Farm Furloughs, Georgia Council of Defense, to Mr. J. O. Sapp, August 1, 1918, Farm Furlough File No. 2, Box 3, GSCD Records.

81. I discuss this in greater detail in "Work or Fight: Selective Service and Manhood in the Progressive Era" (Ph.D. diss., University of California, San Diego, 1992), 80–83, 87–96.

82. John H. Ferguson, Talbotton, Ga., to Governor Hugh Dorsey, September 8, 1918; The daughter of Tom Dorsey to Governor Dorsey, September 1918. unfiled loose papers, Box 1, GSCD Records.

83. R. C. White to Governor Hugh Dorsey, August 14, 1918, Farm Furlough File No. 2, Box 3, GSCD Records.

84. Farm Furlough File, Box 3, GSCD Records.

85. See Shenk, "Work or Fight," 340–345, 358–361, 374–376, 388–392, 551–554, 588–590.

86. R. W. Grow to Governor Dorsey, June 29, 1918, "Farm Furlough" File, Box 3, GSCD Records.

87. Letter from E. R. Griner, Daisy, Ga, August 5, 1917, in records of the Bureau of Farm Furloughs, Farm Furlough File No. 2, Box 3, GSCD Records.

88. R. O. Moore to Marion W. Stump, August 13, 1918, Farm Furlough File No.2, Box 3, GSCD Records.

89. Deborah Gray White, *Ar'n't I a Woman? Female Slaves in the Plantation South* (New York: Norton, 1985), 164, citing the 1969 findings of the National Commission on the Causes and Prevention of Violence.

90. See Wray and Newitz, eds., *White Trash*, 6–8.

91. J. A. Hillis et al., to Joel B. Mallet, Adjutant General, Ga., Feb. 12, 1918, File 54-4, States Files-Georgia, SSS Records, R.G. 163, WNRC.

92. Ibid., Said, *Culture and Imperialism*, 167–168.

93. On the power of "knowing" within systems of domination, see Frantz Fanon, *The Wretched of the Earth* (New York: Grove Press, 1963), 36.

94. Ibid., Hillis to Mallet, February 12, 1918.

95. Unidentified newspaper clipping dated September 5, 1918; Letter from J. D. Gardner, Chairman, Mitchell Co. Council of Defense, to Governor Dorsey, September 7, 1918, File 4, "Farm Furloughs/Negroes," Box 1, GSCD Records.

96. Pink Anderson to Marion W. Stump, Director, Bureau of Farm Furloughs, Georgia Council of Defense, August 2, 1918, Farm Furlough File No. 2, Box 3, GSCD Records.

97. C. D. Marsh to Director, Bureau of Farm Furloughs, July 17, 1918, Farm Furlough File No. 3, Box 3, GSCD Records.

98. Chas. Watt, Jr., Sheriff, Mitchell Co., to Hon. J. J. Brown, Department of Agriculture, April 6, 1918, Adjutant General File, Box 4, GSCD Records.

99. R. W. Grow to Governor Dorsey, June 29, 1918, File "Farm Furloughs," Box 3, GSCD Records.

100. Joel Mallet to Enoch Crowder, October 16, 1918, File 17-167, Box 110, States Files: Georgia, R.G. 163, SSS Records, 1917–1919, WNRC.

101. Scott, *Scott's Official History of the American Negro in the World War*, 9.

102. Ibid., 69.

103. The trial, which had the largest number of defendants of any murder trial in American history, took a single day. Robert V. Haynes, *A Night of Violence: The Houston Riot of 1917* (Baton Rouge: Louisiana State University Press, 1976), is the standard account.

104. *Second Report of the Provost Marshal General* (Washington, 1919), 75–85.

105. J. D. Gardner, Chairman, Mitchell County Council of Defense to Governor Dorsey, August 26, 1918, Labor File, Box 2, GSCD Records. Paula Giddings, *When and Where I Enter: The Impact of Black Women on Race and Sex in America* (New York: Bantam Books, 1984), 141.

106. *Georgia Laws*, 1918, Part I, Title VI, No. 348. "Work Required of Able-Bodied Persons," Act approved August 8, 1918 (Atlanta, 1919).

107. Reverend Henry H. Proctor, Pastor, First Congregational Church of Atlanta, to Governor Dorsey, July 26, 1918, "Negro Organization" File, Box 3, GSCD Records.

108. Tera W. Hunter, *To 'Joy My Freedom: Southern Black Women's Lives and Labors after the Civil War* (Cambridge, MA: Harvard University Press, 1997), 228–229.

109. Walter F. White, "Work or Fight in the South," *The New Republic* XVIII (March, 1919), 144–146.

110. Hunter, *To 'Joy My Freedom*, 230–231.

111. *Report and Opinions of the Attorney General of Georgia, from June 15, 1917, to December 31, 1918*, Clifford Walker, Attorney-General (Atlanta, 1919), 209–210.

112. Gilbert to Clark Howell, August 26, 1918, "Negro Organization File," Box 3, GSCD Records.

113. Constitution of the Negro Workers' Advisory Committee, undated, Negro Organization, Box 3, GSCD Records.

114. George E. Haynes to H. M. Stanley, July 15, 1918, Negro Organization File, Box 3, GSCD Records.

115. Address of Judge Price Gilbert to the "Negro Workers' Advisory Committee," August, 1918, File-"Negroes," Box 4, GSCD Records.

116. Gilbert to William B. Wilson, August 15, 1918; Gilbert to Fleming, August 10, 1918; "Negroes Answer Call of Governor to Stabilize the Race," undated, unidentified newspaper clipping. Negro Organization File, Box 3, GSCD Records.

117. Gilbert to Fleming, August 10th, 1918, Negro Organization, Box 3, GSCD Records. See also, Mark Ellis, " 'Closing Ranks' and 'Seeking Honors': W. E. B. Du Bois in World War I," *The Journal of American History* 79 (June 1992): 96–124, and Steven A. Reich, "Soldiers of Democracy: Black Texans and the Fight for Citizenship, 1917–1921," *The Journal of American History* 82 (March 1996): 1478–1504.

118. Gilbert to Isma Dooley, August 10, 1918, "Negro Meeting" File, Box 5, GSCD Records.

119. Garner to Governor Dorsey, August 10, 1918, accepting his appointment to the Negro Workers' Advisory Committee. "Negro Labor Organization" File, Box 3, GSCD Records.

120. H. M. Hubbard to Price Gilbert, July 29, 1918, Negro Organization File, Box 3, GSCD Records.

121. G. W. Upshaw, Cartersville, Ga., to Governor Hugh M. Dorsey, September 19, 1918; Dorsey cover letter forwarding Upshaw's letter to Gilbert, September 30, 1918; Gilbert to Upshaw, October 4, 1918; and Upshaw to Gilbert, November 11, 1918, correspondence files of Governor Dorsey, 1917–1919, GDAH.

122. Price Gilbert to Hooper Alexander, September 4, 1918; Alexander to Gilbert, September 5, 1918; Gilbert to Alexander, September 7, 1918; Alexander to Gilbert, September 9, 1918. File "Negro Organization," Box 3, GSCD Records.

123. Council of National Defense, "Program for Organization of Negroes by the Southern State Councils," Negro Organization, Box 3, GSCD Records.

124. Giddings, *When and Where I Enter*, 164–170; Jacqueline Jones, *Labor of Love, Labor of Sorrow: Black Women, Work and the Family, from Slavery to the Present* (New York: Basic Books, 1985), 193.

125. Wright, *Old South, New South*, 238; Daniel, *Breaking the Land*, 91–109, 140–142.

126. Telegram from G. B. Clarkson to the Georgia State Council of Defense, January 23, 1918. File 1, Box 2, GSCD Records.

127. Memo from S. J. Slate, dated 1919, on proposed topics for discussion at Council of Defense Conference on Demobilization, "Labor" File, Box 5, GSCD Records.

128. Daniel, *Breaking the Land*, 163; John Dittmer, *Black Georgia in the Progressive Era, 1900–1920* (Urbana: University of Illinois Press, 1977), 203–205.

Chapter Two   Illinois: "A Man Is No Man
That Is Not Willing to Fight"

1. Mrs. Marie Barbee to the War Department, May 23, 1918, File 17-247, Box 118, States Files: Illinois.
2. See Nancy MacLean, "White Women and Klan Violence in the 1920s: Agency, Complicity and the Politics of Women's History," *Gender and History* 3 (Autumn 1991): 287–303.
3. Michael Willrich, "Home Slackers: Men, the State, and Welfare in Modern America," *Journal of American History* 87:2 (September 2000): 460–489.
4. Governor Lowden, Address to the Gentlemen of the Fiftieth General Assembly, State of Illinois, Springfield, June 4, 1917, in Correspondence of Governor Lowden.
5. David F. Wilcox and Judge Lyman McCarl, *Quincy and Adams County: History and Representative Men* (Chicago: The Lewis Publishing Company, 1919), 31.
6. Hon. William H. Collins and Mr. Cicero F. Perry, *Past and Present of the City of Quincy and Adams County, Illinois* (Chicago: The S. J. Clarke Publishing Co., 1905), 255.
7. Geoffrey Perrret, *A Country Made by War: From the Revolution to Vietnam—The Story of America's Rise to Power* (New York: Vintage Books, 1990), 128–129, 132, 136–137.
8. Peter Nabokov, *Native American Testimony: A Chronicle of Indian White Relations from Prophecy to the Present, 1492–2000* (New York: Penguin Books, 1999), 13, 99–101; Collins and Perry, *Past and Present*, 220–221.
9. Collins and Perry, *Past and Present*, 298–299.
10. Wilcox and McCarl, *Quincy and Adams County*, 17.
11. Collins and Perry, *Past and Present*, 255; 220–221.
12. U.S. Statutes at Large, Vol. XXIV, p. 388 ff., Sec. 6. Senator Dawes is quoted at <http://www.law.du.edu/russell/lh/alh/docs/dawesact.html>.
13. *Prairie Farmer's Directory of Adams County, Illinois* (Chicago: The Prairie Farmer Publishing Company, 1918), 80, 276, 280; Draft registration card of Fred Henry Heberlein, Adams County SSS Records, RG 163, NARA, Atlanta.
14. Dorothy Jacobson, who grew up near the Heberlein farm during those years, remembers that German American farm women were more likely to do the same farm work as men. Author's interview with Jacobson, June 9, 1989, Payson, Illinois.
15. Draft Registration Card of Fred Henry Heberlein, Adams County local draft board, SSS Records, RG 163, Atlanta Regional National Archives Branch; PMGO Form 164-A, "List of Men Ordered to Report to this Local Board for Military Duty," Local Board for Adams County, Illinois, September 4, 1917.
16. *Second Report of the Provost Marshal General to the Secretary of War on the Operations of the Selective Service System to December 20, 1918* (Washington, D.C.: GPO, 1919), 505.
17. Booklet of the State Headquarters Selective Service, Springfield, Illinois, States Files-Illinois, SSS Records, RG 163, WNRC; Neighborhood Committees membership card file, and County Executive Committee, Adams County, Illinois State Council of Defense, RG 517, Drawer 77, Illinois State Archives, Springfield, Illinois; Collins and Perry, *Past and Present*, 652; Wilcox and McCarl, *Quincy and Adams County*, 634–635.
18. PMGO Form 185, "Docket Book, District Board for Division No. 3 of the Southern District of the State of Illinois," Local Board for the County of Adams, SSS Records, RG 163, WNRC, Suitland, MD; PMGO Form 164-A, "List of Men Ordered to Report to this Local Board for Military Duty . . .," Local Board for Adams County, Illinois, September 4, 1917, and PMGO Form 4003, "Final Lists of Delinquents and Deserters," State of Illinois, in Binder for local boards code Nos. 12-5-9 through 12-6-27, Section 72, SSS Records, RG 163, Chicago National Archives Branch.
19. *Yearbook of the U.S. Department of Agriculture, 1917* (Washington: GPO, 1918), 546–549.
20. PMGO Forms 164-A, "Lists of Men Ordered to Report to this Local Board for Military Duty," Local Board for Adams County, Illinois, September 4, 1917, September 21, 1917,

and October 26, 1917; Information on farm families is from *Prairie Farmer's Directory of Adams County, Illinois*. See also Table II, p. 38.

21. Form 185-P.M.G.O., "Docket Book, District Board for Division No. 3 of the Southern District of of the State of Illinois, Local Board for County of Adams," SSS Records, 1917–1919, RG 163, WNRC.

22. Occupations of drafted men compiled from the Lists of Men Ordered to Report for Military Duty from Local Board for Adams County, PMGO Forms 1029, March 31, through October 18, 1918. Statistics on exemptions and deferments are from *Second Report of the Provost Marshal General*, 505.

23. Adams County Local Board wire to Enoch Crowder, June 16, 1918, File 27-29, Box 121, States Files-Illinois, SSS Records, 1917–1919, RG 163, WNRC, Suitland, MD.

24. Lists of Men Ordered to Report from Local Board for Adams County, Illinois, PMGO Form 1029, June 27, July 22, and 29, 1918, SSS Records, RG 163, National Archives Branch, Chicago, Illinois.

25. George L. Anderson of Clayton, Illinois, to Provost Marshal General Crowder, June 2, 1918, File 17-350, Box 119, States Files-Illinois, SSS Records, 1917–1919, RG 163, WNRC, Suitland, MD.

26. Guy Franklin Hershberger, *War, Peace, and Nonresistance* (Scottdale, PA: Herald Press, 1969), 53–57, 156–165.

27. Selective Draft Law, Section 4 (Act of May 18, 1917); PMGO Form 1001, "Classification Questionnaire," in Historical Files Box, Selective Service Records, 1917–1919, RG 163, National Archives, Suitland, MD. *Second Report of the Provost Marshal General*, 56–61, lists thirteen officially recognized "peace churches," with a combined male membership of 276,843.

28. Interview with Helen and Herbert Ogle, by the author, June 9, 1989, at Liberty, Illinois. Minutes of District Conference of the Church of the Brethren of Northern Illinois and Wisconsin, held in the Milledgeville Church, August 23, 1917; Minutes of District Meeting of Southern Illinois, held in Astoria Church, October 3, 1917; Minnie S. Buckingham, ed., *Church of the Brethren in Southern Illinois* (Elgin: Brethren Publishing House, 1950), 35–39.

29. Noel Ignatiev, *How the Irish Became White* (New York and London: Routledge, 1995); Karen Brodkin, *How the Jews Became White Folk and What that Tells Us about Race in America* (New Brunswick, New Jersey: Rutgers University Press, 1997).

30. Rufus D. Bowman, *The Church of the Brethren and War, 1708–1941* (Elgin, Illinois: Brethren Press, 1944).

31. Minutes of District Conference of the Church of the Brethren of Northern Illinois and Wisconsin, August 23, 1917; Minutes of District Meeting of Southern Illinois, October 3, 1917.

32. Cover Sheet and file, Lucas C. Akers, Box 4, microfilmed Selective Service Records, Adams County, Illinois, 1917–1918, RG 163, WNRC.

33. PMGO Form 1001, Questionnaire of Lucas C. Akers, Payson, Illinois, submitted December 24, 1917; Affidavit of F. A. Hoecker, December 24, 1917; Affidavit of J. E. Akers and C.P. Johnson, April 1, 1918, all in microfilmed file of Lucas C. Akers.

34. Ibid.; Form 1029, Notice of Induction, Lucas C. Akers, accepted at Jefferson Barracks, St. Louis, Missouri, May 25, 1918.

35. John W. Chambers, Introduction to Walter Guest Kellogg, *The Conscientious Objector* (New York: Garland Publishing, Inc., 1972, Reprint of 1919 edition, published by Boni and Liveright, New York), 9–11.

36. Ibid., 11.

37. Adjutant General of the Army to All Department Commanders in the United States. . . ., Subject: "Conscientious Objectors," July 30, 1918, in Kellogg, *The Conscientious Objector*, 133–138.

38. Ibid., 75–81.

39. Kellogg, *The Conscientious Objector*, 75–81, 127. Guy Franklin Hershberger, *War, Peace, and Nonresistance* (Scottdale, Pennsylvania: Herald Press, 1969), 113–114.

40. William Lynch, Mayor, and David Wilson, Postmaster, Gridley, Illinois, to Crowder, January 17, 1918, File 17-31, Box 117, States Files: Illinois, SSS Records, 1917–1919, RG 163, WNRC.

41. John E. Wall, Adams County Council of Defense Auxiliary Chairman, to Samuel Insull, Chairman, Illinois State Council of Defense, November 27, 1917, reported trouble persuading local committees of the council of defense to meet, blaming "a very strong undercurrent here of a pro-German type;" Wall to Insull, October 24, 1917, reported that only one person attended the meeting of the Adams County Council of Defense; George Jones, Illinois Four-Minute Men, to Ed Friedman, Illinois Four-Minute Man field representative, November 5, 1917, identified Quincy as pro-German hotbed, and Friedman to Jones, November 6, 1917, calls Quincy "the strongest German city in the state;" E. W. Rusk, Adams County Farm Labor Office, to E. K. Moy, Chicago Farm Labor Administration, April 4, 1918, wrote that farmers were "not willing to go outside of the local supply" to solve the farm labor shortage. All correspondence in the Employment Service Correspondence Files, Records of the Illinois State Council of Defense, RG 517.3, Illinois State Archives, Springfield, Illinois; Dorothy Jacobson, interview, Payson, Illinois, June 9, 1989.

42. Landry Genosky, O. F. M., ed. *The People's History of Quincy and Adams County, Illinois: A Sesquicentenial History* (Quincy: Jost and Kiefer Printing Co., 1974), 488. Frederick C. Luebke, *Bonds of Loyalty: German Americans and World War I* (Dekalb, Illinois: Northern Illinois University Press, 1974), 3–24.

43. Quincy had a population of 36,587 in 1910, almost half the county total. *Thirteenth Census of the United States; Population, Part II* (Washington, D.C.: Government Printing Office, 1911), 442.

44. Genosky, *The People's History of Quincy and Adams County*, 491–493. The Council of Defense failed in its repeated attempts to book Four-Minute Men into Quincy theaters. Wall to Insull, March 5, 1918, Illinois State Council of Defense Records, RG 517, Illinois State Archives. On the Provost Marshal General's policy toward the APL, see, "Provost Marshal General to the Governor of (all States), Cooperation of American Protective League, February 7, 1918," in Historical File, document 17–118, Records of the Selective Service System, 1917–1919, RG 163, National Archives, College Park, Maryland.

45. Interview with Dorothy Jacobson; Genosky, *The People's History of Quincy and Adams County, Illinois*, 488–491; *A History of Paloma, Illinois*, typeset manuscript at the Historical Society of Quincy and Adams County, Illinois.

46. The texts of addresses given in Chicago by these men are published in Marguerite Edith Jenison, ed., *Illinois in the World War, Volume VI, War Documents and Addresses*, series editor, Theodore Calvin Pease (Springfield: Illinois State Historical Library, 1923).

47. This material and that in the following three paragraphs is drawn primarily from Luebke, *Bonds of Loyalty*, 164–167. But see also David M. Kennedy, *Over Here: The First World War and American Society* (New York: Oxford University Press, 1980), 67–68.

48. The quotes are from Luebke, 146 and 144. See also pp. 68–69, 140–146; On the anti-hyphenism of Wilson and Roosevelt and the German American political response, see Kennedy, 24–25; Arthur S. Link, *Woodrow Wilson and the Progressive Era, 1910–1917* (New York: Harper Torchbooks, 1963), 231; John Morton Blum, *Woodrow Wilson and the Politics of Morality* (Boston: Little, Brown and Company, 1956), 118–119; and Walter Karp, *The Politics of War: The Story of Two Wars which Altered Forever the Political Life of the American Republic (1890–1920)* (New York: Harper Colophon Books, 1979), 228–229, 231–235.

49. Luebke, *Bonds of Loyalty*, 190–194.

50. Luebke, *Bonds of Loyalty*, 202–205. The following two paragraphs are based on this source. But see also, Kennedy, *Over Here*, 28–29. For opposing interpretations of Wilson's motives during February and March, see Link, *Woodrow Wilson and the Progressive Era*, 252–282; and Karp, *The Politics of War*, 271–278.

51. Lowden to the President, February 7, 1917, contains the text of a telegram from University of Illinois President, Edmund H. Jones, which made the offer. Correspondence of Governor Lowden, Illinois State Archives, Springfield.

52. "Resolutions Adopted at Patriotic Rally, Chicago, March 31, 1917," published in Jenison, ed., *War Documents and Addresses*, 20–21.

53. "Address by Dean Eugene Davenport before Chicago Association of Commerce," April 4, 1917, in Jenison, *War Documents*, 134.

54. "Address by Dean Shailer Mathews before Chicago Association of Commerce," July 18, 1917, in Jenison, *War Documents*, 49, 60.

55. "Resolutions adopted by Springfield Federation of Labor," April 13, 1917, in Jenison, *War Documents*, 29.

56. "Resolutions adopted by Illinois State Bar Association," Danville, June 1, 1917, in Jenison, *War Documents*, 29–30.

57. "Resolutions adopted by the Illinois State Teachers' Association," December 27, 1917, in Jenison, *War Documents*, 81–82.

58. Wharton Clay, Executive Director, Military Training Camps Association of the U.S., Central Department, to "all Members of Advisory Committee," March 14, 1917, Correspondence of Governor Lowden, Illinois State Archives, Springfield. John Garry Clifford, *The Citizen Soldiers: The Plattsburg Training Camp Movement, 1913–1920* (Lexington: University of Kentucky Press, 1972).

59. John Whiteclay Chambers II, *To Raise an Army: The Draft Comes to Modern America* (New York: The Free Press, 1987), 78–85, 136–141. John Milton Cooper, Jr., *The Warrior and the Priest: Woodrow Wilson and Theodore Roosevelt* (Cambridge, Mass.: Belknap Press, 1983) Arthur Link, *Woodrow Wilson and the Progressive Era, 1910–1917* (New York: Harper and Row, 1954), 174–196.

60. Luebke, *Bonds of Loyalty*, 211. A good history of the APL is Joan M. Jensen, *The Price of Vigilance* (New York: Rand McNally and Company, 1968).

61. Luebke, *Bonds of Loyalty*, 217.

62. Quoted in Luebke, *Bonds of Loyalty*, 253.

63. Ibid., 269. The story of the Collinsville lynching is also told in less detail, but in the context of nationwide vigilantism against nonconformists, in Kennedy, *Over Here*, 68.

64. The various reports of registration day are in File 13-23, Box 117, States Files: Illinois. All are dated June 5 or 6, 1917.

65. Correspondence between Illinois officials and Crowder took place in late June and July 1917, and is found in Files of Series 27, Box 121, States Files: Illinois.

66. The Local Board resignation letter of July 22, 1917, and Crowder's response of July 24, 1917, in File 27-6, Box 121, States Files: Illinois.

67. The correspondence in these cases occurred in August and October 1918, and is found in Files 39–78, and 39–86, Box 122, States Files: Illinois.

68. Crowder to Governor of Illinois, May 28, 1917, File 13-8, Box 117, States Files: Illinois.

69. Clerk of Chicago Local Board No. 4 to Crowder, August 9, 1917, File 15-2, Box 117, States Files: Illinois.

70. Smith to the Provost Marshal General, April 4, 1918, and note from PMGO, referred to State Dept., File 17-74, Box 117, States Files: Illinois, SSS Records, 1917–1919, RG 163, WNRC.

71. Series of letters and telegrams between Gigliotti and the PMGO are found in File 39-42, Box 122, States Files: Illinois.

72. Correspondence describing the Rockford riots and subsequent prosecutions is in File 186233–72, DOJ Correspondence, 1910–1920.

73. Crowder to Adjutant General, Springfield, May 8, 1917, Clabaugh, Dept. of Justice Division Superintendent, to June C. Smith, May 9, 1918, File 39-53, Box 122, States Files: Illinois. These six men must have been U.S. citizens or resident aliens who had declared their intention to become citizens, since all other aliens were exempt from induction. (They were not exempt from registration.)

74. Luebke, *Bonds of Loyalty*, 239–240.
75. Brodkin, *How the Jews Became White Folks*, 103–137.
76. Mrs. R. A. Alexander to the Editor, *Literary Digest*, July 23, 1917, and B. P. Adams, *Literary Digest*, July 28, 1917, File 21-31, Box 119, States Files: Illinois.
77. Rock Island County Local Board to the District Board Chairman for Division I, Southern District, October 10, 1917, Re: Henry Arp, File 17-15, Box 117, States Files: Illinois, SSS Records, 1917–1919, RG 163, WNRC.
78. Records of this case, including correspondence and the investigative report by June C. Smith, Illinois Military and Naval Department, March 6, 1918, are in File 17-39, Box 117, States Files: Illinois, SSS Records, 1917–1919, RG 163, WNRC, and File 186233–72–28, DOJ Correspondence.
79. Report of Agent Louis Loebl, February 24, 1918, "In Re: All. Discrimination of Local Board of Monroe County," File 10101–150, MID Files, RG 165, National Archives, Washington.
80. Report of BI Agent, J. M. Hooper, April 24, 1918, File 17-163, Box 118, States Files: Illinois.
81. Ibid.
82. Circular Letter to Registration Boards and Mayors from F. S. Dickson, May 31, 1917, FIle 13-11, Box 117, States Files: Illinois.
83. I. Bonillas to Lansing, August 21, 1917, and related correspondence in File 17-8, Box 117, States Files: Illinois.
84. E. K. Pierce, Chief Clerk, McHenry County Local Board, to Dickson, March 20, 1918, Local Board No. 19, Chicago, to Dickson, March 28, 1918, and C. A. Hope, for Crowder, to Adjutant General, Illinois, April 9, 1918, File 17-62, Box 117, States Files: Illinois, SSS Records, 1917–1919, RG 163, WNRC.
85. The "Slacker Raids" are described in File 17-265, Box 117, States Files: Illinois. The quotes and statistics in the following account are taken from B. W. Bielaski to Crowder, July 16, 1918, Crowder to Governor Lowden, July 16, 1918, and F. S. Dickson to the Governor, July 20, 1918.
86. Jensen, *The Price of Vigilance*, 195–196.
87. Dickson to PMGO, June 11, 1917, File 13-14, Box 117, States Files: Illinois, SSS Records, 1917–1919, RG 163, WNRC.
88. Mrs. Charles McNeely to Committee on Public Information, June 14, 1918, File 17-292, Box 118, States Files: Illinois.
89. Myrtle Williams to Mr. Wilson, July 13, 1918; Secretary of Local Board for Marion County, Illinois, to Adjutant General, August 14, 1918, File 17-307, Box 119, States Files: Illinois.
90. Mrs. Reid to "Dear Sir" (addressee not otherwise indicated), January 22, 1918, and Alexander Johnson, for Enoch Crowder, to Mrs. John Reid, March 1, 1918, File 17-40, Box 117, States Files: Illinois.
91. Illinois was probably the leading destination of African American males who left the South between 1915 and 1920. Of the many treatments of this migration, see James R. Grossman, *Land of Hope: Chicago, Black Southerners, and the Great Migration* (Chicago: University of Chicago Press, 1990), and Carole Marks, *Farewell—We're Good and Gone: The Great Black Migration* (Bloomington: Indiana University Press, 1989).
92. Melba Darensbourg White to War Department, July 29, 1918, and Knox County Local Board to Illinois Adjutant General, September 27, 1918, File 17-325, Box 119, States Files: Illinois.
93. These letters are contained in File 17-243, Box 117, States Files: Illinois. The form letter identified the complainant as "the wife of the registrant [name of registrant] and alleges that he should be placed in Class I Division b, as a registrant whose wife and children are not mainly dependent on his labor for support for the reason that the registrant has habitually failed to support them . . . [and] that he has been making no bona fide attempt to support them in the past and can not be relied upon to do so in the future."

94. Crowder to Bielaski, December 29, 1917, File 16-1, Box 117, States Files: Illinois. Assistant United States Attorney General John Lord O'Brien forwarded Crowder's demand for prosecutions to Edward C. Knotts, the United States Attorney in Springfield, but without any indication of whether he agreed with Crowder. Charles F. Clyne, United States Attorney for Eastern Illinois, apparently persuaded the Attorney General not to pursue such prosecutions. He wrote, "it is inconceivable that they [the examining physicians] could have gained anything. [They] gave their services gratuitously and are impelled by patriotism." File 186233–72–34,-46, DOJ Correspondence Files, RG 60, National Archives, Washington.

95. Local boards, however, defended themselves against Crowder's criticisms by citing differences in the standards contained in the regulations used by local board physicians and those used by Camp authorities. Dickson to PMGO, February 21, 1918, File 32-17, Box 121, States Files: Illinois. That defense does not refute other explanations. The local board for Vermilion County made an argument for following the spirit of the regulations rather than the letter. A registrant it had drafted failed the physical examination at training camp, leading the board to lodge this protest with the adjutant general: "The only thing the matter with this man was when he was young he had his arms broken near the elbow, and they did not make a good job of setting the same, so, when he extends his arms straight before him, his hands turn out slightly and his elbows in slightly, but this has never incapacitated him from labor in any respect. He has been a machinist's helper and slung a sledge all day. Any person that can do that, we believe is fit for service." Local Board, Div. 1, Vermilion County, to Dickson, August 12, 1918, File 42-9, Box 122, States Files: Illinois.

96. Numerous reports of this sort were made by A. E. Lord, Surgeon, 129th Infantry, dated November and December 1917, File 16-1, Box 117, States Files: Illinois.

97. A. E. Lord, Surgeon, 129th Infantry, "Complaint: Enuresis, nocturnal and diurnal," November 17, 1917, File 16-1, Box 117, States Files: Illinois.

98. A. E. Lord, Surgeon, 129th Infantry, Memo Re. Pvt. John F. Sheridan, November 17, 1917, File 16-1, Box 117, States Files: Illinois.

99. Esther Newton has explored some of the Progressive Era portrayals of women with masculine bodies. It is in some ways parallel to this example, although in no case does it appear that women with manly bodies were considered as bizarre as men with womanly bodies. But the similarity of descriptions is uncanny: "Masculine features, deep voice, manly gait, without beard, small breasts," was one psychologist's portrayal of a manly woman. A novelist of the period wrote of women "narrow-hipped and wide-shouldered, muscular, small compact breasts," and a "strangely ardent yet sterile body." Newton, "The Mythic Mannish Lesbian: Radclyffe Hall and the New Woman," in Martin Duberman, Martha Vicinus, and George Chauncey, Jr., eds, *Hidden From History: Reclaiming the Gay and Lesbian Past* (New York: Penguin Books/Meridian, 1989), 287–289.

100. Samuel Insull, address of January 18, 1919, in Jenison, *War Documents*, 456–457, 465.

Chapter Three   New Jersey: "He's His Mother's Boy; Go and Get Him"

1. The debate over this issue in various states, its connection to the preparedness movement and to Progressive ideology, and the role of professional educators in promoting military training is described by Timothy P. O'Hanlon, in "School Sports as Social Training: The Case of Athletics and the Crisis of World War I," *Journal of Sport History* 9 (Spring, 1982), 5–29.

2. *Report of the Commission on Military Training and Instruction in High Schools to the New Jersey Legislature*, Session of 1917, reprinted as a pamphlet by the American Union Against Militarism, entitled, *New Jersey Says "No!"* (Washington, D.C., 1918), copy found in the records of the Military Intelligence Division, Bureau of Investigation, Department of Justice, File 10101–10, RG, 165, National Archives, Washington, D.C.

3. Ibid., 3,5. Differentiation, as Joan Scott has argued, is the key to understanding how people construct and experience their social identities. Thus, as in Georgia, where the differentiation of race was essential to white males' experience of themselves as men, these New Jersey politicians constructed their identity as men in part by attempting to differentiate sharply between boyhood and manhood. Age differentiation may have been less crucial for men and boys in the rural South where often males assumed many of the functions of men at about the same time as the onset of puberty. This is supported by the findings of Joseph Kett and Anthony Platt that age distinctions, especially between children, adolescents, and adults, became more important as people became more regimented by the time demands of industrial society. Scott, *Gender and the Politics of History* (New York: Columbia University Press, 1988), 2, 45; Kett, *Rites of Passage: Adolescence in America, 1790 to the Present* (New York, 1977), 124–127; Platt, *The Child-Savers*, 56–61.

4. *Report of Commission on Military Training*, 9.

5. Donna Haraway, *Primate Visions: Gender, Race, and Nature in the World of Modern Science* (New York London: Routledge, 1989), 42.

6. *Report of Commission on Military Training*, 6–7; Proclamation of President Woodrow Wilson, May 18, 1917, copy in "Historical Files of the Selective Service System," 1917–1919, RG 163, WNRC.

7. David Kennedy, *Over Here: The First World War and American Society* (New York: Oxford University Press, 1980), 30–36. See also Roland Marchand, *The American Peace Movement and Social Reform, 1898–1918* (Princeton: Princeton University Press, 1973); and Peggy Lamson, *Roger Baldwin, Founder of the American Civil Liberties Union: A Portrait* (Boston: Houghton Mifflin Co., 1976), 67–73. On the marginalization of radical women who challenged the dominant gender order, see Kathleen Kennedy, " 'We Mourn for Liberty in America:' Socialist Women, Anti-Militarism, and State Repression, 1914–1922" (Ph.D. diss., University of California, at Irvine, 1992), 10, as quoted in Frances H. Early, "New Historical Perspectives on Gendered Peace Studies," *Women's Studies Quarterly* 3 and 4 (1995): 26. I am grateful to Frances Early for her critique of my original analysis, which had suggested that the peace movement was disorganized. She rightly pointed out that although the peace movement was tiny, it was organized as a movement (27). Nevertheless, Selective Service Records suggest widespread, but unorganized, and unfocused opposition to the war, and I believe that failure to mount an organized challenge to the fundamental class/race/sex/gender structure of society fatally compromised most opposition.

8. Army Adjutant General Memo, July 30, 1917, file 9317–4, Adjutant General Documents Files, War College Division, RG 165, National Archives; Lewis B. Hershey, *Outline of the History of Selective Service (From Biblical Times to June 5, 1965)* (Washington: Government Printing Office, 1965), 2; Arthur Ekirch, Jr., *The Civilian and the Military: A History of the American Antimilitarist Tradition* (New York: Oxford University Press, 1956), 188.

9. Paterson Friends of the Great Falls, at <http://patersongreatfalls.com/>.

10. Herbert G. Gutman, "The Reality of the Rags-to-Riches 'Myth,' " and "Class, Status, and Community Power in Nineteenth-Century American Industrial Cities: Paterson, New Jersey: A Case Study," in *Work, Culture, and Society in Industrializing America: Essays in American Working-Class and Social History* (New York: Vintage Books, 1977), 211–260. See also, Charles A Shriner, *Four Chapters of Paterson History* (Paterson: Lont & Overkamp Publishing Co., 1919), ch. 4; Levi R. Trumbull, *A History of Industrial Paterson* (Paterson: Carleton M. Herrick, Book and Job Printer, 1882); and W. Woodford Clayton, *History of Bergen and Passaic Counties, New Jersey* (Philadelphia: Everts & Peck, 1882); Maury Klein, *Prisoners of Progress: American Industrial Cities* (New York: Macmillan, 1976); Steve Golin, *The Fragile Bridge: Paterson Silk Strike, 1913* (Philadelphia: Temple University Press, 1988).

11. Gutman, "The Reality of the Rags-to-Riches 'Myth,' " 220–221. But see Klein, *Prisoners of Progress*, for a different interpretation.

12. Gutman, "The Reality of the Rags to Riches 'Myth,' " 240. David J. Goldberg, *A Tale of Three Cities: Labor Organization and Protest in Paterson, Passaic, and Lawrence, 1916–1921* (New Brunswick and London: Rutgers University Press, 1989), 20.

13. United States Census, *Population Reports; Thirteenth Census of the United States Taken in the Year 1910*, Vol. II (Washington: Government Printing Office, 1911); *Abstract of Census Returns for the County of Passaic, 1915*, loose pages of partial document in historical files, Paterson Free Library. By 1910 seventy-six percent of Paterson's residents were either immigrants or the children of immigrants. See also, Golin, *The Fragile Bridge*, 20–21, 25–28, 30–31, 39, and Goldberg, *A Tale of Three Cities*, 26–31.

14. For a concise description of Italian immigrant families and work in New Jersey see Dennis J. Starr, *The Italians of New Jersey: A Historical Introduction and Bibliography* (Newark: New Jersey Historical Society, 1985), 28–29. For studies of Italian immigrants elsewhere in the U.S. during the Progressive Era see Judith Smith, *Family Connections: A History of Italian and Jewish Immigrant Lives in Providence, Rhode Island, 1900–1940* (Albany: State University of New York Press, 1985), 41, 44–60; Virginia Yans-McLaughlin, *Family and Community: Italian Immigrants in Buffalo, 1880–1930* (Urbana: University of Illinois Press, 1982); and John Bodnar, Roger Simon, and Michael P. Weber, *Lives of Their Own: Blacks, Italians and Poles in Pittsburg, 1900–1960* (Urbana: University of Illinois Press, 1982), 99–100.

15. This nationwide movement has been thoroughly detailed in Anthony Platt, *The Child Savers: The Invention of Delinquency* (Chicago: University of Chicago Press, 1977).

16. "Annual Reports of City Officers, 1911–1912"; *Annual Report of the Board of Education of the City of Paterson, New Jersey, for the Year Ending June 30, 1914* (Paterson: The Press-Chronicle Co., 1915), 46.

17. *Annual Report of the Board of Education of Paterson, New Jersey, for the Year Ending June 30, 1910* (Paterson: The Press Chronicle Co., 1911), 58–60; *Annual Report of the Board of Education of Paterson, New Jersey, for the Year Ending June 30, 1914* (Paterson: The Press Chronicle Co., 1915), 45–46; "Report of the Principle of School No. 25, Disciplinary School," in *Annual Report of the Board of Education of Paterson, New Jersey, for the Year Ending June 30, 1915* (Paterson: The Press Chronicle Co., 1916), 175–178.

18. "Annual Reports of City Officers," 1911–1912, 1912–1913, 1919. General age proportions for the City of Paterson are derived from the *Abstract of Census Returns for the County of Passaic, 1915*.

19. Bederman, *Manliness and Civilization: A Cultural History of Gender and Race in the United States, 1880–1917* (Chicago: University of Chicago Press, 1995), 84, 92–93. See also, Thomas Dyer, *Theodore Roosevelt and the Idea of Race* (Baton Rouge: University of Louisiana Press, 1992).

20. I am indebted to John W. Chambers, of Rutgers University, for an excellent collection of documents and brief essays on the Paterson silk strike prepared for classroom use by Delight W. Dodyk and Steve Golin. The unpublished collection is entitled "The Paterson Silk Strike of 1913: Primary Materials for the Study of the History of Immigrants, Women, and Labor," and was produced in 1987 by the Garden State Immigration History Consortium. See pages 20–21 for workers' changing attitudes toward law enforcement officials.

21. Golin, *A Fragile Bridge*, 13–41; Goldberg, *A Tale of Three Cities*, 33–34.

22. Golin, *A Fragile Bridge*, 20–21.

23. Melvyn Dubovsky, *We Shall Be All: A History of the IWW* (New York: Quadrangle, 1969), 270, 275–276, 281–283.

24. Goldberg, *A Tale of Three Cities*, 13.

25. Ibid., 6–18.

26. *Paterson Evening News*, April 4, 1917.

27. *Paterson Evening News*, April 2, 1917.

28. *Paterson Evening News*, April 2, 5, 1917.

29. *Paterson Evening News*, April 5, 1917.
30. The war did give workers additional leverage in their demands for wage increases, but, as David J. Goldberg has found, the cost of living increases outstripped wages. Workers felt especially victimized by rents that rose as an influx of new workers arriving to take advantage of munitions jobs created a housing shortage. *A Tale of Three Cities*, 8–9.
31. *Paterson Evening News*, April 7, 1917.
32. *Paterson Evening News*, June 9, 1917.
33. *Paterson Morning Call; Paterson Evening News*, May 5 through June 8, 1917.
34. Based on occupational listings for local board members found in the *Paterson City Directory, 1917* (Paterson: Price and Lee Co., Publishers, 1917).
35. *Obituary Notices Book Number 27*, scrapbook in the collection of the Paterson Free Library. The biographical information is from the obituary of Peter D. Westerhoff, dated August 17, 1923, p. 44. William Nelson and Charles Shriner, *History of Paterson and Its Environs (The Silk City)*, Vol. II (New York: Lewis Historical Publishing Co., 1920), 430, and *Paterson City Directory, 1917* (Paterson: The Price and Lee Company, Publishing, 1917), 806. Westerhoff's draft card is with others from local board number three in the Selective Service Records held at the National Archives Branch, Atlanta, GA.
36. *Paterson Morning Call*, and *Paterson Evening News*, June 5, 6, 1917.
37. *Paterson Evening News*, June 8, 9, 1917.
38. *Evening News*, June 11, 12, 1917.
39. The documents in this case are contained in Files 186233–897 and 186233–686, DOJ Correspondence Files, 1910–1920, RG 60, National Archives, Washington, D.C.
40. Feeney to Lynch, November 11, 1917, File 186233–897, DOJ Correspondence Files, 1910–1920.
41. Lynch to the United States Attorney General, April 5, 1918, File 186233–686, DOJ Correspondence Files, 1910–1920.
42. "Casual Officer, Fort Jay, New York, to Adolph Keppler, October 28, 1918, and Keppler to Adjutant General, United States Army, October 28, 1918, File 17-310, Box 195, SSS Records, 1917–1919, RG 163, WNRC.
43. See File 19, Box 2, New Jersey Department of Defense Records, State Archives, Trenton, for general descriptions of APL investigations of silk manufacturers.
44. The Weidmann dye workers had been central in the strikes of 1894, 1902, and 1913. Golin, *The Fragile Bridge*, 24, 26, 37. Again, in 1918 the dye workers walked out in a pay dispute. The dye companies were probably considered the most likely source of labor unrest and radical activity during the war. They were among the lowest paid of Paterson's silk workers and endured miserable workplace conditions. Furthermore, they had been unable to break the manufacturers' open shop policy because the two largest dye companies, National and Weidmann, "had been able to standardize wages and to work in concert on labor matters." Goldberg, *A Tale of Three Cities*, 7, 11–12, 22–23.
45. "Confidential" memo from Archie M. Palmer, Intelligence Officer, Camp Merritt, to Intelligence Officer, Camp Dix, June 4, 1918, and APL report "In the matter of Ralph M. Fischer," February 26, 1918, both in File 10101–560, Files of the Military Investigative Division, Records of the War Department, National Archives, Washington.
46. APL report, December 20, 1917.
47. C. R. Rice to Col. R. H. Deman, General Staff, Military Investigative Bureau, April 2, 1918, File 10101–560, MID Records, National Archives, Washington.
48. APL report on Ralph Fischer and Henry Rosen, Paterson, N. J. December 20, 1917, File 10101–560, Military Investigative Division Files, Records of the War Department, National Archives, Washington.
49. Rice to Col. R. H. Deman, General Staff, MIB, April 2, 1918, File 10101–560, MID Records; and Palmer, "Confidential" memo, June 4, 1918. The dates given on the April reports of Westerhoff and Rice are not consistent with the chronology of events established by the other records. Since Fischer was inducted by the local board on April 1, and

accepted by Camp Dix on April 5, the date given on Rice's letter to Deman cannot be correct. It would have to be sometime after April 5.

50. APL Report, Newark, October 22, 1918, "Re Agler Reinhardt," File 10101–823, MID Records, National Archives, Washington.

51. Charles H. Rice, APL agent, to Col R. H. Van Deman, "Re. Henry Rosen," July 1, 1918, File 10101–823, MID Records, National Archives, Washington.

52. E. T. Drew, "Alleged Bribery to Secure Enlistment in Non-Combatant Service," report of June 12, 1918, File 10101–813, Military Investigative Division, Records of the United States Adjutant General, National Archives, Washington.

53. "Memos for Captain Busby, Re: Samuel B. Thomson, August 23, 24, 26, 27, 1918. The association of Jewish immigrants from Russia and Poland with labor radicalism went back to at least 1905 in Paterson and may have deepened the xenophobia that officials already felt toward them as a result of cultural differences. See Goldberg, *A Tale of Three Cities*, 29–30.

54. L. B. Dunham, Intelligence Officer, Port of Embarkation, Hoboken, to Director of Military Intelligence, November 12, 1918; and Emmett T. Drew, Special Agent, Department of Justice, to L. B. Dunham, November 17, 1918.

55. Thomas G. Bailey, "Cover sheet," Box 78, Microfilmed Cover Sheets, Records of the Selective Service System, RG 163, WNRC. On the desirability of women as operatives in silk factories, from the perspective of manufacturers, see Golin, *The Fragile Bridge*, 17.

56. See "labor News," *Paterson Evening News*, April 3, 1917.

57. A random selection of names from the registrant cards for the board showed that eleven percent of its registrants were employed in silk factories and among those drafted between February and October 1918 silk workers constituted twelve percent. Subtracting the students inducted at their request into the Student Army Training Corps at the end of the war reverses the percentages. The random selection yielded 339 cases, or approximately ten percent of Local Board No. 3 registrants. They were drawn from the draft cards which are arranged alphabetically by local boards. These are in the Selective Service Records, 1917–1919, National Archives Branch, Atlanta. Draftees and their occupations are from the induction lists, PMGO Form 1029, for Paterson Local Board No. 3. These forms cover all inductions between February 8, 1918 and November 11, 1918, and are held in Selective Service Records, 1917–1919, National Archives Branch, Bayonne, New Jersey. Induction lists for Paterson before February 1918 are missing. Therefore the conclusions here must be tentative since the registration data covers the entire period from the first draft in 1917 to the final registration. The local board's deferment policies might well have changed between September 1917 when the first calls were issued and February 1918 when those used here began.

58. See Crowder, *Final Report of the Provost Marshal General to the Secretary of War on the Operations of the Selective Service System to July 15, 1919* (Washington: Government Printing Office, 1919), Table 20.

59. The continued strong presence of a variety of radical labor and political organizations in Paterson during the war probably stimulated the ideological policing function of the Selective Service System and related agencies. On wartime radicals in Paterson, see Goldberg, *A Tale of Three Cities*, 15–16, 27–31.

60. Compare these women with the white Georgia women in the 1920s, described by Nancy MacLean, who turned to the Ku Klux Klan for similar reasons. In both cases, women's actions, which admittedly improved their immediate condition, enhanced the effectiveness of institutions that otherwise constructed gender hierarchies that subordinated women to men. MacLean, "White Women and Klan Violence in the 1920s: Agency, Complicity and the Politics of Women's History," *Gender and History*, 3 (Autumn 1991): 287–303.

61. Mrs. John A. Dotterweich to General Crowder, June 12, 1918, File 17-178, Box 195, SSS Records, 1917–1919, States Files: New Jersey, SSS Records, 1917–1919, RG 163, WNRC.

62. On team metaphors and teaching young men to play by the rules see Dominick Cavallo, *Muscles and Morals: Organized Playgrounds and Urban Reform, 1880–1920* (Philadelphia: Temple University Press, 1981), 61, 70, 89–95, 109–117. Also, Paul Boyer, *Urban Masses and Moral Order in America, 1820–1920* (Cambridge: Cambridge University Press, 1978), 214–233.

63. Dotterweich to Crowder, June 12, 1918.

64. Ibid.

65. Ibid.

66. Slater to Frederick Gilkyson, Adjutant General, Trenton, July 1, 1918, File 17-178, Box 195, States Files: New Jersey, SSS Records, 1917–1919, RG 163, WNRC.

67. War Department, PMGO Forms 44 and 45, to Mrs. John A. Dotterweich, both dated June 18, 1918, File 17-178, Box 195, SSS Records, 1917–1919, RG 163, WNRC.

68. Mrs. Wm. J. Porter to Governor Walter E. Edge, July 29, 1918, File 31, Box 1, Passaic Complaints, Correspondence of Governor Edge, State Archives, Trenton. The capitalization here conforms to the original letter. I have added punctuation in brackets where necessary. The Mr. Ferrary referred to in the letter was Secretary of Paterson Local Board No. 2.

69. Secretary to the Governor to Mrs. Porter, July 31, 1918, File 31, Box 1, Passaic Complaints, Correspondence of Governor Edge, State Archives, Trenton.

70. Ferrary to Provost Marshal General Crowder, December 18, 1918, File 20-16, States Files: New Jersey, SSS Records, 1917–1919, RG 163, WNRC.

71. R. L. Watkins, M. D., New York City, to Governor Edge, March 12, 1918, File 29a, Box 3, Correspondence of Governor Edge, 1917–1919, NJSA.

72. Governor Edge to Fred P. Greenwood, Massachusetts House of Representatives, May 6, 1918, File 29a, Box 3, Correspondence of Governor Edge, 1917–1919, New Jersey State Archives, Trenton.

73. "Statement" at the end of the Compulsory Labor Bill, contained in the File 29a, Box 3, Correspondence of Governor Edge, 1917–1919, NJSA. The bill was introduced January 14, 1918.

74. "Rules and Regulations Issued by the Commissioner of Labor at the Request of the Governor in Accordance with Provisions of the Compulsory Work Law, Chapter 55, Laws of 1918," File 29b, Box 3, Correspondence of Governor Edge, 1916–1918, State Archives, Trenton. On the state as masculine and the nation as feminine see Catharine A. MacKinnon, *Toward A Feminist Theory of the State* (Cambridge, MA: Harvard University Press, 1989), 155–170.

75. Daniel F. Hendrickson, Sheriff, Gloucester County, to Governor Edge, March 26, 1918, File 29a, Box 3, Correspondence of Governor Edge, 1917–1919, NJSA.

76. David M. Bowen, Sheriff, Cumberland Co., to Governor Edge, June 1, 1918, File 29a, Box 3, Correspondence of Governor Edge, 1917–1919, NJSA.

77. Alfred J. Perkins, Sheriff, Atlantic Co., to Governor Edge, August 8, 1918, File 29a, Box 3, Correspondence of Governor Edge, 1917–1919, NJSA.

78. George Eckhardt, Sheriff, Warren County, to Governor Edge, May 7, 1918, ibid.

79. Charles Anderson, Sheriff, Middlesex County, to Governor Edge, May 4, 1918, "Re. Compulsory Work Act," File 29a, Box 3, Correspondence of Governor Edge, 1917–1919, NJSA.

80. John Magner, Sheriff, Hudson County, to Governor Edge, July 9, 1918, ibid.

81. John R. Flavell, Sheriff, Essex County, to Governor Edge, May 3, 1918, ibid.

82. Letter from unidentified correspondent to Governor Edge, March 18, 1918, ibid. According to a notation in the file this letter was referred to the Sheriff of Passaic County under the category "compulsory work."

83. W. Penn Carson, Sheriff, Camden County, to Governor Edge, May 6, 1918, ibid.

84. Ellsworth Brokaw, Sheriff, Somerset County, to Governor Edge, undated, ibid.

85. John W. Courter, Sheriff, Bergen County, to Governor Edge, May 3, 1918, ibid.

86. A. Engle Haines, Sheriff, Burlington County, to Governor Edge, May 3, 1918, ibid.

87. Walter L. Burnell, Attorney, Westfield, New Jersey, to Governor Edge, April 2, 1918, ibid.

88. Thos. F. Carey, Jersey City, to Governor Edge, March 9, 1918, ibid.

89. F. B. Stratford to Governor Edge, April 22, 1918, File 29b, Box 3, Correspondence of Governor Edge, 1916–1918, NJSA.

90. E. S. Woodward, Esq., to Governor Edge, May 29, 1918, and Edge to Woodward, May 31, 1918, File 29a, Box 3, Correspondence of Governor Edge, 1916–1918, NJSA.

91. "A Citizen of Jersey City" to Governor Edge, March 9, 1918, ibid.

92. Mrs. Joseph Williams, Long Branch, New Jersey, to Governor Edge, undated, received March 9, 1918, Ibid.

93. Mrs. F. M. Steck, Union, New Jersey, to Governor Edge, March 5, 1918, File 29a, Box 3, Correspondence of Governor Edge, 1917–1919, NJSA.

94. Stephen Colon, Passaic, to Governor Edge, April 2, 1918, File 31, "Passaic Complaints," Box 1, Correspondence of Governor Edge, 1917–1919, NJSA. The files indicate no response from the Governor.

95. Form letter of J. O. H. Pitney, Chairman, District Board for Division No. 2 of New Jersey, to various industrial employers, July 1, 1918; Pitney to Major H. C. Kramer, PMGO, July 5, 1918, File 22-21, States File—New Jersey, SSS Records, 1917–1919, RG 163, WNRC. Pitney's form letter also asked the employers to report (1) The percentage of work their firm was doing under direct Government contract (2) The percentage of work being done indirectly for the government (specifying for whom the work was being done and the nature of materials furnished), and (3) The total number of employees in the firm and the number engaged in Government.

96. Reynolds, *Testing Democracy*, 7.

97. Gilkyson, Acting Adjutant General, to the Provost Marshal General, October 22, 1917, "re: men reported on Form 146-A," File 101-5, Box 38, States File: New Jersey, SSS Records, 1917–1919, RG 163, WNRC. The procedures required for these men are spelled out in "Supplemental Rules and Regulations No. 1, Prescribed by the President for Local and District Boards, Governing The Disposition of Persons Called for Examination Who Fail to Report for or Submit to Examination," August 1, 1917 (Washington: GPO, 1917).

98. On the Progressives' concern for fairness, see Warren S. Tyron, "The Draft in World War I," *Current History*, 54 (June 1968): 341. That fairness had gendered significance is suggested by Hugh Johnson: "There is no reason why one woman's son should go out and defend another woman's son who refuses the tasks of training." (Quoted by Tyron.) See also John Kennedy Ohl, "Hugh S. Johnson and the Draft, 1917–18," *Prologue* 8 (Summer 1976): 92, 96; and Robert K. Griffith, *Men Wanted for the U.S. Army* (Westport, CT: Greenwood Press, 1982), 6, 11.

99. Lynch to the U.S. Attorney General, October 6, 1917; Lynch to the U.S. Attorney General, October 9, 1917; O'Brian to the U.S. Secretary of War, October 10, 1917; Provost Marshal General to O'Brian, October 11, 1917; and Lynch to the U.S. Attorney General, October 23, 1917, all in File 186233-489, DOJ Correspondence, RG 60, National Archives, Washington.

100. Ibid.

101. Gilkyson to Crowder, "re COLORED ALLOTMENT," file 27-38, Box 196, States Files-New Jersey, SSS Records, 1917–1919, RG 163, WNRC. For newspaper accounts of the "colored" draft, see "Entrainments for Colored Men Bound for Camps Dix and Upton," *Newark Evening News*, July 19, 1918; "City to Send 181 More Colored Men to Camp," *Newark Evening News*, August 1, 1918.

102. Clerk of the Board, Selective Service Local Board, Division No. 2, Bergen County, Hackensack, New Jersey, to Chairman, Local Board, County of Elizabeth, Hampton, Va., November 25, 1918, loose sheets in file series 17, States Files: New Jersey, SSS Records, 1917–1919, RG 163, WNRC.

103. Local Board for the County of Elizabeth City, Virginia, to the Provost Marshal General, December 3, 1918, and Local Board for the County of Elizabeth City, Virginia, to Chairman, Local Board, Division 2, Hackensack, N.J., December 3, 1918, loose sheets in file series 17, States Files: New Jersey, SSS Records, 1917–1919, RG 163, WNRC.

104. W. C. Cabell, Secretary, Local Board No. 2, Passaic County, to Gilkyson, July 16, 1918, reported several registrants from his board apparently had gone to Cuba or Brazil to avoid the draft; Roscoe Conkling to Governor Edge, July 25, 1918, reported men could not be extradited from these countries. Both letters in Series 17, Box 195, States Files: New Jersey, SSS Records, 1917–1919, RG 163, WNRC.

105. The papers and correspondence in this case are found in File 17-241, Box 195, States Files: New Jersey, SSS Records, 1917–1919, RG 163, WNRC.

106. Ibid.

107. See letters to Governor Edge in Files by county, labelled "complaints," Box 1, Correspondence of Governor Edge, 1917–1919, New Jersey State Archives, Trenton. For example, File 31, "Passaic County Complaints," contains a number of such letters beginning in the Spring of 1917.

108. Crowder, *Second Report*, 187–188.

109. The New Jersey Department of Defense files in the State Archives contain hundreds of reports from these volunteer secret police. See Box 2, Miscellaneous Correspondence—Post Spanish-American War, Military Records, New Jersey Department of Defense, NJSA. For this study I have relied mostly on those files, supplemented by APL reports that found their way into the records of the United States Military Investigative Division of the Bureau of Investigation. The latter organization was the forerunner of the Federal Bureau of Investigation (FBI), and its records are held as Justice Department documents (RG 60) by the National Archives in Washington, D.C.

110. Report of John A. Barnshaw and Charles Ernest, American Protective League, copy sent to Wm Frank Sooy, Director of Public Safety, Atlantic City, April 27, 1917, Book 19, Box 2, Miscellaneous Correspondence—Post Spanish-American War, Military Records, New Jersey Department of Defense, State Archives, Trenton.

111. Ibid.

112. Report of Charles Ernest and John A. Barnshaw, APL, attached to letter from commanding officer, Second New Jersey Infantry to New Jersey Adjutant General, April 18, 1917; Form letter prepared by New Jersey Adjutant General, May 1917, for use in reporting suspected German sympathizers to local authorities and the United States Department of Justice. By July the adjutant general's office was receiving many reports on these forms from volunteers for the APL "secret service." See Book 19, Box 2, Miscellaneous Correspondence—Post Spanish-American War, Military Records, New Jersey Department of Defense, NJSA.

113. "Slacker Hunt Gets Thousands Without Cards," *Newark Evening News*, September 3, 1918; "Flow of Slackers to Dix Is Started," *Newark Evening News*, September 4, 1918.

114. The correspondence and various investigative reports relating to "slacker raids" made by the Interstate Detective Agency are in Files 17-235, 17-314, 17-323, 17-325, and 17-327, States Files: New Jersey, SSS Records, 1917–1919, RG 163, WNRC.

115. The investigative reports which describe much of this case are contained in File 17-325, States Files: New Jersey.

116. Capt. W. F. Lent, Investigator Draft Desertion Cases, to Commanding General, Camp Dix, N. J., March 6, 1919, and H. L. Scott, Maj. General, Commanding, Camp Dix, N. J., to the Adjutant General of the Army, March 6, 1919, File 17-325, States Files: New Jersey, SSS Records, 1917–1919, RG 163, WNRC. A handwritten note on the bottom of the latter document reads, "File—Boards about to be disbanded." The Army apparently did not want to pursue the investigation since the Selective Service apparatus was about to cease functioning.

117. Frank R. Stone, Special Agent, APL, to Chief, Bureau of Investigation, March 14, 1919, File 17-235, States Files: New Jersey.
118. Stone to Chief, Bureau of Investigation, February 14, 1919, File 17-323, States Files: New Jersey.

Chapter Four   California: "Please Forward Chinese, Japanese and American Indians, but no Negroes"

1. Circular letter No. 81, State of California, the Adjutant General's Office, Sacramento, 5-18, October 2, 1917. In *Compiled Circulars No. 4* (December 26, 1917), RG 163, Records of the Selective Service System, 1917–1919, States Files—California, National Archives, College Park, MD.
2. Ian F. Haney Lopez, *White by Law: The Legal Construction of Race* (New York: New York University Press, 1996).
3. The other states were: Arizona, Colorado, Delaware, Nebraska, Nevada, New Mexico, Texas, and Washington. See State Board of Control, *California and the Oriental: Japanese, Chinese and Hindus (Report to Gov. Wm. D. Stephens)* (Sacramento: California State Printing Office, 1922), 45.
4. Quoted in, "U.S. Supreme Court to Decide Citizenship Case," *San Francisco Chronicle*, June 1, 1917. 10. For a detailed analysis of the Ozawa case, see Haney Lopez, *White by Law*, 80–86.
5. The views of both Governor Stephens and Japanese leaders are found in the Report of the State Board of Control of California, *California and the Oriental*. See The Japanese Association of America, "Memorial Presented to the President While at San Francisco on September 18, 1919." The Governor Stephens quote is from page 12.
6. Gary Okihiro, *Common Ground: Reimagining American History* (Princeton, New Jersey: Princeton University Press, 2001), 76.
7. Okihiro, 78.
8. Ibid., 69.
9. *California and the Oriental*, 8–10.
10. Ibid., 223–229.
11. Ralph P. Merritt to E. H. Crowder, May 30, 1917, and Crowder to State Bureau of Registration, May 31, 1917, RG 163, Records of the Selective Service System, 1917–1919, States Files—California, Box 90, Folder 13, National Archives, College Park, MD.
12. "Japanese Will Not Be Recorded as Mongolians," *San Francisco Chronicle*, Tuesday, June 5, 1917. 3
13. See *San Diego Union*, June 6, 1917, and June 7, 1917, for complete lists of draft registrants in San Diego County, grouped according to "white" and "colored" races.
14. Hard copies of draft registration cards for all draft boards and all registrations in 1917 and 1918 are held as part of Record Group 163 in the National Archives Atlanta Regional Branch, East Point, Georgia. All National Archives regional branches hold microfilm of the registration cards, as do most Mormon family research centers.
15. PMGO Form 164A, "List of Men Ordered for Induction," Local Board No. 2, San Diego County, September 28, 1917. States Files—California, box 30, RG 163, Records of the Selective Service System, 1917–1919, NARA, College Park, MD.
16. Manuscript Population Schedule, Thirteenth Census of the United States, County of San Diego, San Diego City, Enumeration District 141, Sheets 17B and 18A, taken May 5, 1910.
17. When Maxine Hong Kingston named a book, *China Men* (New York: Ballantine Books, 1981), she showed how profoundly a single typographical space can alter meaning. In separating the two parts of that term, she simultaneously rescued the dignity of Chinese American racial identity and undermined the power of historically feminized images of Chinese American men to designate an inferior form of manhood.

18. For example, a California law that prohibited Indians and Negroes from testifying against white men in criminal cases was interpreted by the California Supreme Court to apply to Chinese as well. See *People v. Hall* Supreme Court of California, 1854 [4 Cal 399].

19. An excellent general treatment of Indian-Spanish relations in southern California during this period is Douglas Monroy, *Thrown Among Strangers: The Making of Mexican California in Frontier California* (Berkeley: University of California, 1990).

20. Castillo as quoted in James J. Rawls and Walton Bean, *California: An Interpretive History* (New York: McGraw-Hill, 2003), 19.

21. Robert F. Heizer and Alan F. Almquist, *The Other Californians: Prejudice and Discrimination under Spain, Mexico, and the United States to 1920* (Berkeley: University of California Press, 1971), 2–3.

22. Act of Feb. 8, 1887 (24 Stat. L. 388), Sec. 6.

23. "An Act for the Relief of the Mission Indians in the State of California," January 12, 1891 (26 Stat. 712). See also various documents identifying tribal patents in the 1890s in RG 75: Records of the Bureau of Indian Affairs, Records of the Pala Superintendent, National Archives Regional Branch, Laguna Niguel. For a more detailed description, see Rader, " 'So We Only Took 120 Acres,' " 356–362.

24. Helen Hunt Jackson, *Ramona* (1884; Avon Books Reprint: New York, 1970); Kevin Starr, *Inventing the Dream*, 55–63, 344; Rader, " 'So We Only Took 120 Acres,' " 288–297.

25. Ed Fletcher to G. W. Henshaw, 7-26-1912, Fletcher papers, Folder 4 (Helm, Franklin), Mandeville Special Collections, University Library, University of California, San Diego.

26. Testimony of a "Mr. Cosgrove," testifying for the City of San Diego, June 1917, Fletcher Papers, Box 11, Folder 1, Mandeville Special Collections, University Library, University of California, San Diego.

27. *San Diego Historical Society*, San Diego Biographies, *"Colonel Ed Fletcher (1872–1955),"* adapted from Carl Heilbron, History of San Diego *(1936)* <*http://sandiegohistory. org/biofletcher.htm*>.

28. Emily Rader, " 'So We Only Took 120 Acres,' " (302–331) describes this process in detail for the northern San Diego County area around the town of Escondido.

29. See, for example, Fletcher's letter to H. P. Bard, San Diego City Council, September 18, 1917, stating that if the City did not accept his offered rate of six cents, the price would be withdrawn and raised to ten cents. Fletcher Papers, Box 1, Folder 34.

30. "An Act for the Relief of the Mission Indians in the State of California"; Tribal Patents, Records of the Pala Superintendent, Records of the Bureau of Indian Affairs, RG 75, NARA, Laguna Niguel.

31. I have pieced together this account from several sources. The Ed Fletcher Papers at the Mandeville Special Collections Library, University of California, San Diego, contain a letter from Ed Fletcher to Wm Henshaw, November 27, 1917 that describes the meeting with Harper, linking Fletcher's assistance with young Scripps' exemption to the elder Scripps' opposition to the San Diego City water projects. Numerous articles in the Spreckels-owned newspaper, the San Diego *Union* from late 1917 through the end of the war in 1918 reveal the political fault lines that complicate this case; and the Selective Service Records in the National Archives, both the regional branch at Laguna Niguel, California, and at College Park, Maryland, contain allusions to the case, and some of the official records relating to it.

32. Fletcher to William Henshaw, November 27, 1917, Folder 13, Box 11, Ed Fletcher Papers, Mandeville Library Special Collections, University of California, San Diego.

33. "Despite Denial, Scripps Still Seeks Exemption," *San Diego Union*, March 14, 1918.

34. Ibid.

35. "Scripps Exemption Appeal Turned Down Hard by Board," *San Diego Union*, March 19, 1918. The Thomas Scripps case was reported in the *San Diego Union*, September 12, 1917.

36. Ibid.

37. "One of Scripps Boys Ought to Get Into War, Says Allen," *San Diego Union*, March 19, 1918, quoting the *San Diego Tribune*.
38. Wire from PMGO Crowder to Governor, Sacramento, May 11, 1918, unnumbered file, Box 1, California District Appeals Granted and Denied, 1917–1919, Records of the Selective Service System (WW I), RG 163, National Archives, San Bruno, California.
39. Fletcher's various negotiations are described in detail in his voluminous correspondence with W. G. Henshaw, Box, 11, Folder 13, Ed Fletcher Papers, Mandeville Special Collections, University of California, San Diego.
40. Ed Fletcher, *Memoirs of Ed Fletcher* (San Diego: Col. Ed Fletcher, 1952), 683–686.
41. Fletcher to F. W. Henshaw, March 19, 1914, and F. W. Henshaw to Fletcher, March 21, 1914, Folder 5 (Henshaw, F. W., 1914–1918), Box 11, Ed Fletcher Papers, Mandeville Special Collections, University of California, San Diego.
42. See Fletcher's response to H. E. Wadsworth, Superintendent, Indian Reservation, San Jacinto, Calif., September 30, 1916, Folder 17, Box 31, Ed Fletcher Papers, Mandeville Special Collections, University of California, San Diego.
43. Act of Feb. 8, 1887 (24 Stat. L. 388), Sec. 6.
44. Superintendent, Pala Indian School, to the Commissioner of Indian Affairs, August 9, 1918, Records of the Pala Superintendent, Selective Service Records, 1917–1919, RG 75, Records of the Bureau of Indian Affairs, National Archives, Laguna Niguel, California; Act of May 8, 1906 (34 Stat. 182).
45. Superintendent, Pala Indian School, to Local Registration Board for San Diego County, September 21, 1918.
46. James Wilson, *The Earth Shall Weep: A History of Native America* (New York: Grove Press, 1998), 300, 311–316; Peter Nabokov, *Native American Testimony* (New York: Penguin Books, 1999), 215–218; Ward Churchill, *Perversions of Justice: Indigenous Peoples and Angloamerican Law* (San Francisco: City Lights, 2003), 13.
47. Memorandum of Decisions Under Circular #1305-M, undated (most likely August 1918) on Form 5-1142, Department of the Interior, United States Indian Service, Records of the Pala Superintendent, Selective Service, 1917–1919, RG 75, National Archives, Laguna Niguel, California.
48. Abraham J. Shragge, " 'I Like the Cut of Your Jib': Cultures of Accommodation between the U.S. Navy and Citizens of San Diego, California, 1900–1961," UCSD Civic Collaborative, University of California, San Diego, September 29, 2001. Manuscript provided by the author.
49. Cato Sells, Commissioner of Indian Affairs, to Superintendents, Circular No. 1305-G, February 20, 1918.
50. Cato Sells, Commissioner of Indian Affairs, to Superintendents, Circular No. 1305-M, July 19, 1918.
51. Sells to Superintendents, August 15, 1918, Circular No. 1305-N.
52. Superintendent, Pala Indian School, to Commissioner of Indian Affairs, December 29, 1917, Circular No. 1305-E.
53. Undated document with June 10, 1918 "List of Indians who should have registered from Pala Indian School, in Records of the Pala Superintendent, Selective Service Records, 1917–1919".
54. Superintendent, Pala Indian School, to Local Registration Board, Fallbrook, Cal., September 12, 1918.
55. Crowder to Governors of Texas, New Mexico, Arizona, and California, May 29, 1917, Folder 16, Box 90, States Files, Records of the Selective Service System, 1917–1919, RG 163, National Archives, College Park, MD.
56. "Second Call in San Diego Necessary to Fill Quota," *San Diego Union*, August 11, 1917.
57. *San Diego Sun* to E. H. Crowder, August 8, 1917, document 22-6, Box 91, States Files, SSS Records, College Park.
58. "Alien Residents Decline to Serve Country of Adoption," *San Diego Union*, August 21, 1917.

59. Department of Commerce and Labor, Bureau of the Census, *Thirteenth Census of the United States: Taken in the Year 1910*, Vol. II, Population (Washington, D.C.: Government Printing Office, 1913), 157, 174.
60. Calculated from the registration lists published in the *San Diego Union*, June 15 and 16, 1917.
61. G. C. Woodward, American Consul, Matamoros, to U.S. Secretary of State, November 2, 1917, document 17-50, States Files-CA, Box 95, SSS Records, College Park, MD.
62. The letter from Spreckels to Julius Kahn is dated October 31, 1917. Complete correspondence in this case is in California File 117, States Files-CA, Box 95, SSS Records, College Park, MD.
63. "Slackers Taken on High Seas," *San Diego Union*, September 11, 1917.
64. "Slackers Drift from Coast Town," *San Diego Union*, April 6, 1918.
65. Charles Mills, *The Racial Contract* (Ithaca and London: Cornell University Press, 1997), 81.
66. "Japanese and Irish Questions Stir Conference," *San Francisco Chronicle*, June 1, 1917. 15.
67. "Registration in State Exceeds Total Forecast," and "Enrollment for Draft Quiet and Orderly Throughout City," *San Francisco Chronicle*, Wednesday, June 6, 1917. 2
68. Walter G. Beach, *Oriental Crime in California: A Study of Offenses Committed by Orientals in that State, 1900–1927* (Stanford: Stanford University Press, 1932), 459–460.
69. War Dept., P. M. G. O., June 20, 1918—To the Adjutant General of California, Sacramento, Cal., California File 17-76, States Files, R. G. 163, Records of the Selective Service System, 1917–1919, NARA, College Park, MD.
70. Frank Yeo Lee to Crowder, May 1918, Folder 17, Box 90, States Files—California, Records of the Selective Service System, 1917–1919, RG 163, NARA, College Park, MD.
71. Leitch, Camp Fremont, Calif., to Provost Marshal General, March 5, 1918, Folder 17, Box 90, States Files—California, Records of the Selective Service System, 1917–1919, RG 163, NARA, College Park, MD.
72. Since the Selective Service System categorized them as "white," official draft records do not provide aggregate data on how Japanese or Chinese men of draft age actually responded to the draft. The lists for San Diego and Monterey Counties, where there were small but significant Chinese and Japanese communities name very few Chinese or Japanese. Out of 170 names on the San Diego lists, there are three apparent Japanese and six apparent Chinese names. See "Delinquent Classification List," PMGO Form 1013-a, and "Lists of Men Ordered to Report to This Local Board," PMGO 164 and PMGO1029, in Records of the Selective Service System, 1917–1919, RG 163. For Monterey, these forms are at the NARA Regional Branch, San Bruno, CA, and for San Diego, they are at the NARA Regional Branch, Laguna Niguel.
73. See Records of the District Board for Division Two of Southern District of California, Presidential Appeals, R. G. 163, Records of the Selective Service System, 1917–1919, NARA Regional Branch, Laguna Niguel, CA; and Records of the District Board, Division Two, for Northern California, Presidential Appeals, Box 1, R. G. 163, Records of the Selective Service System, 1917–1919, NARA Regional Branch, San Bruno, CA.
74. Tomas Almaguer, *Racial Faultlines: The Historical Origins of White Supremacy in California* (Berkeley: University of California Press, 1994); Martha Menchaca, *The Mexican Outsiders: A Community History of Marginalization and Discrimination in California* (Austin, TX: University of Texas Press, 1995); Neil Foley, *White Scourge: Mexicans, Blacks, and Poor Whites in Texas Cotton Culture* (Berkeley: University of California Press, 1997, 1999).
75. "Registration of Mexicans," Crowder form letter to governors of Texas, New Mexico, Arizona and California, May 29, 1917: "Advices received through the State Department indicate misapprehension among Mexicans in border States concerning registration. Most Mexicans do not understand that only those between twenty-one and thirty inclusive are required to register and those who do understand suspect some sinister motive. These misapprehensions may cause serious exodus of labor and interfere with registration. It is

suggested that an explanatory proclamation by you in Spanish, the publication thereof in newspapers printed in Spanish and such other publicity as you can give to it would go far to cure this situation. . . ." Records of the Selective Service System, RG 163, Box 90, Folder 14-16.

76. J. J. Borree, The Adjutant General, Circular No. 84, State of California, The Adjutant General's Office, October 16, 1917, in *Compiled Circulars No. 4*, Records of the Selective Service System, 1917–1919, California, RG 163, NARA, College Park, MD.

77. In its front page report on the final registration numbers two days after the first registration, the *San Francisco Chronicle* gave only figures for "white citizens and those with their first naturalization papers." June 7, 1917, 1. Inside the paper, a table showed numbers for both "white" and "colored." "Draft Registration Classified: Zemansky Gives out Figures."

78. Provost Marshal General, *Second Report of the Provost Marshal General on the Operations of the Selective Service System, to December 1918* (GPO: Washington, D.C., 1918), 458–459.

79. "Report of the Women's Committee of the State Council of Defense," 137–138.

80. Nancy Ordover, *American Eugenics: Race, Queer Anatomy, and the Science of Nationalism* (Minneapolis: University of Minnesota Press, 2003), 15–20.

81. "City Quiet as Young Men Enroll for Grim Work of War Overseas: Passive Objectors Are Arrested in Attempt to Influence Eligible Men from Registry," June 6, 1917, 1.

82. "Opposition to Draft Charge Is Brought," *San Francisco Chronicle*, June 6, 1917, 2.

83. "Slacker Raid Brings 26 to City Prison," June 17, 1917, 1.

84. "Hotel Man Held for Throwing Anti-Draft Papers from Train," *San Francisco Chronicle*, June 4, 1917, 1.

85. "Conferences on War Called by California," *San Francisco Chronicle*, May 12, 1918, 4; War History Department of the California Historical Survey Commission, *California in the War: War Addresses, Proclamations and Patriotic Messages of Governor William D. Stephens* (ND), 33–34.

86. "California War Conference at L. A. Begins," *San Francisco Chronicle*, May 14, 1918, 8.

87. Frank Ray Davis *Ricardo Flores Magon: the Man who Saw Tomorrow* (Sharp Press, 2001).

88. "Eight Arrested in a Raid on I. W. W., *San Francisco Chronicle*, May 10, 1918, 3.

89. "California War Conference at L. A. Begins," *San Francisco Chronicle*, May 14, 1918, 8.

90. Carey McWilliams, *Factories in the Fields: The Story of Migratory Farm Labor in California* (Little, Brown, & Company: Boston, 1939).

91. "Men to Harvest Big State Will Be Problem," *San Francisco Chronicle*, June 8, 1917, 15.

92. "Men Cannot Evade Draft By Retreat to Farms," *San Francisco Chronicle*, June 13, 1917, 1.

93 "Squirrels Are an Expensive Luxury," *Salinas Daily Index*, July 10, 1917.

94. State Councils Section, 14-D2, Weekly Reports of Activities, p. 5, undated document. Council of National Defense, State Councils Section, RG 62, Box 784.

95. "Angelenos Wage War on Idlers," *San Diego Union*, August 9, 1917.

96. "Vagrants Turned Over To Ranchers: Labor Shortage Thereby Partially Solved; Wages Average $2 Daily and Board," *San Diego Union*, May 15, 1918.

97. "California War Conference . . . ," May 14, 1918.

98. "Idlers Must Get Jobs or Don Uniforms," *San Francisco Chronicle*, May 24, 1918, 2.

99. Ibid.

100. "Registration Continues Under Sacramento Order," *San Francisco Chronicle*, June 8, 1917, 3.

Chapter Five   "The Final Report"

1. *Final Report of the Provost Marshal General to the Secretary of War on the Operations of the Selective Service System to July 15, 1919* (Washington: Government Printing Office, 1920), 9.

2. Crowder, *The Selective Service System: Its Aims and Accomplishments, Its Future* (Washington: Government Printing Office, 1917), 5.

3. Ibid., 12–13.

4. On the mental segmentation of American men through the use of the Army "Alpha" test, an early version of the Stanford-Binet IQ test, see Richard T. Von Mayrhauser, "The Manager, the Medic, and the Mediator: The Clash of Professional Psychological Styles and the Wartime Origins of Group Mental Testing," in *Psychological Testing and American Society, 1890–1930,* Michael M. Sokal, ed. (New Brunswick and London: Rutgers University Press, 1990), 128–157.

5. *Second Report of the Provost Marshal General to the Secretary of War on the Operations of the Selective Service System to December 20, 1918* (Washington: Government Printing Office, 1919), 460.

6. *Final Report,* 12.

7. Gerald E. Shenk " 'Work or Fight': Selective Service and Manhood in the Progressive Era, " Ph.D. diss. (San Diego: University of California, 1992).

8. *Second Report of the Provost Marshal General,* 16–17; David Kennedy, *Over Here: The First World War and American Society* (New York: Oxford University Press, 1980), 57.

9. *Final Report,* 8.

10. *Final Report,* 10.

11. *Final Report,* 16.

12. *Final Report,* 9.

13. *Final Report,* 11–12.

14. *Final Report,* 9.

15. Vicente L. Rafael, *White Love and other Events in Filipino History* (Manila: Ateneo de Manila University Press, 2000), 29.

16. *Final Report,* 14–15.

17. For the concept of "a field of engagement," see Genja SenGupta, "Elites, Subalterns, and American Identities: A Case Study of African-American Benevolence," *American Historical Review* 109 (October 2004): 1107.

INDEX